Benjamin Chapman Burt

A Brief History of Greek Philosophy

Benjamin Chapman Burt

A Brief History of Greek Philosophy

ISBN/EAN: 9783743351011

Manufactured in Europe, USA, Canada, Australia, Japa

Cover: Foto ©ninafisch / pixelio.de

Manufactured and distributed by brebook publishing software (www.brebook.com)

Benjamin Chapman Burt

A Brief History of Greek Philosophy

A

BRIEF HISTORY

OF

GREEK   PHY.

Entered according to Act of Congress, in the year 1888, by
B. C. BURT,
in the Office of the Librarian of Congress at Washington.

TYPOGRAPHY BY J. S. CUSHING & CO., BOSTON.
PRESSWORK BY GINN & CO., BOSTON.

TO

H. G. B.

AND

E. S. McK.

PREFACE.

THE following work had its beginning in a series of essays written for one of the ethico-religious periodicals of the country. To these — at the suggestion of friends whose counsel seemed to be as valuable as that of any could possibly be and could not well be disregarded — others were added to make a brief account of Greek speculation from its beginning to its end. This account has been prepared in the belief that the problems of philosophy are in a large measure always the same, and that the Greek solutions of the cardinal problems, by reason of their simplicity and freshness (for they are solutions that were found when the world's thought was comparatively in its youth, and are, in larger measure than those unacquainted with the history of thought begin to suspect, the only *original* solutions of those problems), and by reason of their remoteness from the prejudices of the present, have a certain value not possessed by any others, particularly for the beginner in philosophical thinking. Most of the works treating of the subject of which this volume treats are learned and extensive, overwhelming the general reader, and even the student, almost, with a sense of the superabundant wealth of the ancient thought in particular and the world's thought in general. It is hoped that the present work will render accessible in convenient form and quantities some of the noblest portions of the intellectual wealth of Greece. An attempt is here made not merely to expound and elucidate, but also to present in their historical connection, and give a just estimate of the validity of, the leading standpoints and categories of Greek thinking. Much reading and not a little original study have been given to the task.

The writer takes the liberty to express here his sense of obligation to G. S. Morris, Professor of Philosophy in the University of Michigan, and formerly Lecturer on Philosopy in the Johns Hopkins University, and to G. S. Hall, late Professor of Psychology in the Johns Hopkins University, and now President of Clark University, for suggestions and encouragement received from them. A word of thanks is due also to John Dewey, now Assistant Professor of Philosophy in Michigan University, and Professor Elect of Philosophy in the University of Minnesota; and to a college-classmate who has become a life-companion.

ANN ARBOR, June, 1888.

GENERAL TABLE OF CONTENTS.

INTRODUCTORY PARAGRAPH, p. 1.

I. NATURALISM, pp. 1-34.

§ 1.

THE HYLICISTS, HYLOZOISTS, OR EARLY IONIC NATURAL PHILOSOPHERS: *Thales*, p. 1; *Anaximander*, p. 2; *Anaximenes*, p. 3; Result, p. 3.

§ 2.

THE PYTHAGOREANS, p. 4: *Pythagoras* and the Pythagorean Society, pp. 4-6; Pythagorean Philosophy, p. 6; Number-Theory and Doctrine of Contraries, pp. 6-7; Theories not purely Pythagorean, pp. 7-9; Miscellaneous Theories, p. 9; Result, p. 9.

§ 3.

THE ELEATICS, p. 10: Life of *Xenophanes*, p. 10; Philosophy of Xenophanes, p. 11; Result, p. 11; Life of *Parmenides*, p. 12; Philosophy of Parmenides, pp. 13-14; Result, p. 15; Life of *Zeno*, p. 16; Philosophy of Zeno, p. 16; Result, pp. 17-18; *Melissus*, p. 18; General Result, p. 19.

§ 4.

HERACLITUS: Life of Heraclitus, p. 20; First Principle, pp. 20-21; Physical Doctrine, p. 22; The Soul and Reason, p. 22; Result, p. 23.

§ 5.

LATER NATURAL PHILOSOPHERS, p. 23: Life of *Empedocles*, p. 24; Theory of Nature, pp. 24-25; Theory of Knowledge, p. 26; Result, p. 26; Life of *Anaxagoras*, p. 27; Theory of Nature, pp. 27-28; Theory of Nous, or Mind, and Knowledge, p. 29; Result, p. 29; The Atomists, *Leucippus* and *Democritus*, p. 30; Theory of Nature, pp. 30-31; Theory of the Soul, etc., pp. 31-32; Result, pp. 32-33.

§ 6.

GENERAL CHARACTER OF THE FIRST PERIOD IN THE HISTORY OF GREEK PHILOSOPHY, pp. 33-34.

II. RATIONALISM, pp. 34-263.

§ 7.

THE SOPHISTS, p. 34: Life of *Protagoras*, p. 35; Theory of Protagoras, pp. 35-36; Life of *Gorgias*, p. 36; Theory of Gorgias, pp. 36-37; Result, p. 37. *Hippias* and *Prodicus*, p. 38; The Sophists as a Class (Result), pp. 38-40.

§ 8.

SOCRATES: The Sophists and Socrates, p. 41; Special Sources of Information regarding Socrates, p. 42; Life of Socrates, pp. 42-45; Personality of Socrates and its Relation to the Subsequent History of Greek Philosophy, pp. 45-47; Philosophy of Socrates, p. 47; Spirit of the Socratic Philosophizing, pp. 48-50; The Socratic Method, pp. 50-54; The Doctrines of Socrates (their general character), p. 54; Physical Philosophy of Socrates, p. 55; (Ethical Philosophy of Socrates) Relations between Knowledge and Virtue, p. 56; General Consequences of the Unity of Knowledge and Virtue, p. 57; Classification of the Virtues, p. 58; Temperance, p. 58; Friendship, p. 59; Right Citizenship and Justice, p. 60; Piety, p. 61; Wisdom, p. 62; Beauty, p. 63; General Result, pp. 63-64.

§ 9.

THE FOLLOWERS OF SOCRATES, p. 65.

§ 10.

THE LESSER SOCRATICS, p. 65: *The Megarians* (*Euclid, Eubulides, Diodorus, Stilpo,* and their doctrines), pp. 66-67; *The Cynics* (*Antisthenes, Diogenes,* — their doctrines), pp. 67-69; *The Cyrenaics* (*Aristippus, Theodorus, Hegesias, Anniceris,* — their doctrines), pp. 69-71; Result, p. 71.

§ 11.

PLATO: Life of Plato, pp. 72-75; Plato's Works, pp. 75-78; Plato's General Conception of Philosophy, pp. 78-81; The Divisions of Philosophy, p. 81; Dialectic as a Twofold Science, p. 82; Dialectic as a Theory of Knowledge and Method, pp. 82-84; (Dialectic as a System)

Thought and Being, pp. 84-85; The World of Ideas, pp. 85-87; Relation of the Ideal, to the Phenomenal, World, pp. 88-90; (Physics, or the Theory of Nature) The Method of Physical Speculation, p. 90; The Cosmos, pp. 91-93; Body and Soul, pp. 93-97; (Plato's Ethics) General Basis, p. 98; The Method of Ethics, p. 98; Nature and End of the State, p. 99; The Parts of the State and the Virtue of Each, pp. 99-101; Virtue in the Individual, p. 101; State Administration, p. 102; False Forms of the State and their Genesis, pp. 104-107; The Eternal Life, p. 107; Beauty and Art, p. 108; Later Form of Plato's Philosophy, pp. 109-113; Result, pp. 111-113.

§ 12.

THE DISCIPLES OF PLATO, p. 113.

§ 13.

THE OLD ACADEMY, p. 114: *Speusippus*, p. 114; *Xenocrates*, p. 115; Other Members of the Old Academy, p. 116.

§ 14.

ARISTOTLE: Life of Aristotle, p. 116; General Character of Aristotle's System, and His Chief Philosophical Works, pp. 118-122; Theory of Knowledge, p. 122; Kinds of Knowledge, p. 122; Scientific, or Philosophical, Knowledge, p. 122; Demonstration, p. 123; The Syllogism (Deductive), pp. 123-125; Definition and Predicables, p. 125; The Categories, p. 126; Syllogism (Inductive), pp. 127-128; Probable Proof and Dialectical and Rhetorical Method, p. 129; First Philosophy, or Metaphysics, p. 130; Being and Plato's Ideas, p. 131; Matter and Form, Potentiality and Actuality, p. 132; Causes, or First Principles (ἀρχαί), pp. 133-134; Kinds of Real Substance, Immovable Substance, God, p. 135; Physics, or the Philosophy of Nature, p. 136; Essential Character of Nature, pp. 136-137; Method of the Philosophy of Nature, p. 137; Motion, Space, and Time, p. 138; The Visible Universe, p. 139; Graduated Scale of Being in Nature, p. 140; Psychology as a Science, p. 140; Body and Soul, p. 141; Parts, or Faculties, of the Soul, p. 142-147; (General Analysis, p. 142; Sense-Faculties, p. 143; Phantasy and Memory, p. 144; Reason, pp. 144-146; Desire and Locomotion, p. 146); Practical Philosophy, p. 147; Method of Practical Philosophy, p. 147; End of Practical Philosophy, or "Political Science," pp. 148-149; Psychological Basis of Ethics, p. 149; Sources and Conditions of Virtue, pp. 150-152; Definition of Virtue, p. 152; Deliberate

Choice, p. 153; The Ethical Virtues, pp. 154-157; Right Reason, Prudence and the Intellectual Virtues, Generally, pp. 157-158; Self-Control and its Opposite, p. 158; Friendship, p. 159; Pleasure and Happiness, p. 160; "Practical" Ethics, p. 160; Origin of the State, p. 161; The Family, p. 162; Criticism of Certain Theories and Forms of State (Plato and Others), pp. 162-165; The End of the State, p. 165; The Nature of the Citizen, p. 165; A Polity and its Kinds, p. 166; Who Should be Rulers, p. 167; The Best Polity, pp. 168-170; Characteristics of Different Polities, pp. 170-174; Methods of Establishing and Maintaining the Various Forms of State, pp. 174-177; Causes of Political Revolutions, pp. 177-180; The Most Permanent Polities, p. 181; Plato's Theory of Revolutions, p. 181; Rhetoric, pp. 181-182; Poietical Philosophy, p. 183; Sources and Genesis of Aristotle's Philosophy, pp. 185-190; Substantial Unity of Plato and Aristotle, p. 191; Result, pp. 191-194.

§ 15.

THE PERIPATETIC SCHOOL, p. 194: *Theophrastus*, p. 195; *Strato* of Lampsacus, p. 196; *Dicæarch* of Messene, p. 196.

§ 16.

THREE LEADING POST-ARISTOTELIAN SCHOOLS, p. 196.

§ 17.

THE STOICS AND STOICISM: *Zeno, Cleanthes, Chrysippus*, and Others — Lives, pp. 197-199; Stoic Conception of the Nature and Parts of Philosophy, p. 199; Stoic Logic, p. 200; Origin of Ideas, pp. 200-201; The Criterion of Truth in Ideas, p. 202; System and Logical Method, p. 202; The Categories, p. 203; Physics, or the Theory of Nature, pp. 204-206; Ethics and its Parts, p. 206; The Chief Good, — Life according to Nature, p. 207; Nature of Virtue, p. 207; Classes of Virtue, p. 208; Classes of Goods, — the *Summum Bonum*, pp. 209-211; The Wise Man, pp. 211-212; The Stoics, and the Popular Religion, p. 213; Historical Sources of Stoicism, p. 213; Result, pp. 214-215.

§ 18.

THE EPICUREANS AND EPICUREANISM: *Epicurus* and his School, pp. 216-218; The Parts of Philosophy, p. 218; (Canonics) Criterion of Truth in Ideas, pp. 219-220; Method of the Study of Nature, p. 220; Physics — Aim and General Character, p. 221; First Principle, p. 221; Atoms, pp. 222-224; Properties of bodies, p. 224; The Visible Universe, pp. 224–226; The Gods, p. 227; The Human Soul, pp. 227–229; Ethics — First Principle (Pleasure), p. 227; Kinds of Pleasure, p. 230; The Wise Man, pp. 230–232; Friendship, p. 232; The State, p. 233; Religion, p. 233; Historical Sources of the Epicurean Doctrines, p. 234; Result, pp. 234–235.

§ 19.

THE SCEPTICS, p. 235: *Pyrrhonists — Pyrrho, Timon of Phlius, Æneside-mus, Agrippa, Sextus Empiricus*, p. 236; Theories of the Earlier Pyrrhonists, p. 236; The Later Pyrrhonists — The "Tropes," p. 237; The Impossibility of Demonstration, Sign, and Cause, p. 239; Pure Negativism of the Pyrrhonists, p. 240; *Middle and New Academies*, p. 240; *Arcesilaus*, p. 241; *Carneades*, pp. 241–243; Result, pp. 243–245.

§ 20.

THE COMMON GROUND OF THE STOICS, EPICUREANS, AND SCEPTICS, pp. 245–247.

§ 21.

PHILOSOPHY IN ROME: ECLECTICISM, p. 247.

§ 22.

THE LATER PERIPATETICS, pp. 248–250; *Andronicus of Rhodes, Boëthus of Sidon*, an *unknown* author, *Alexander of Ægæ, Aspasius and Adrastus of Aphrodisias, Aristocles, Alexander of Aphrodisias.*

§ 23.

THE LATER ACADEMICS, pp. 250–251; *Philo of Larissa*, p. 250; *Antiochus of Ascalon*, p. 250.

§ 24.

THE LATER STOICS, pp. 251–261; *Boëthus*, p. 251; *Panætius of Rhodes*, p. 252; *Posidonius*, p. 252; *Varro*, p. 253; *Cicero* — Life, pp. 253–254; General Conception of Philosophy, p. 255; Theory of Knowledge, p. 255; Physics, p. 256; Ethics, pp. 256–258; *Seneca* — Life, p. 258; Philosophy, pp. 258–260; *Musonius Rufus, Epictetus, Marcus Aurelius*, p. 260; Cynicism, p. 261.

§ 25.

GENERAL CHARACTER OF THE SECOND PERIOD, pp. 261–262.

III. SUPRA-RATIONALISM (AND SUPRA-NATURALISM), pp. 263-296.

§ 26.

STANDPOINT AND SCHOOLS OF THE THIRD AND LATEST PERIOD OF GREEK PHILOSOPHY, p. 263.

§ 27.

JEWISH-ALEXANDRIAN SCHOOL, p. 264: *Aristobulus*, p. 264; *Philo-Judæus*, General Attitude, p. 264; Theory of Knowledge, p. 265; God, p. 266; The Logos, p. 266; The Sensible World and Matter, p. 267; Man, p. 267; Result, p. 268.

§ 28.

NEO-PYTHAGOREANISM, p. 269.

§ 29.

THE ECLECTIC PLATONISTS, p. 269.

§ 30.

NEO-PLATONISM: *Ammonius Saccas*, p. 270; *Plotinus* — Life, p. 270; Dialectic, pp. 271-274; Reason, Intellect or Nous (Realm of Ideas), pp. 274-276; The One, The First, The Good, pp. 276-278; Intellect, Reason, or Nous, as an Emanation, pp. 278-280; Soul, pp. 280-281; Soul and Body, pp. 281-284; Individual Soul and Soul of the World, p. 284; The Sensible World and Matter, pp. 284-286; Virtue, p. 287; Historical Sources of the System of Plotinus, p. 288; Result, pp. 289-291. *Porphyry* and Others, p. 291; *Jamblichus*, p. 291; *Proclus* — Life, p. 292; Philosophy of Proclus, pp. 293-295; Result, p. 296.

BRIEF BIBLIOGRAPHY.

FOR the convenience of the student a list is here given of the principal easily-accessible works referred to in the following pages or consulted in the preparation of them. The names of other works are to be found in foot-notes throughout the volume.

Xenophon's Memorabilia of Socrates (Fielding's trans.).
Plato's Works (Jowett's trans., with Analyses and Introductions).
Aristotle's Works : —
  Organon (trans. by Owen in Bohn's Class. Lib.).
  Metaphysics (trans. by McMahan in Bohn's Class. Lib.).
  Psychology (trans. by E. Wallace, with Introd., and Notes and Text).
  Nicomachean Ethics (trans. by Browne in Bohn's Class. Lib., and by Peters).
  Politics (trans. by Welldon).
  Rhetoric and Poetic (trans. by Buckley in Bohn's Class. Lib.).
Lives of the Philosophers, by Diogenes Laertius (trans. by Yonge in Bohn's Class. Lib.).
Cicero's De Officiis (trans. by Edmonds in Harper's Class. Lib.).
Seneca's Works (Lodge's trans.).
Select Works of Plotinus (trans. by T. Taylor).
Five Books of Plotinus (trans. by Taylor).
Zeller's Outlines of the History of Greek Philosophy (trans. by Alleyne and Abbott).
Zeller's Pre-Socratic Philosophy, 2 vols. (a translation by S. F. Alleyne from Zeller's *Die Geschichte der Philosophie der Griechen*.
Zeller's Socrates and the Socratic Schools (trans. by Reichel).

Zeller's Plato and the Older Academy (trans. by Alleyne and Goodwin).
Zeller's Stoics, Epicureans, and Sceptics (trans. by Reichel).
Zeller's The Eclectics (trans. by Alleyne).
Lewes's Biographical History of Philosophy.
Ueberweg's History of Philosophy (Morris's trans.).
Schwegler's Handbook of the History of Philosophy (Stirling's trans.).
Ritter's History of Ancient Philosophy (trans. by Morrison).
A. W. Benn's The Greek Philosophers, 2 vols.
Grote's Plato.
Grote's Aristotle.
E. Wallace's Outlines of the Philosophy of Aristotle.
Grant's Aristotle.
Grant's Ethics of Aristotle, 2 vols.

GREEK PHILOSOPHY.

GREEK PHILOSOPHY had its beginning in the seventh century B.C. As distinguished from the theogony and cosmogony of the poets, its natural precursors, it was, in its beginning, an attempt to explain the sensible world — its origin and constitution — upon the basis of definite, natural fact, or what was regarded as such, instead of supernatural existences, such as gods and goddesses. In this attempt observation and reflection played the part played by imagination or fancy in the earlier; science and speculation, crude and false, though, no doubt, they in large measure were, took the place of mythology.

I. NATURALISM.

§ 1.

The Hylicists, Hylozoists, or Early Ionic Natural Philosophers.

Thales. — The earliest of the Greek philosophers was Thales, born at Miletus, a city on the western coast of Asia Minor, about the year 640 B.C. Thales was distinguished for political and ethical wisdom, for his knowledge of arithmetic, geometry, and astronomy, and for his Egyptian and Eastern lore. Several propositions in elementary geometry have been attributed to him, and he was reputed to have predicted an eclipse of the sun.[1] He declared the source of all things to be water; having, perhaps, been led to this hypothesis by the observation of the fact that water plays a great part in the economy of nature, or, as Aristotle says, by the idea that the seeds and nutriment of all things have a watery character. Thales held that nature is not merely material and mechanical, but animate; that water, the primal matter, is filled with life or soul. He may have believed in the existence of a world-soul, but probably not in the existence of an independent, world-ordering mind: dualism originated later in the history of philosophy.

Anaximander. — Next, chronologically, to Thales was Anaximander, also of Miletus, born 611 B.C., whose work, *On Nature* (περὶ φύσεως), was the earliest of many works of the same class written by the early Greek philosophers. Like Thales, he was a "scientist," being a geographer and astronomer. He affirmed that all things arise out of, and return into, an infinite entity, indeterminate in character, which he termed τὸ ἄπειρον, the Infinite (indefinite), and ἀρχή, "first principle." He was, it appears, the first philosopher who employed the term ἀρχή in this sense. Out of the Infinite, which he called "the Divine" and conceived as an eternal and living, though not immaterial, being, he supposed actual existences to have sprung by the generation, first, of the "contraries," "the warm" and "the cold," "the moist" and "the dry," then, by an eternal motion, of the universe of worlds, in the centre of which is the earth, fixed in position and cylindrical in form. From the original

---

[1] Ueberweg's *History of Philosophy* (Morris's translation), Vol. I. pp. 34 and 35.

moisture all things were generated by heat. Animals and men were evolved from fishes. The soul he declared to be aëriform. Anaximander may be called the earliest "evolutionist."

Anaximenes. — Nearly contemporary with Anaximander was another Milesian, named Anaximenes (588–524 B.C.). He assumed *air* to be the ἀρχή of things, conceiving it as infinite in extent and as animate, having within itself, to employ a modern phrase, "the promise and potency of life." From air, he held, fire, winds, clouds, water, and earth were generated by the processes of "thinning" (fire) and "thickening"—rarefaction and condensation.

Result. — Aristotle, in the first chapter of his account of early Greek philosophy, — the third chapter of the first book of his *Metaphysics*, — affirms that scientific knowledge is the knowledge of causes, which he divides into four classes: the formal cause, or that which constitutes the essence of a thing; the material cause; the efficient cause, or "first principle of motion"; the final cause, or the end. He affirms, and rightly, that the earliest philosophers were occupied with the consideration of the material cause of things, *i.e.*, the material source and constitution of the universe. Because of this they have been called *Hylicists* (ὕλη, *hyle*, = *matter*); and because they held matter to be, not dead, but living, they have received the name of *Hylozoists* (ζωή, = *life*). It should be noted, however, that in the Infinite of Anaximander there is the germ of a principle not merely physical but metaphysical; for the Infinite, as such, cannot be grasped by the imagination or sensuous thought, but must be apprehended by abstract and pure thought, though it is only virtual and negative, not actual and positive, conception. It should be noted, also, that there are in the speculations of Anaximander and Anaximenes the suggestion of processes by which the original worldstuff becomes actual concrete things; though this part of their theories must be regarded as having been of secondary importance in their thoughts. Crude as their speculations must now appear to every one, Thales, Anaximander, and Anaximenes must be looked upon as philosophers, because they sought to determine the universal permanent element in what was for them the universe. They are commonly spoken of as the *Early Ionic Natural Philosophers.*

§ 2.

The Pythagoreans. — The next step in Greek speculation was taken by Pythagoras and his followers, regarding whom and the theories of whom it is difficult to arrive at clear, consistent, unquestionable views.[1]

Pythagoras and the Pythagorean Order. — Pythagora was born on the island of Samos, near the coast o Asia Minor, about the year 580 B.C., dying at Metapon tum in Lower Italy about the year 510 B.C. Possibly he was a pupil of Anaximander, and familiar with his scientific and philosophical views. Possibly, also, he travelled in Egypt, making additions to the store of his scientific knowledge, and receiving a new religious and ethical impulse through contact with the learned priesthood there. He was regarded by Heraclitus, a philoso-

---

[1] See *Zeller's Pre-Socratic Philosophy* (a translation by S. F. Alleyne of a portion of Zeller's *Geschichte der Philosophie der Griechen*), Vol. I. pp. 306-308.

pher of the next century, as very learned, but not very profound. He either founded or contemplated founding an ethico-religious order in his native place. Such an order he did found in Crotona, Lower Italy, whither some of his countrymen had migrated and he himself went in 529 B.C. This order was, it may be conjectured, such an embodiment as was possible to be made by a Grecian on Grecian soil, of the idea of monasticism which Pythagoras, if he visited Egypt, had brought from that country. The discipline of the society was, particularly in the later period of its existence, of the rigid, aristocratic sort, out of harmony, as Hegel remarks, with the democratic spirit of Greece. Habitual silence, implicit obedience to the authority of the master, fidelity to friends, abstinence, self-scrutiny, non-proselytism, were required of all its members. Physical, as well as intellectual, moral, and religious, culture was aimed at. Pythagoras professed to be, not σοφὸς, *wise*, but φιλόσοφος, *lover of wisdom;* and we may regard the society he founded as an organization intended to furnish the conditions for a philosophic life. He was, it appears, a man capable of leading such a life and of inspiring others to do so. He was looked upon as a very Apollo in his appearance, character, and gift of inspiration; and fabulous stories gathered about his name. By his personal dignity and worth, and by his teachings, he was able to show — and was perhaps the first among the Greek philosophers who did show — that wisdom is an affair of character and life as well as of knowledge. The maxims of the so-called "Wise Men" savor of a moral utilitarianism not to be found in the doctrine and practice of Pythagoras and his followers. But the ideal of

Pythagoras was not that of pure asceticism; nor was the society, at least in the earlier part of its existence, narrowly monastic: the earlier Pythagoreans were, says Grote, men of "practical efficiency of body and mind." The society became large, and strong, not merely by its influence upon the lives of its members, but also by its influence in the political affairs of Lower Italy. It was the prototype of many societies in other cities in Lower Italy. It existed for more than a century; having been finally broken up by the opposition it aroused in the democratic element of the population because of its too decided espousal of the principles of the aristocratic party.

The Pythagorean Philosophy. — We come now to the Pythagorean philosophy, the speculations, that is to say, of Pythagoras and his followers. It has been found impossible to distinguish those of Pythagoras from those of his followers.

The Number-Theory and the Doctrine of "Contraries." — According to Aristotle,[1] the Pythagoreans, having especially cultivated the mathematical sciences, fancied that they discovered the patterns, or archetypes, of things, not in any sensible thing, as fire, earth, or water, but in number, and asserted that the principles of number were the principles of being, and that the "whole heaven was a harmony and number." They did not distinguish between the affirmation that the principles or laws of number are the principles or laws of things, and the affirmation that numbers themselves are things or the substances of things; between number as a "formal cause," and number as a "material cause,"

[1] *Metaphysics*, Bk. I., ch. 5.

of all things. Now number is odd or even, *one* being both odd and even. The odd is finite; the even infinite. The number *ten* was held to be perfect. Some of the Pythagoreans, Aristotle states, asserted that the first principles were ten in number — ten pairs of " contraries " : the finite and infinite, the odd and the even, unity and plurality, right and left, male and female, rest and motion, straight and crooked, light and darkness, good and bad, square and oblong. There seems at first to be no direct connection between this crude table of "categories" and the number-theory. The uniting link between them may, however, be the thought that the truth is the union of a contrariety of elements, *i.e.*, a harmony. Such seem to be the main features of the Pythagorean theory in its earlier form.

Theories not purely Pythagorean. — Other theories have been, though to some extent wrongly,[1] attributed to the Pythagoreans. In one of these the number *one* represents the Deity, and, again, the principle of unity or continuity in things, *two* represents the principle of variety or difference, *three* the union of the two, *four* (as the square of *two*) the "perfection" of mere difference, and *ten*, "the perfect number" (the sum of *one*, *two*, *three*, and *four*), the complete organic unity and harmony of the world. Again: " The author of a work ascribed to Philolaus [a Pythagorean of the fifth century B.C.] sees in the principles of number the principles of things. These principles are 'the limiting' and 'illimitation.' They converge to harmony, which is unity in multiplicity and agreement in heterogeneity. Thus they generate in succession, first, unity, then the series

[1] *Zeller's Pre-Socratic Phil.*, Vol. I. pp. 386 and fol.

of arithmetical or monadic numbers, then 'geometrical' numbers or 'magnitudes,' *i.e.*, the forms of space: point, line, surface, solid; next material objects, then life, sensuous consciousness, and the higher psychical forces, as love, friendship, mind, and intelligence. Like is known by like, but it is by number that things are brought into harmonious relations to the soul. The understanding, developed by mathematical study, is the organ of knowledge. Musical harmony depends on a certain numerical proportion in the lengths of musical strings. The octave, in particular, or harmony in the narrow sense, depends on the ratio 1:2, which includes the two ratios of the fourth (3:4) and the fifth (2:3 or 4:6). [This fact was discovered by Pythagoras himself.] The five regular solids — the cube, the tetrahedron, the octahedron, icosahedron, the dodecahedron — are respectively the fundamental forms of earth, fire, air, water, and the fifth element, which encompasses all the rest. The soul is united by number and harmony with the body, which is its organ, and at the same time its prison. From the Hestia, *i.e.*, from the central fire around which the earth and counter-earth[1] daily revolve, the soul of the world spreads through the spheres of the counter-earth, the earth, the moon, the sun, the planets Mercury, Venus, Mars, Jupiter, Saturn, and the fixed stars to 'Olympus,' the last sphere, which includes all the others. The world is eternal and

---

[1] Supposed to be under the earth and moving around the central fire with it. *Ten* being the perfect number, there must, it was thought, be ten bodies "borne through the heaven." There being, says Aristotle, only nine apparent, the Pythagoreans assumed a tenth, calling it *Counter-Earth* (ἀντίχθων).

ruled by the One, who is akin to it, and has supreme might and excellence. The director and ruler of all things is God; he is one and eternal, enduring and immovable, ever like himself and different from all things beside him. He compasses and guards the universe."[1]

Miscellaneous Theories. — Certain other discoveries and theories of Pythagoras and the Pythagoreans may be here mentioned for interest's sake; some of them bear relation to the number-theory, others do not. Pythagoras is said to have discovered two important truths in geometry: one relating to the triangle inscribed within a semicircle, and another to the square of the hypothenuse of a right-angled triangle. The discovery of the latter is said to have elated him so much that he sacrificed a hundred oxen and made a great feast. Some of the Pythagoreans, if not Pythagoras himself, fancied that the supposed celestial spheres were arranged at intervals corresponding mathematically to the intervals of the octave. Some of the Pythagoreans believed that the earth rotated upon an axis. Pythagoras held the doctrine of the transmigration of souls, — believed that his own soul had inhabited the body of Euphorbus, a Trojan hero. The noblest education for a youth he thought to be that which would fit him to be the citizen of a well-regulated state.

Result. — From the foregoing it appears that though the Pythagorean order was primarily religious and ethical, the Pythagorean philosophy was cosmical, a philosophy not of conduct and of God but of the sensible universe; it appears, also, that, as Aristotle pointed out, the first principle, the ἀρχή, of the Pythagorean theory

[1] Ueberweg's *Hist. of Phil.* (trans.) Vol. I. p. 49.

is not "material" but "formal" or primarily so. The subject of the Pythagorean speculation was, that is to say, not the original world-stuff or material source of things but the order stamped upon phenomena. These speculations must be regarded as a step in advance of those of the Hylicists. The Pythagorean theories, we shall hereafter see, largely influenced subsequent speculation, particularly that of Plato and the Platonists.

§ 3.

The Eleatics. — Nearly contemporaneous with the Pythagoreans was a school of thinkers known in the history of philosophy as the Eleatics, being so named from the city of Elea in Lower Italy, where they taught. The leaders of this school were *Xenophanes, Parmenides, Zeno,* and *Melissus.*

Life of Xenophanes. — Xenophanes, who was born about the year 570 B.C., was a native of Colophon a town near the coast of Asia Minor, and not far from Miletus and Samos, the birth-places of Thales and his followers, and of Pythagoras. He was an elegiac and gnomic poet, a wandering rhapsodist, in whom the mystery of nature awakened a profound religious and speculative impulse. He was, it seems, very decidedly at variance with popular religious and ethical views, and, like many another intellectual radical, was obliged to suffer on account of his convictions, becoming a fugitive or an exile (it is uncertain which of the two) because of them. He settled at Elea, there founding the Eleatic school, distinguished and influential, as we shall have abundant occasion to note, in the history of Greek thought. He wrote a didactic poem, *On Nature.*

Philosophy of Xenophanes. — Xenophanes took his start apparently from the Infinite of Anaximander. Instead, however, of attempting to supplement and perfect this conception by uniting it with its opposite, the Finite, as did the Pythagoreans, he lifted it above all opposition and held (more or less unconsciously perhaps) the real infinite to be not existent in or for anything other than itself, either as source of being or as ground of harmony, but existent simply in and for itself. He affirmed, says Aristotle, that the universe is one, and "looking wistfully at the whole heaven he declared that the One is God." In other words, he held that "the Many," multiplicity, is, as such, non-existent, and that all things are parts or forms or aspects of the One. The One, he held, is beyond human comprehension, and yet he called it God, saying, "God is all ear, all eye, all intellect; without effort he sways all things by the force of his thought." He combated the popular anthropomorphic dogmas concerning the gods by such arguments as the following: If oxen and lions had the requisite skill, they would picture their gods as animals, like themselves. He condemned Homer and Hesiod for representing the gods as doing those things which men would be treated as criminals for doing — as lying, stealing, committing adultery. Although Xenophanes did not, so far as we know, explicitly affirm the One to be either material or spiritual — the explicit and clear distinction, familiar to us, between the material and spiritual was probably of later origin in the history of thought — he held it to be essentially what we call spiritual. Without mentally separating mind and matter he declared reality to be *one* (the Many being phenomenal). The One as one is not a subject of generation or decay, of multiplicity or change: it is eternal, infinite, imperishable. Regarding the Many, *i.e.*, the gods and the multitude of visible phenomena, Xenophanes seems to affirm that man's knowledge is mere opinion. Speaking hypothetically, he said that all things have as their elements earth and water; the earth extends indefinitely in space below us, the air indefinitely above; the stars are fiery clouds.

Result. — Compared with the speculations of earlier philosophers those of Xenophanes present two new features: first, they are not materialistic nor mathematico-idealistic but theistic, — Xenophanes, though a nature-philosopher, was a theological and rationalistic nature-philosopher; secondly, they contain an element of scepticism, — the mental attitude of Xenophanes towards phenomena, or the universe as immediately known to us, is negative.

Life of Parmenides. — Of the life of Parmenides, the greatest of the Eleatics, who was born in the latter part of the sixth century B.C., very little is known. He was a man of striking appearance and impressive personality. Plato[1] represents Socrates as having in his youth met Parmenides and as remembering him in later life as quite an old man, "with grey hair and a handsome and noble countenance." The Pythagorean views of culture were familiar to him and were in part adopted and practised by him, through the influence, it would appear, of intimate friends of his who were Pythagoreans. Like the Pythagoreans, he engaged actively in public affairs; and is said to have drafted for his native city, Elea, a

[1] *Parmenides*, p. 127.

code of laws to which the citizens, annually, for a considerable period of years, swore fidelity. He was, in all probability, a pupil of Xenophanes ; it is certain that he adopted the latter's views and developed them, in writing and in public lectures and discussions. He wrote a philosophical poem, entitled *On Nature*, and having three parts : the first, which is merely introductory to the second and third, being an allegory representing the poet as being transported to the realm of the "goddess who knoweth all things " ; the second, a logical exposition of the conception of Being, entitled *On Truth;* the third, a mythological representation of the generation of the world of sense, entitled *On Opinion.*[1]

Philosophy of Parmenides. — Parmenides begins the exposition of his theory by opposing to Opinion, as the mental correlate of Phenomena, Conviction, as the mental correlate of Being, — Conviction, upon whose "footsteps Truth closely follows." The One, which he denominates Being, is known by thought or reason. Thinking and Being are thus one (the One) and in such a way that it matters not with which you begin in thought, — you must always arrive at the same result, since all things are one. But Being is only of what *is:* there is *no* not-Being. Not-Being cannot even be conceived, for the very conception of it converts it into Being. The idea of not-Being (nothing) is a spurious conception, a mere fancy. Being, and Being only, *is:* it is

Whole and only begotten, and moveless and ever-enduring:
Never it was or shall be ; but the All simultaneously now is
One continuous one."[2]

[1] See the *Journal of Speculative Philosophy*, Vol. IV. No. 1. (1870); also W. L. Courtney's *Studies in Philosophy.*
[2] *Jour. Spec. Phil.*, Vol. IV., etc.; Courtney's *Studies*, etc.

It cannot have been generated, for, if so, it must have sprung from not-Being; but there could have been in not-Being (pure nothing) no power or necessity to cause its production. Being must be wholly or wholly must not be.[1] Nor does anything absolutely other than itself spring from Being; for that so-called other must itself *be*, and so be identical with Being.

"Nor is there ought of distinct; for the all is self-similar alway;
Wherefore the all is unbroken, and Being approacheth to Being."

Such being the case, we return to our starting-point —

"One and the same are thought, and that whereby there is thinking.
Never apart from existence wherein it receiveth expression
Shalt thou discover the action of thinking, for naught is or shall be
Other besides or beyond the existent."

Being is, therefore, self-determined. It is, moreover, not infinite, or indefinite, as Anaximander and Xenophanes had held: an inner necessity renders it self-contained and definitely thinkable. It is the knowing and the known One; self-caused and self-thought. It may be compared to a sphere, — it is perfect in its homogeneity and continuity and in the regularity and definiteness of its limit. Of the phenomenal universe, our knowledge of which is mere "opinion," the account given by Parmenides is that it was created by the "goddess that governeth all things," by the mixture of two entirely contrary elements, one of which is like light and fire, and the other is dark, dense, and cold. The first-created of the gods was Love. The mind of the individual man

---

[1] This seems to be the first enunciation in the history of Greek Philosophy of the so-called Law of Excluded Middle.

is such an organic entity as the body, with its members, is; and the character of the human individual's thought depends upon which of the two elements predominates in his bodily constitution — mind that is to say, is a function of body.

Result. — Comparing the philosophy of Parmenides with that of Xenophanes, we observe, first, that the thought theologically and poetically enunciated by the latter was, by the former, abstractly and logically propounded and developed. Instead of the term *God*, employed by Xenophanes, Parmenides employs the term *Being;* he does not dogmatically assert but reasons; he affirms the existence of, and employs, a *method* of knowledge. We observe, secondly, that although Parmenides acknowledges no absolute not-Being, he draws sharply a distinction not so drawn by Xenophanes, between reality and phenomena, Being and relative not-Being; between what is given by "reason," the organ of truth and conviction, and what is given in "opinion." By virtue of the fact that he was the first among the Greek thinkers to state and logically deduce the notion of absolute being, he is the first purely *philosophical thinker* among the Greeks; by virtue of the fact that he was the first to point out and demonstrate the unity of Thought and Being, he is the father of idealism. His statement of idealism is, however, we must note, incomplete, because Thought, though recognized by him as an essential moment of Being, is not distinctly recognized as the (for us, and, in fact, absolute) *prius* of Being.

Life of Zeno. — In some respects the most remarkable of the Eleatics is Zeno. His birth may be placed at about the year 500 B.C. Plato represents him [1] as a fine-appearing man of forty when Socrates saw him with Parmenides, who was about twenty-five years his senior. He was a favorite pupil and, perhaps, the adopted son of Parmenides. Though a devotee of speculative science, he held not aloof from public affairs; was, indeed, a most enthusiastic patriot and a bitter hater of tyranny. There is a story that, when tried for conspiring with others against the tyrant of his native city, Elea, he showed his hatred and disdain of the tyrant by biting off his tongue and spitting it in his face. The brilliancy of his intellect, the genuineness of his moral fibre plainly, even now, mark him as one of the select spirits of Grecian antiquity.[2]

Philosophy of Zeno. — Zeno's main thesis is, in substance, Not-Being is not; hence only Being is. Now as Being is one and unchanging, not-Being must be conceived as the many and changing. But the notion of the many is self-contradictory, and, therefore, false. The One, only, *is*, the Many are not, *i.e.*, multiplicity and change are unreal, phenomenal. Against the notions multiplicity and change he advanced eight arguments, — four against the former, four against the latter.[3] The substance of one of the arguments against mult'plicity is as follows: If Being were absolute multiplicity, then it must be both infinitely great and infinitely small; for, first, it must have an infinite number of parts, and,

---

[1] *Parmenides*, p. 127.
[2] See the life of him by Diogenes Laertius (trans. in Bohn's Class. Lib.).
[3] See Mullach's *Fragmenta Philosophorum Graecorum*, Vol. I. pp. 269 and 270; *Zeller's Outlines of the Hist. of Greek Philos.* (trans.), pp. 63 and 64; *Pre-Socratic Philosophers*, Vol. I. pp. 608-627.

secondly, each part must be infinitely small, *i.e.*, without magnitude. Another of the arguments is, in substance, that, if a bushel of grain when shaken out produces a sound when it strikes the floor, each grain and part of a grain must produce a sound, which is not the fact. Against change (of place) one argument is the following: "Motion cannot begin because a body in motion cannot arrive at a new place without passing through an infinite number of intermediate places"—which is impossible. Another argument against motion is, "The flying arrow is at rest; for it is at every moment only in one place." It is always in one place, Zeno argues, because time is perfectly continuous—is not to be conceived as a series of distinct "nows"; but if we suppose movement through distinct spaces or places, we must suppose distinct times. There is, therefore, no motion; the flying arrow is at rest.

Result. — If mere multiplicity is the first principle of the universe, then there is nothing but an infinity of, so to say, particles or points of nothingness; for the principle of multiplicity, taken as absolute, is not satisfied if there be anything that is one and indivisible. But of such points of nothingness, infinite in number though they be, nothing can be constituted; continuity and identity, which are objects of reason, cannot spring from infinite discontinuity and multiplicity. Multiplicity is, therefore, purely phenomenal: not-Being is not. *As such*, *i.e.*, as a "fact," it is not denied by Zeno. Nor are the arguments against motion tantamount to the denial of motion as a fact presented to us by sense: it would have been no "answer" to Zeno to point to a moving object, for he simply denied motion as absolute. If motion were absolute, then (absolute) change in Being would be possible, which is absurd, because, as Parmenides declared, Being is

"Whole and only-begotten, and moveless and ever enduring."

Translated into the language of modern theology or of modern science Zeno's argument would mean "God, only, *is;* He is the same yesterday, to-day, and forever," or "The laws of nature are unalterable." To treat the arguments of Zeno merely as word-puzzles or even as "fallacies," "material" or "formal," is to miss their point. The peculiar method employed by Zeno in the above-cited arguments — that of maintaining a position by the demonstration of the inherent absurdity of its opposite — was termed the dialectic method; and because of his peculiar mastery in it, he was called the inventor of dialectics, though the same method had been employed by Xenophanes (to some extent) and Parmenides. Zeno gave no account of this method.[1] Zeno's position, compared with that of Parmenides, is indicated with sufficient accuracy by the statement that he holds the *re*verse side of the position of which Parmenides holds the *ob*verse, the two being in substance the same, and that he had a fuller consciousness than Parmenides of the significance of method in and for itself. Zeno did not, so far as is now known, put forth a theory, mythological or other, of the visible universe.

Melissus. — Of Melissus, who flourished a little later than Zeno and wrote a treatise in prose entitled *On*

---

[1] This mode of arguing should be carefully discriminated from that of overthrowing a position merely by adducing some fact that does not lie immediately in the given position but which tells against it nevertheless.

Nature, it is sufficient to say that his position was that of Parmenides, qualified by the affirmation that Being is unlimited *in space*. This seems to be a relapse towards the *quasi*-materialism of the Hylicists; but Melissus, while holding this, affirmed the entire oneness of Being. Diogenes Laertius states that Melissus was "greatly occupied in political affairs," was "held in great esteem among his fellow-citizens," and, in consequence, elected admiral by them, and "was admired still more on account of his private virtues."

General Result. — The Eleatic philosophy is twofold in character: it is a theory (though an elementary one) of knowledge as well as of Being. (It is the earliest theory of knowledge.) It is primarily, however, a theory of Being, Thought being treated as, primarily, dependent upon Being, not Being upon Thought, though the two are inseparable. It is, therefore, to be classed among the nature-philosophies, though the term *nature* given in this philosophy what is, practically, a new interpretation, the Eleatic notion of nature verging on that of mind. The Eleatic doctrine of Being is, as has been said, that it is one; of knowledge, that it is a product or function of reason, Thought and Being being organically one. The Eleatic theory is, therefore, ostensibly monistic. Practically, however, it is not quite so. No intelligible account is given by it of phenomena, the relatively non-existent; a fact which, we may here properly surmise, we shall find to have been discovered and pointed out by contemporaneous or succeeding thinkers. And there is, of course, the same dualism in their theory of knowledge as in their account of Being, for they held reason to be trustworthy and sense to be illusory;[1] a view which, also, must have had its consequences among contemporaneous or later thinkers.

§ 4.
Heraclitus.

Life of Heraclitus. — Nearly contemporary with Parmenides was Heraclitus of Ephesus, who flourished not earlier than 500 B.C., nor later than 450 B.C. He belonged to the nobility of the place. He was in temperament aristocratic, melancholy, and meditative; and gave up public office for contemplative retirement, holding the world in contempt. Mostly self-taught and independent in his views, he studied and freely criticised those of others, and was probably the profoundest of the early Greek thinkers. A work of his entitled *On Nature* won for him, by the crudity of its style and, also, we may suspect, by the depth and paradoxical character of its contents, the sobriquet of The Obscure. Diogenes Laertius relates that Socrates, when asked what he thought of a certain work of Heraclitus, replied, "What I have understood is good; and so, I think, what I have not understood is; only the book requires a Delian diver to get at the meaning of it."[2]

Heraclitus's First Principle. — Heraclitus is sometimes treated as a Hylicist and Hylozoist. He did, it is true, assume a physical principle (fire) and affirmed the universal presence of life in matter. The central

---
[1] It is important here to discriminate between a scepticism that denies, or gives up the belief in, the possibility of a knowledge of the real, and a scepticism that consists merely in distrusting the "reports of the senses."

[2] *Lives of the Philosophers* (Bohn's Class. Lib.), p. 65.

point in his speculations, however, was not the universal material source of things, but the universal process of things. Emphasizing the aspect of change in Nature, he held that existence was an absolute process, a continual flux: πάντα χωρεῖ, "all things flow," is his real first principle. Instead of affirming, as did the Eleatics, Only Being is, he affirms or seems to affirm, Only not-Being is; Becoming or not-Being is the object of his thought. But what is Becoming? Is it mere change? Another of his dicta runs, All is and also is not: Becoming, that is to say, is the union of Being and not-Being. Being and not-Being are involved one in the other. Our human bodies, for example, undergo a process of growth and decay: we live and die continually, — live because we die, die because we live. Moreover, what we call the actual death of the body is but the birth of a new life: "Both life and death are in our life and our death"; "While we live our souls are buried in us, but when we die our souls are restored to life." Time — to take another example — cannot be conceived as now existent or now not. In time as in all reality, continuity and discontinuity, Being and not-Being are inseparable. Opposite qualities co-exist in the *real*, not merely in the phenomenal, as the Eleatics declared. "Strife is the father of all things." "Unite the whole and the not-whole, the consentient and the dissentient, the consonant and the dissonant and there arises one from all, all from one." There is a continual conversion of the Many into the One, and *vice versa*. The harmony of the One and the Many, which the Pythagoreans asserted but did not explain, is brought about through the notion of Becoming, — activity, life.

Physical Doctrine of Heraclitus. — Now the omnipresent element or medium in which this process is realized and which is hardly to be distinguished from the process itself is, according to Heraclitus, fire, which in its purest form is spirit. By a process subtler than the "condensation" of Anaximenes, fire is transmuted into air, air into water, water into earth; air, water, and earth being, though "opposites," but stages in the *in*volution of fire. This is called the "downward way." The two "ways" are inseparable or organic members of one process. This process must be conceived, not as a mechanical process, but as a vital organic process, in which opposite forces are held as one. In the vast process by which the visible universe is maintained there is alternately a kindling and an extinguishing of the elemental fire.

The Soul and Reason. — The human soul is but a mode of the universal fire. The dry soul is best; moisture in the soul obscures reason. By respiration and the action of the organs of sense, the soul is nourished with the universal fire. "Souls enter the body from a higher state of existence, and after death, when they have proved themselves worthy of their privilege, they return as dæmons into a purer life."[1] Eyes and ears are bad witnesses to those who have "barbarous souls." The senses deceive by giving the appearance of fixedness to things not fixed. The reason is the real source of knowledge. By reason man ceases to be a dreaming individual and becomes a waking universal. It is by participation in the universal reason, the κοινὸς

---

[1] *Zeller's Pre-Socratic Philos.*, Vol. II. p. 87.

λόγος, that we know and do that which is true and right.

Result. — It is obvious that Heraclitus attained to a riper and richer conception of nature than any of his predecessors had attained to. The Eleatic notion of the One and the Pythagorean notion of the harmony of the One and the Many are realized more perfectly in the Heraclitean doctrine, in which they are subordinate, than in those theories in which they are principal. Heraclitus recognizes no phenomenal world, however shadowy, as separate from, and irreconcilable to, the realm of Being, and the One and the Many are not, in his notion, merely in harmony, they are the *same thing*, by virtue of the power of motion, or life, and reason.[1] And if the material source of things is to be found among the "elements" fire, air, earth, and water, certainly it must be that which is subtlest and capable of the most manifold transformations. There is, even in this latest age of the world, beauty in the Pythagorean conception, a certain loftiness and splendor in the Eleatic ; but there is infinite vigor and pregnancy in the Heraclitic. There does not appear immediately in the after-course of Greek speculation an intellectual midwife — to borrow a Socratic metaphor — skilful enough to bring to the birth its entire significance.

§ 5.

The Later Natural Philosophers. — The speculations of Heraclitus, the Eleatics, and earlier philosophers,

[1] The philosophy of Heraclitus has been called "the philosophy of the logical law of the identity of contradictories."

established, practically, certain fundamental points for the philosophers whose views we have next to consider and who may be called the Later Natural Philosophers or Nature-Philosophers. One point was, that there is no absolute change, no real "generation" or "decay": *ex nihilo nihil fit.* Another point was, that there is a becoming, nature is a process. A third point, which may be regarded as the (imperfect) synthesis of the two, was that the process of nature is a mechanical process. In place of the monism of the earlier theorists, we shall, accordingly, find a more or less distinct dualism, of matter and force, of the material world and reason. Speculation now practically turns upon the inquiries, What causes and maintains the process of nature? What is the character and end of that process? Of these Later Nature-Philosophers, the chief are *Empedocles, Anaxagoras, Leucippus,* and *Democritus.*

Life of Empedocles. — Empedocles was a native of Agrigentum in Sicily, and lived *circa* 495-535 B.C. He took the active interest usually taken by the early Greek philosophers in political affairs, and was a leader of the democratic party in his native city. He was not only a statesman and a philosopher, but an orator, a poet, a physician, a prophet, and a thaumaturgist. His character and personal influence are said to have been similar to those of Pythagoras.

Theory of Nature. — Holding fast to the Eleatic idea that generation and decay are impossible, he yet holds, in a certain way, to the notion of Becoming; and attempts to account for changing nature by the hypothesis of a continued process of combination and separation of certain (supposed) original, imperishable, unchangeable, purely material elements or "roots," — fire, air, water, earth. Fire, air, and water, it has been seen, had been separately posited as " principles" by earlier philosophers. Empedocles was the first who assumed these four as the primal elements. Now the question arises — and this is the first appearance of such a question in the history of Greek philosophy — What is the cause of the combination and separation of the elements? The elements we have just seen are purely material; the combining and separating forces are Love and Hate, — the ancient mythological analogues of the modern scientific "attraction" and "repulsion." By Love the elements are bound indistinguishably together in one all-embracing sphere; Hate penetrating from the outside to the centre drives the elements asunder, thus giving rise to the world of individual existences. In the eternal process of nature, Love and Hate alternately rule. Variety in the world of individual existences arises, of course, from variety in the combination of elements: flesh and blood, for example, are composed of the four elements united in equal proportions, whereas bones are one-half fire, one-fourth earth, and one-fourth water. Animals are formed by the combination by Love of parts that existed separately, having sprung out of the earth. The monstrosities that were the result of the earliest combinations, such as bodies of men united to horses' heads, bodies of oxen with human heads, etc., gradually gave way to higher forms, until eventually the present mode of generation was established. Empedocles, it thus appears, was, like Anaximander, an "evolutionist."

Theory of Knowledge. — Even knowledge is explained

by Empedocles as the result of mixture. Sense-perception is the effect of an efflux of particles from external bodies entering pores corresponding in size to them, in the body of the percipient. In the case of sight there is a double efflux, — an efflux from the eye as well as from the body perceived, sight being a consequence of the intermingling of effluences.[1] The efflux *from* the eye is an efflux of particles of water and fire. The elements in things are known through like elements in us, — earth through earth, water through water, etc. Thought also depends, for its character, on the character of the mixture of elements. Quickness and acuteness of perception and thought result from mixtures different from those from which their opposites result. The psychological organ of truth is not perception but reflection.

Result. — The sources and essential character of the theory of Empedocles are apparent. Conceptions borrowed from, or suggested by, the Eleatics, Heraclitus, and earlier speculators, are combined to produce what is almost a purely mechanical explanation of natural phenomena. The system is mechanical because of the want of organic conception or affinity between the posited original elements and powers of nature. But for the anthropomorphic elements, Love and Hate, the system would be entirely mechanical. We may reasonably expect to encounter in the history of early Greek speculation a system from which such anthropomorphic elements are entirely absent.[2]

---

[1] In modern "psychological" phraseology this would mean that sight is both "objective" and "subjective."

[2] See p. 32 *infra.*

Life of Anaxagoras. — Anaxagoras was a native of Clazomenæ in Asia Minor. Though born somewhat earlier than Empedocles he flourished a little later. Giving up wealth and social position for philosophy, he went in early manhood to Athens, and remained there, as thinker and teacher, till near the close of his life, a period of about fifty years. His sojourn at Athens was the beginning of that magnificent course, hereafter to be delineated, which philosophy ran there in the most capacious intellects of antiquity. Parmenides and Zeno may have visited Athens, but Anaxagoras was the first philosopher who made that city of culture and individuality his home and the chief outward abode of philosophy. His presence in Athens during the period of her greatest glory under the statesmanship of his personal friend (and disciple), Pericles, was, no doubt, opportune for philosophy, and particularly for a system that placed in the forefront of the universe νοῦς, or intelligence. Among the pupils of Anaxagoras there were — besides Pericles — Euripides and Socrates. Because of the unpopularity of his doctrine — he was accused of atheism — and his connection with Pericles, he was obliged, when the latter fell temporarily into disfavor with the Athenian populace, to pay a fine and leave Athens. He died at Lampsacus on the Hellespont, 428 B.C., at the age of seventy-two. He wrote a work entitled *On Nature.*

Theory of Nature. — To account for the order and beauty of the world Anaxagoras assumes two principles, one material, the other spiritual or *quasi*-spiritual. The material principle is an infinite medley, a chaos, of an infinite number of qualitatively different elements, which he terms σπέρματα, or the "seeds" of things. The elements, however, must, though different, be conceived as organically the same; *i.e.*, each element must have in it, potentially, all others, for we cannot conceive the union of things *absolutely* different. The spiritual, or *quasi*-spiritual, principle is just the opposite in nature to the material — perfectly "unmixed" and "pure," the "finest and purest of all things," an independent, intelligent power, since we cannot conceive order and beauty as the offspring of mere necessity or chance. Out of the original mixture, or chaos, the world was formed by a rotatory motion produced by the action of the original mind, a movement which, beginning at a single point and gradually extending, caused a universal separation of unlike, and union of like, seeds, the dense and moist moving to the centre, the rare and warm to the circumference of the world. This process of differentiation goes on forever, becoming ever more refined. Differences in bodies result from differences in the character of the seeds that predominate in their constitution. From the hypothesis that certain substances, *e.g.*, gold, blood, bones, were formed only of seeds like themselves, the name *homœomeriæ* (ὁμοιομέρειαι = *like parts*) was applied by later writers (not by Anaxagoras) to the original elements, or "seeds" of things. The earth he conceived to be a cylinder resting on the air, in the centre of the universe. The sun is not a blessed god, as the multitude believe, but an immense glowing mass of stone — as large as the Peloponnesus, — one of the doctrines, probably, that gave ground for the charge of atheism that was brought against him. The moon is like the earth and is inhabited. Plants and animals spring from germs communicated to moist or slimy earth by the air and the æther; they have souls, and feel pleasure and pain.

Theory of Mind or Nous (νοῦς) *and of Knowledge.* — The world-mind has been described as a nature that is perfectly "pure" and "unmixed," "the finest and purest of all things," and independent of the material universe. All derivative minds are essentially the same with it, and with one another, differing from it and from one another only in degree. Sense-perception, which is dependent upon the structure of the bodily organs, is not of "like by like," as Empedocles asserted, but of "like by unlike," as of heat by cold: that which is equally warm with ourselves makes no impression upon us. The senses do not afford real knowledge; that comes through reason. Man's highest satisfaction lies in the pursuit of wisdom.

Result. — The mechanicalness that is so conspicuous in the theory of Empedocles is less conspicuous here; for there is, in the very essence of the "principles" of the system — the "seeds," which, though different, are potentially the same and virtually synthesizable, and the world-ordering mind, — the beginning of an organic conception of the universe. For if chaos be a mass of potentially organizable, though not actually organized or articulated elements, it just verges upon mind, which is the actually determining, organizing element in the universe. The system of Anaxagoras is mechanical, therefore, in part because it offers no statement of this connection between matter and mind. For another reason, also, it fails of being organic and completely rational, viz., Anaxagoras's conception of mind was, though fundamentally correct, but rudimentary. A developed conception of mind belongs, in fact, to a later period in the history of thought. Plato and Aristotle, the latter of whom, comparing him with other nature-philosophers, likened him to a sober man coming in among the drunken, properly enough found fault with the theory of Anaxagoras, because in it mind was treated as a mere mover of matter. Anaxagoras, as Plato points out in his dialogue *Phædo* (pp. 97-99), just missed grasping fairly the idea of the final cause, or of end-determined causation, in nature.

Leucippus and Democritus, the Atomists; their Lives. — Of Leucippus's life nothing is known. He was the originator of the essentials of the theory expounded in the writings of Democritus, who was a pupil of his. Democritus was born in Abdera in Thrace about the year 460 B.C. Possessed of great wealth, he was able to gratify to the fullest extent his passion for knowledge, which impelled him to travel very extensively in Egypt and the East, and, upon his return home, to devote himself to philosophical research. He was the most learned of the early Greek philosophers, an encyclopædist, worthy of the admiration freely bestowed upon him by the still greater master of knowledges, Aristotle. His numerous works, of which only fragments have been preserved, were written in prose instead of didactic verse, such as most of his predecessors had employed. They were greatly admired among the ancients for their style as well as their doctrine. Democritus lived about a century.

Theory of Nature. — Μὴ μᾶλλον τὸ δὲν ἢ τὶ μὴ δὲν εἶναι: "No more is Thing [Being] than no-Thing [not-

Being]," says Democritus, recognizing the respective claims of the Eleatics and Heraclitus. This implies that Democritus accepted, and attempted to explain, change as a fact. To do the latter, he conceived Being to consist of innumerable eternal, infinitesimal, movable, material elements, which he termed ἄτομα (indivisibles), *i.e.*, atoms. With Being thus constituted (termed the "full," "plenum") is coeval not-Being, empty space (the "void"). Thing and no-Thing, the "full" and the "void" constitute absolute reality: all else is phenomenal. Unlike the four elements of Empedocles and the "seeds" of Anaxagoras, they are not qualitatively, but only quantitatively, different, — different as regards figure, size, weight, order, and position. The world of individual existences is produced by the eternal falling (!) and collision of the atoms, due to an inherent necessity. By a rotatory motion thus generated the heavenly bodies were produced. The qualitative as well as quantitative properties of things depend merely upon the figure, size, weight, arrangement, position, and number of the atoms constituting them. Though atoms are imperishable, the bodies composed of them are not.

Theory of the Soul, of Knowledge, and of the Good. — Soul, or spirit, in the external world and in man, is composed of fine, round, smooth, fiery atoms. The exhalation and inhalation of these is the source of life in the human body. In the brain the motion of such atoms produces thought, in the heart anger, in the liver desire. Sense-perceptions are the effects of impressions made upon the organs of sense by particles of air set in motion by effluences from objects. The sensation of sight, however, is a resultant of the meeting of emanations from the eye with incoming impulses. Dreams are effects of enfeebled and distorted images (εἴδωλα) that have found their way from objects and persons to our minds. The character and degree of trustworthiness of sense-perceptions depend upon the character of external impressions. Sense gives conflicting reports and is deceptive. Thought, which is a result of a symmetrical motion of atoms, is alone the source of knowledge. The true method in knowledge is to proceed from the known to the unknown. Ethically considered, man's real being lies in nobility of soul: his real good is happiness, which is not sensuous enjoyment but peace and contentment springing from measure and moderation in living. The highest happiness is the pleasure of knowledge. The seat of morality is not in the act performed but in the will. Democracy is the best form of government. The wise and good are citizens of the whole world. The popular gods are beings in the air similar to man but far higher in degree. The truly divine element in the world is the fiery atom or totality of fiery atoms.[1]

Result. — The theory of the Atomists is doubtless the most perfect of the merely mechanical, non-anthropomorphic,[2] theories of nature of the early Greek philosophers: it has a simplicity and an inner consistency not possessed by any other. The conceptions of quantity and natural necessity, which are the ruling conceptions of the theory, are harmonious and easily grasped, and seem all-sufficient, until problems of soul and life are confronted, when it becomes necessary to recognize

---

[1] See *Zeller's Pre-Socratic Philosophy*, Vol. II. pp. 207–321.
[2] See *supra*, p. 26.

mind as an absolute. The Atomists are unable to derive, theoretically, knowledge and feeling from the nature and motion of atoms, and the conception of natural necessity is poor in content compared with that of mind. This being the case, while in one direction the Atomistic philosophy is the most highly developed of all the early nature-philosophies, the philosophy of Anaxagoras is, on the whole, nearer the truth: the philosophy of nature is naturally and necessarily linked with that of mind. It should be noted before leaving Democritus that he entered more largely than did any of his predecessors into anthropological and ethical questions, topics belonging to the philosophy of man as distinct from merely physical nature. In this respect he has greater affinity with the philosophers of the next period than any of the very early Greek philosophers.

§ 6.

General Character of the First Period in the History of Greek Philosophy. — We have now, as will presently appear, finished the first great epoch in the history of Greek philosophy. Before going further we must briefly sum up its characteristics. As to subject-matter, thought has in this epoch been occupied chiefly with external nature, — man and the supernatural receiving but little consideration. As to its method, it has been speculative, hypothetical, and deductive rather than observational, inductive, "scientific," — *rather than* because, in any case, something must be "given" or assumed at the start, and where this is true, there is room for *rough* induction at least. The greatest achievement in method is, doubtless the "dialectic" of the Eleatics and the Heraclitic "unity of opposites," which are "possessions for all time." Of these we shall hear again, farther on. Finally, as to the general attitude of thought in this epoch, there has been a change from simple unsophisticated confidence in the power of the mind to know nature to a kind of scepticism, — scepticism, indeed, not with reference to the scope of reflection but with reference to sense-perception. This scepticism reached its highest degree in the Atomists, with whom even the power of thought reached the minimum, *i.e.*, the power to know just the "void," "atoms," and the motion of atoms. This seems to be the natural consequence of regarding reality as external to mind, and, viewed as such, may be considered one of the best lessons to be gathered from the study of very early Greek speculation. A higher thought, the obverse of this, is virtually contained in the theory of Anaxagoras, the reality and unity of all things in mind.

II. RATIONALISM.

§ 7.

The Sophists. — There arose in Greece in the fifth century B.C. a class of persons to whom, on account of their peculiar pretensions to wisdom, was especially applied (and generally with opprobrium) the term "Sophist," this term having been previously applied to any who were preëminent among men in the knowledge of human affairs. For certain reasons, somewhat peculiar (as we shall see), these men must be included among philosophers. The leading Sophists were *Protagoras of Abdera, Gorgias of Leontini, Hippias of Elis,* and *Prodicus of Ceos.* Others among the most eminent Sophists are those named *Polus, Thrasymachus,* and *Euthydemus.*

Life of Protagoras. — Protagoras of Abdera in Thrace (*circa* 490–415 B.C.) was first in Athens about the middle of the fifth century B.C. He was the first of the Sophists to take a fee for instruction given by him, — a practice that was condemned by Socrates and Plato. Protagoras, however, as it would appear, charged only a moderate fee and deserved not the contempt with which the money-getting Sophists after him were richly rewarded. He was a man of learning, character, and intelligence — whom even Plato did not always sneer at — and was much sought after. He had the "courage of his convictions" and held and taught doctrines, religious and political, which caused him to be condemned as an atheist, and his works (one of which was on Truth) to be publicly burned. He is said to have prepared laws for one of the Athenian colonies. He was an embryo etymologist and a rhetorician ; he affirmed, however, that rhetorical art consists in "making the worse appear the better reason."

Theory of Protagoras. — " The measure of all things," says Protagoras, " is man " : " of things that are, that they are ; of things that are not, that they are not." To this dictum, which is in itself equivocal and may mean that the human mind is adequate to the attainment of absolute objective truth or that what is true to one individual is true for him only, Protagoras gave the latter meaning, and thus human knowledge was reduced by him to a "knowledge" of subjective appearances. This doctrine, it will be perceived, is simply the Heraclitean doctrine (superficially interpreted) of the eternal flux of things in general transferred from nature to man. Strictly applied, it would signify not only that no two persons think or perceive the same thing, but that no person thinks or feels twice alike; it would mean also that there is and can be no real fixed object of knowledge. Contradictory opinions are equally true; right and wrong are merely matters of subjective opinion; the state is a compact based on force. The existence of the gods is uncertain,— the subject being too difficult and life being too short to admit of our learning anything certain about the matter.[1]

Life of Gorgias. — Gorgias of Leontini in Sicily (*circa* 480-395 B.C.) began teaching in Athens about the year 427 B.C., and acquired as a teacher of rhetoric "greater celebrity than any man of his time." His reputation as a rhetorician — he was an orator as well as a teacher of rhetoric — seems to have overshadowed his character as an acute thinker.

Theory of Gorgias. — In a work entitled *On Nature or the Non-Existent* Gorgias denied objective reality. He argued :— Nothing is ; if anything were, it would be unknowable ; and if knowable, not explicable in words. One branch of his argument to prove that nothing is is substantially as follows :— If anything were, it must be derivative or eternal. It cannot be derivative, for, as

---

[1] The doctrine of the "relativity of knowledge," it is thus to be seen, is quite ancient. Plato's criticism of it, which will be cited later on, is as good now as it was when first made.

the Eleatics maintained, there is no becoming. It cannot be eternal, for it would then be infinite; but the infinite is nowhere, for it can neither be in itself nor in any other, and what is nowhere is not. To prove that if anything were it would be unknowable, Gorgias argues that thought and being are incommensurable, since if they be not, whatever is thought must *be*, as, for example, a contest with chariots, on the sea. Finally, knowledge, even if possible, could not be communicated because the sign of an idea and the idea itself have no natural necessary connection.[1]

Result. — The method of Gorgias is the dialectic of Zeno, and his sceptical conclusions seem to flow from the fact that he treats conceptions that are valid only in relation to certain others that are correlative with them, as if they were themselves absolute, and excluded those others, *e.g.*, the conceptions of being and not-being, one and many, thought and being, infinite and finite, word and idea. *One* has no meaning absolutely out of relation to *many;* we cannot assume that only the *one* is. The same holds true of being and not-being, infinite and finite, word and idea. The argumentation of Gorgias points, by the absurdity of its result, to the conclusion that what is is a union of opposites, and we are, just on this account, indebted to him; holding to the principle of identity (not of opposites but of each thing in and by itself) he forces us to acknowledge the dualistic character of consciousness. Gorgias, however, seems to have had no higher than a purely sceptical aim in so doing. The real lesson of his argumentation is that the

[1] See *Zeller's Pre-Socratic Philosophy*, Vol. II. pp. 452–455.

truth is not simple and abstract but complex and concrete.

Hippias and Prodicus. — Hippias of Elis and Prodicus of Ceos were younger contemporaries of Protagoras and Gorgias. Because of the extent and variety of his learning, Hippias was styled "the polymathist." He declared that law is a tyrant compelling men to do many things contrary to nature, a saying that reflects a tendency then existing in Athens towards social and political disintegration. Prodicus was a moralist, and seems to have been considered by Socrates as a sage adviser of youth, but no dialectician, or scientific thinker. In the Second Book of Xenophon's *Memorabilia* there is to be found an allegory that Socrates is represented as borrowing from the "Wise Prodicus." In this the hero Hercules is pictured as exposed to the respective charms of two female personages of opposite character, — Pleasure and Virtue. The allegory was greatly admired among the ancients. Prodicus is said to have investigated the subject of synonyms.

The Sophists as a Class; Result. — Strictly speaking, the Sophists should, perhaps, be regarded as philosophers only in a negative way : for they were interested primarily not in universal science but in individualistic culture ; they were moulders of men rather than investigators and expounders of ideas. They were shrewd enough to see, however, that the pretension to the possession of wisdom which the professional educator necessarily puts forward must be supported by at least a modicum of philosophy as such. Very much of the real thing would doubtless have hindered, instead of promoting, the realization of their main purpose, which seems to have been to fashion what Plato calls the "narrow, keen, little legal mind."[1] Their principal business was the fitting of ambitious youths for political careers in a democracy. The young Athenian who must distinguish himself before a body of dicasts, or judges, was supposed to need all possible skill in rhetoric and dialectic, and the appearance of being wise on all subjects, particularly those relating directly to social and political matters; the young Athenian required, and the Sophist prepared himself to teach, not the philosophy of the schools, which he considered merely as a juvenile discipline, but a "practical" philosophy. But the Sophist, though not a genuine philosopher, did something to prepare the way for philosophy. He was, as Grote says, the "professor" or public teacher; by him "higher education" was offered to Grecian youth; to him the young man who in the schools had been trained in gymnastics, had gotten the cream of the poets and moralists, had learned to recite fittingly from their works and to take part in dramatic choruses, went for instruction in "philosophy," including mathematics, astronomy, dialectics, oratory, and criticism. And the Sophist not only gave instruction; he stimulated his pupils, if not to profound inquiry, at least to the practice of analysis and criticism before which merely superficial traditional views and customs were not always strong enough to stand, — in other words to something like free and independent, if not sober, thinking. In saying this, we do not forget that the practices of the later Sophists were not above mere

[1] *Theætetus*, p. 175 (Jowett's trans.).

verbal trifling and charlatanry.[1] The philosophical findings of the Sophists, though slender from a positive point of view, were yet, in certain respects, marked and important. They were certainly peculiar. If we compare them as regards subject of speculation, method, or point of view with those we have already considered, we shall discover what proves to be the beginning of a new epoch in the history of Greek speculation. Not Nature but Man is the principal theme of the Sophists; they profess and practise everywhere a certain method (the dialectical or *quasi*-dialectical); and their mental attitude, instead of being that of confidence or scientific circumspectness, is, wholly and on principle, sceptical, as is well illustrated even in the very title of Gorgias's work, *On Nature, or the Non-Existent.* And it will appear as we proceed that their successors are very largely occupied in developing and transcending their point of view, correcting and further perfecting their method, and investigating their theme. In its psychological aspect the philosophy of the Sophists was pure sensationalism; in its ethical, pure individualism, the philosophy of mere "private judgment," "private right." As Hegel puts it, — the Sophists introduced the principle of subjectivity into philosophy.

[1] For the most extended and authoritative accounts of the Sophists see Grote's *Hist. of Greece*, Chap. LXVII.; *The Journal of Sacred and Classical Philology*, Vols. I., II., and III., arts. by E. M. Cope; *Zeller's Pre-Socratic Philosophy*, Vol. II. pp. 462-469.

§ 8.

Socrates.[1]

The Sophists and Socrates. — The philosophical successor of the Sophists, though a contemporary of the earliest and chief ones, is *Socrates*. Like them, he maintained a sceptical attitude towards the physical speculations of the early nature-philosophers, and was driven, in part at least, by the unsatisfactoriness of those speculations, to the almost exclusive contemplation of human nature. But to him "man" in the Protagorean dictum meant man not merely in his individual, but also and primarily in his universal, nature, man the thinker and the natural participator in the life of his fellow-men. For the showy rhetoric and false dialectic of the Sophists he sought to substitute scientific method, adequate to fact and universal truth; and for their doctrine of external pleasure and utility, the idea of inherent justice and happiness. Like the Sophists, he questioned existing beliefs and institutions — theological, ethical, political — but he sought to discover and preserve their universal element, or truth. As to his external methods, neither love of publicity or popular favor, nor ostentation of learning or skill in words, nor any desire to reap pecuniary reward, had any part in them. In a word, he sought the "simple truth": in the spirit of the truth he sought the truth first of all, in its own proper form, universality and accessibility to all intelligence. What Hegel calls the principle of subjectivity was, as introduced and employed by the Sophists, largely an empty

[1] See especially Zeller's *Socrates and the Socratic Schools* (trans. from Zeller's *Die Geschichte der Philos. der Griechen*).

form; Socrates gave to it a definite, full, and enduring content.

Special Sources of Information regarding Socrates.— Socrates wrote no philosophical treatise. What is known of him and his teachings has been learned chiefly from the writings of Xenophon, Plato, and Aristotle. Owing to the discrepancies between the presentations of Xenophon and of Plato, there arises a question as to which of the two affords the better view of Socrates and his philosophizing. Xenophon's superiority, so far as he possesses any, is due to his evident historical intent. It has been urged, however, that he wrote largely as an apologist, that he lacked the speculative insight necessary for the appreciation at its full value of the Socratic philosophizing, and that he has pictured Socrates regarded as a pattern of manhood, rather than Socrates the speculative inquirer. Plato's presentation, on the other hand, though undoubtedly an idealization, is, in the earlier dialogues, sufficiently faithful to external fact, and probably represents, more truly than the Xenophontic, the spirit, method, and tendency, if not the outward doctrines and circumstances, of the Socratic philosophizing: the student who is especially interested in the *continuity* and *development* of Greek philosophy will, no doubt, derive, as regards Socrates, more satisfaction from Plato than from Xenophon, for the simple reason that Plato's mature views were shaped with reference to the whole course of Greek thought preceding him, being or containing, therefore, the development of Socratic as well as other earlier doctrines.

Life of Socrates.— Socrates was born near Athens, about the year 469 B.C., his parents being Sophroniscus, a sculptor, and Phænarete, a midwife. Of his early years nothing is known, save that he must have received the usual education in gymnastics, poetry, and music. He was self-instructed in geometry and astronomy; and doubtless heard the lectures of some of the Sophists, with whom, in all probability, he frequently measured dialectical swords. It is conjectured that with some regular instruction or other assistance from others, he made a special study of the theories of the Pythagoreans, the Eleatics, Heraclitus, and Anaxagoras. If he really did so, he undoubtedly formed original opinions of them, and regarded much in them as problematical and futile. It is sometimes said that he followed for a while his father's occupation, and that a work of his, "representing the Graces attired, was standing at the entrance to the Acropolis" as late as 150 A.D. Not long after he was thirty years of age he entered upon what he regarded as a divine calling, that of a seeker of wisdom and searcher of men. He professed to know only his own ignorance; to be, not a teacher, but an intellectual "midwife." In this vocation he spent most of the remaining forty years of his life; but instead of travelling extensively, as did most of his predecessors in philosophy, and of affecting a learned cosmopolitanism, as did some of the Sophists, he remained continuously at Athens, with the exception of three or four intervals when he was absent on a holiday trip or with the army. His astonishing indifference to hardship while in military service, his bravery, his self-forgetfulness, his sagacity, and, withal, his periods of rapt meditation, are forever memorable. Public office he cared less for than did any philosopher who had lived before him, and accepted it only once, and then not till near the close of his life and only from a sense of duty. Once when in office, and again when merely a private citizen, he defied tyranny by refusing to violate at its bidding the law of the state. Standing aloof from participation in political affairs, he held firmly and, as he declared, patriotically, to his calling; and in the pursuit of this he might be found in the gymnasium, the market-place, the workshop, conversing with boys, men, and women, of all sorts and conditions, putting to them keen questions, and quickening the pulse of moral and intellectual life. He was concerned almost as little about his own family affairs as about affairs of state; and if Xanthippe was really the scolding wife that tradition represents her to have been, she certainly had occasion for so being. Socrates was, in fact, so absorbed in his calling that he neglected to exercise common prudence not only for his family, but for himself. It was food and raiment to him to probe the conceit and foolish ignorance of men, to search their consciences and expand their shrivelled individualities; in short, to awaken them to the life of true self-consciousness. In doing this he made them, now his friends and helpers, now his bitter enemies, but always, — frequently in spite of themselves, — his enlightened pupils. It was no part of his business or purpose to fill the ears of men with a specious wisdom, and to send them away self-complacent and ready to appear wise for a price; it was not primarily his business or purpose to *inform* those with whom he conversed, but to render them thoughtful, critical, and, if need were, even sceptical. He became an object of ridicule and hatred to the lovers of the old ways and times, and was, by the poet Aristophanes, in his comedy of *The Clouds*, satirized as a Sophist and a charlatan of the worst description. At last, certain of the "conservatives," exasperated at seeing themselves and their favorite institutions exposed to the light of truth by Socrates and by others whom he had stimulated to *think*, formally charged him with discarding the national gods, introducing new gods, and corrupting the youths of Athens. His defense was bold and sharply critical, and he was (though by only a small majority) condemned to be, according to law, imprisoned, heavily fined, or banished; and when he refused, somewhat haughtily indeed, to acknowledge any guilt, and claimed, on the contrary, that he ought to be publicly entertained in the Prytaneum, or City Home, as a benefactor to the state, he was by a majority of eighty votes adjudged worthy of death. He went to prison, and, after a delay of thirty days, during which, partly, as it would seem, from pride, but mostly from the spirit and habit of obedience to regularly constituted authority, he scornfully refused a proffered opportunity of escape, he suffered the penalty by drinking hemlock (399 B.C.). The moral sublimity of his last hours appears from Plato's dialogue *Phædo*.

The Personality of Socrates and its Relation to the Subsequent History of Philosophy.— Of the personality of Socrates, which seems to have satisfied Greek notions of completeness and symmetry of character in every item but one, namely, as regards harmony between exterior appearances and interior reality (for Socrates was not handsome in aspect), it is necessary to say only so much here as will direct attention to three aspects of it that appear to bear special relation to his doctrines, to have particularly influenced his contemporaries, presenting to his followers (according to their various capacities) ideals of mental and moral excellence, and exemplifications of various portions of his doctrines, and thus to have determined in large measure the subsequent course of philosphy in its history. It is, probably, to the character quite as much as to the teaching of Socrates that we must look for the source of the explanation of the effects of the Socratic philosophizing, and hence of the influence of Socrates in the history of philosophy. In the first place, then, may be noticed his critical insight and analytic faculty, which enabled him to understand at a glance and expose plainly to view, if need were, the inward condition of those about him. It was the pure genius of inquiry and discovery directed, not to external things, but to the things of the mind and conscience. This appears in almost all the reported conversations of Socrates with his contemporaries; and there is evidence of it in the fact that Socrates made possible, or it may almost be said, discovered two such intellects as Plato and Aristotle, not to mention, individually, at this point, certain acute minds among the so-called *Lesser Socratics*, of whom we shall have to speak hereafter. In the second place, we notice his moral vigor and equipoise, the balance of strong emotions and animal faculties under the rule of a superb will. Socrates, generally and on principle, practised self-restraint, was even abstemious; and, on the other hand, he at times far outdid his fellows in convivial indulgence, but without losing self-control. Socrates, the abstemious, was the ideal of one class of philosophers; Socrates, the easy master of self, the ideal of another. In the third place, and finally, there was his "dæmon," or warning voice, and the ever-present consciousness of the supernatural. Of the real nature of this it is difficult to form a satisfactory opinion. Socrates himself did not identify it with reason or with conscience, he did not attribute to it a scientific character or importance. Nor, on the other hand, does he seem to have viewed it as a familiar spirit, an attendant personality. It was to him, rather, an inner oracle, which, instead of giving him a standard of truth or rule of life, warned and restrained him on particular occasions.[1] To the general mission of his life it seems to have been related only in so far as it gave increased vitality to the idea or feeling of subjectivity or close relation to an inner reality. Especially did it hold him aloof from public affairs, thus contravening the whole spirit of Greek life; and it helped to add internal significance to what had hitherto been too much a matter of external observance, namely, piety and the religious life. In the eyes of those about him he was by it rendered more sacred and more authoritative as a teacher; they felt that in their converse with him they held communion with a seer and a man of God.[2]

Philosophy of Socrates. — Coming now to the Socratic philosophy, or, more correctly speaking, since Socrates framed no system, — the Socratic philosophizing, — we have to notice its spirit, its method, its content, or doctrines, and its general character and result.

[1] Xenophon's *Memorabilia*, Bk. I. ch. 1.; Bk. IV. ch. 8.
[2] On Socrates's personality, see particularly, Xenophon's *Memorabilia* (especially at the end) and Plato's *Symposium*. Schwegler's account is brief, comprehensive, and very forcible. See his *Handbook of the History of Philosophy* (Stirling's trans.), pp. 39, 41.

Spirit of the Socratic Philosophizing. — Regarding the spirit of the Socratic philosophizing, it is to be remarked, in the first place, that it was, as has been already stated, in an important sense and a marked degree, *sceptical.* He freely criticised prevailing beliefs, customs, and institutions. He discredited the early physical speculation on the ground that it was unprofitable, and even impious.[1] He encouraged the study of geometry and astronomy, for example, only in so far as they served the most utilitarian ends. He discredited the "wisdom" of the Sophists without always putting forward palpable and positive doctrines in its stead. He discredited, if we may say so, himself, asserting that he knew only that he knew nothing. He made no pretension to being a teacher at all, not to say a teacher of philosophy.[2] It was, indeed, not without apparent reason that he was considered by some of his contemporaries as a Sophist, or even worse than a Sophist. Superficially regarded, at least, Socrates was one of the most pronounced negativists of his age. And if we look below the surface for what was positive in him, we shall find it, not in the positing of an ἀρχή of all existence, but in his affirmation of the necessity and all-sufficingness of self-knowledge for the practical purposes of human life, in his love of true manhood, and in his assumption that the essence, or, rather, essences of things, can be expressed in a definition valid for all human intelligences. The position of Socrates was equivocal; he knew that he did not know,[3] and yet he felt that he had a deeper

---

[1] Xenophon's *Memorabilia*, Bk. I. ch. 1, and Bk. IV. ch. 7.
[2] *Ibid.*, Bk. I. ch. 2.
[3] Plato's *Apology*, p. 21.

sense of reality than any other man of his age. And this brings us to a *second* element in the spirit of the Socratic philosophizing, namely, the *profound irony* that pervades much of it. This is not that playful and sarcastic irony that appears immediately on the surface and belongs rather to the external manner and method of Socrates; that habit of pretending to be ignorant in order the better to draw out or put to confusion a pupil or disputant. It was, the rather, a certain equivocality of speech begotten of the consciousness of the possession of superior insight and of the existence of a gulf between himself and his hearers. It was the irony of his situation, and did not proceed from humor or whim. When he professed ignorance, — though, from one point of view he spoke the literal truth, for he had a deeper insight than he could give adequate and scientific utterance to, — he seemed to be giving the lie in words to the well-known effects of his manner and teaching, his well-known power over men's minds. This was sometimes perplexing and exasperating to his associates, and more than anything else, perhaps, was the cause of his death. *Thirdly:* This irony was softened in a measure by a large geniality (proceeding from bodily and spiritual health) — by what, in its superficial aspect, has been termed by Hegel and others after him "Attic urbanity,"[1] but seems to be nothing more nor less than *love of true self-hood, regard for essential human nature.* If, indeed, the leading idea of the teaching of Socrates is, as we shall see, the prime importance of self-knowledge, a large element in its spirit is self-love or the love of the true self, very like what in recent years has been termed

[1] Hegel's *Geschichte der Philosophie*, Vol. II. p. 50.

the "enthusiasm of humanity." The Greeks, generally, were lovers and admirers not of humanity in general, but of Greek humanity; Socrates was broader in his insights and sympathies than his fellows were. But, *finally*, the *principal* element in the spirit of the Socratic philosophizing was a love of the truth,—a love rooted in a profound sense of reality and a pretty clear insight into the fundamental form of truth. This was, no doubt, qualified by his attitude toward the existing philosophy of nature and his predilection for man; and Socrates was, consequently, not a philosopher in the fullest sense of the term; he was an ethical inquirer. But within the sphere of human interests he never for long nor in any essential regard turned aside from the search for truth for its own sake.

The Socratic Method.—As to the method of the Socratic philosophizing, we must observe that it was not grounded upon the conception of any fully conceived principle of all existence, and that, on the other hand, it was not mere subjective groping after the "truth." It was not merely a logical mode of procedure but was also pedagogical. It was a method of bringing into consciousness, by any and every true psychological expedient, clearly and effectively, true conceptions. Such being the case, it is chiefly a necessity of exposition merely that warrants the separation here of the spirit and the method of this philosophizing. *Logically regarded*, the Socratic method was a compound of simple induction and definition — "two improvements in science which one might justly ascribe to Socrates"[1] — and reasoning upon the principle of analogy. Socrates,

---

[1] Aristotle's *Metaphysics*, Bk. XIII. ch. 4.

Xenophon tells us,[1] was always stimulating his companions to inquire into the essence or nature of things, and to class them properly. He did *not*, however, frame a *systematic theory* of logical (or pedagogical) processes or method. But, again, the Socratic "method" was a process, the outcome of which depended upon insight, sympathy, tact, quite as much as upon logic. It was an ethical conference, the presiding spirit of which was the love of the truth, intellectual and moral. Informal conversation was the natural outward aspect of it, both on account of the state of the Greek mind and Greek society and on account of the character of the truth (chiefly ethical) that was the subject of the Socratic inquiries. Crude individualism had begun to prevail; interchange of opinion was necessary and natural; the Greeks were a social, talkative people; the raw material for ethical science or edification had to be gathered and wrought up by dialogue (whence "dialectic"). And, we may observe in passing, the truth that was in Grecian life must have been brought to life and made effective in the Socratic conferences, for at them were present some of the very flower of that life: Euripides, Xenophon, Pericles the Younger, Critias, Alcibiades, Phædo, Chærephon, Plato, Euclid, and others, most of whom came to Socrates "not," to quote Xenophon, "that they might become public speakers in the assembly or the courts,[2] but that they might become noble and good, capable of discharging properly their duties to their families, their servants, their relatives, their friends, the state, and

[1] *Memorabilia*, Bk. IV. ch. 5.
[2] See above, § 7, p. 39.

their fellow-countrymen."[1] Some of them, as Plato and Euclid, came, no doubt, for intellectual training also — to understand and catch, if possible, that wonderful mastery of conceptions which made Socrates the king of dialectic. Now, in these conferences with fresh, earnest, active minds — and some not fresh, active, and earnest — Socrates delighted to practise what he was pleased to call his maieutic or obstetric art, — his art of bringing ideas or conceptions to the birth, for he saw that the minds of the Grecian youths were in labor. In the practice of this art he assumed that truth is native to the mind, — not to be poured into it, but, the rather, to be drawn out of it.[2] Now, sometimes, he feigned, the ideas that he by his art brought to the birth were not "worth keeping and rearing," and must be "exposed" in real Spartan fashion, the only important consequence of the "birth" being increased self-knowledge on the part of those who had been relieved of the ideas with which their minds had been pregnant. Sometimes, however, the ideas were sound and vigorous, and, if well cared for, might be reared into something worth the trouble of rearing them. The Socratic dialectic — for, as has been intimated, the dialogue became dialectic — was, accordingly, twofold, destructive and constructive. On the whole it was, perhaps, more *frequently* the former than the latter, with a net result, however, of what was positive and enduring; as the one fact, Plato, man and philosopher, is sufficient to prove.[3] And

[1] *Memorabilia*, Bk. I. ch. 2.
[2] See Plato's *Meno*, pp. 81-83.
[3] If Critias and Alcibiades turned out badly we are obliged to assume that it was hardly in them to do otherwise, whoever had been their master.

if we look more closely into the nature and effect of the Socratic dialectic, we find that the majority of those who were, willingly or unwillingly to themselves, subjected to it were, in the beginning, unripe for the perception of the naked truth : they could not appreciate logical distinctions, pure and simple, nor could they understand fact. They were filled with false sentiments and opinions ; some of them were stuffed with the learning of the Sophists and were full of conceit. Before they could be brought to the perception and appreciation of positive and constructive truth they must be relieved of their ignorance, false sentiment, and conceit. They must be encouraged in their right opinions and their keen appetite for knowledge. These services Socrates could perform for them thoroughly and well. The young man who was confident that he was just, and understood what justice was, lost confidence in himself and his ideas of justice, after being compelled to contradict himself several times within a few breaths ; and he simply desired to know himself and how to make himself capable of understanding what he had in vain long labored to understand. Such is a case, reported by Xenophon,[1] of the use of destructive dialectic and its effect. In dialectic of this sort a false general statement was overthrown by being shown to be inconsistent with an admitted general truth or well-known particular facts. In the opposite process, the constructive dialectic, some truth or right opinion held by the learner was confirmed, or some new truth was brought to light ; induction, defini-

[1] *Memorabilia*, Bk. IV. ch. 2. Perhaps the happiest example of the Socratic dialectic, destructive and constructive, is given in the *Meno* of Plato.

tion, and reasoning by analogy constituting the *logical* elements of the process. On the whole, the most valuable result of the Socratic dialectic was the begetting, in those who took part in the conferences, of the spirit of Socrates himself, — modesty, the habit of circumspection, a sense of the differences in things, an intelligent love of the truth and of wholeness or integrity of mind and character; what, in short, may be termed the philosophic spirit.

The Doctrines of Socrates; their General Character. — The doctrines of Socrates, it has already been intimated, were chiefly ethical in content. Whatever there may have been — and doubtless there was much — in what we have termed the Socratic conferences, to suggest to a mind like that of Plato, or of Euclid, who was afterwards a leader of one of the Socratic schools, a science of the soul (psychology), or of ultimate being (ontology), the fact is that the old and popular maxim which Socrates adopted as the expression of the leading thought of his teaching, γνῶθι σεαυτόν, "Know thyself," was given by him an application principally practical, or ethical (and in a rather narrow sense): Man should know himself — in order to be good and do the good. Though he assumed that truth was native to the mind and that human knowledge is at bottom self-knowledge, he did not make the nature of the mind or soul as such a subject of scientific investigation, nor did he wholly or in part identify self-knowledge with the knowledge of absolute intelligence or reality. To judge from the *Charmides*, one of the earliest and doubtless one of the most purely Socratic of Plato's dialogues, Socrates was sceptical in regard to the possibility of constructing a *science* of absolute knowledge or being, it being impossible for him to separate in thought the form of knowledge from the content.

Physical Philosophy of Socrates. — But Socrates did not abstain entirely from speculation concerning things not human. For though he hesitated on the threshold of the science of ultimate intelligence and reality, and cast aside as futile and impious the early nature-philosophy, he was not without a theory of nature. In his youth he was, according to a representation in one of the dialogues of Plato,[1] always agitating himself with questions relating to the mechanical causes and constituents of things. Anaxagoras, though not completely satisfactory to him, had helped him to get beyond mechanical to final causes, in which alone he found complete satisfaction. Whether Plato's representation be perfectly authentic or not, we find, as we turn the pages of Xenophon, that a favorite theme with Socrates is the beautiful and wise adaptation and order in nature, showing the care of the gods or providence (for polytheistic and monotheistic points of view are blended in the accounts) for the human family. The Socratic interpretation of nature is, however, not a philosophical deduction. It does, indeed, subordinate nature to the idea of the Good, but the mechanistic conception exists side by side with, and practically prevails over, the teleological and organic: nature, though held to be animated by a soul, is conceived as a wise contrivance, for man's benefit chiefly, rather than as a living self-realizing organism,[2] in which man holds a superior place because of his superior power of assimilating and synthetizing

[1] See the *Phædo*, pp. 97, 98, 99.
[2] See especially *Memorabilia*, Bk. I. ch. 4, and Bk. IV. ch. 3.

the "elements" of reality. This latter conception of nature we shall have occasion to examine when we reach Aristotle. The Socratic theory, which is theological (in not the largest sense) rather than philosophical, is the beginning, historically speaking, of what is commonly termed Natural Theology.

Ethical Philosophy of Socrates.

Relations between Knowledge and Virtue. — Coming now to the doctrines that are most characteristically Socratic,[1] we find the first and most important to be this: All virtue is knowledge. *Knowledge* here means, according to the express testimony of Aristotle,[2] as well as the whole tenor of the Socratic discussions everywhere, (not mere "prudence" or practical insight, but) science, correct definition. The man of virtue is not he who performs his duties to self and the state, half-reflectively, but he who possesses, and consciously realizes in act, the exact conception of each of his relations to self and the state. Socrates meant that scientific knowledge is not only *a* condition to virtue, but the *sole* condition; and, conversely, that vice is simply ignorance: to do wrong wittingly is better than to do right ignorantly.[3] Character and deliberate choice, consequently, were not regarded by Socrates as elements of virtue. He did not admit that there was any merit or virtue in the overcoming of evil inclinations by force of character or will. Given knowledge, thought he, and there follows, necessarily and immediately, virtue. "Now the rest of the world are of the opinion that knowledge is a principle

---

[1] Aristotle's *Metaphysics*, Bk. I. ch. 6.
[2] See Aristotle's *Nicomachean Ethics*, Bk. III. ch. 8; Bk. VI. ch. 11.
[3] Xenophon's *Memorabilia*, Bk. III. ch. 9; Bk. IV. ch. 6.

not of strength or of rule, or of command; their notion is that a man may have knowledge, and yet that the knowledge which is in him may be mastered by anger, or pleasure, or pain, or love, or perhaps favor, — just as if knowledge were a slave and might be dragged about anyhow. Now, is that your view? Or do you think that knowledge is a noble and commanding thing, which cannot be overcome, and will not allow a man, if he only knows the difference of good and evil, to do anything contrary to knowledge, but that wisdom will have strength to help him?"[1]

General Consequences of the Unity of Knowledge and Virtue. — From the unity of virtue and knowledge it follows that the virtues are not many, merely, but one also. They are related to each other, not as the "parts of the face" but "as the parts of gold," which are like one another, and like the whole of which they are parts. One implies the rest; there is a necessary relation between them through knowledge.[2] Possessing a common essence, they possess a power of giving rise one to another: the man who, in one relation is temperate, will in another be just, or holy, or courageous, as the case may require. From the unity of virtue and knowledge, it follows, also, that the virtues can be taught. They are not, as the Sophists thought, so many particular knacks, or little arts, that can be caught and practised by instinct: they are the offspring of conception, scientific apprehension. Hence the importance, constantly emphasized by Socrates, of comprehending in every instance the exact nature of what is required to be done,

---

[1] Plato's *Protagoras*, p. 352 (Jowett's translation).
[2] *Protagoras*, pp. 349, 360.

and of a right training of the mind to the forming of conceptions, *i.e.*, scientific education.

Classification of the Virtues.—But, now, what virtues are there? and of what are they the knowledge? To these questions Socrates gives no scientific answer. Virtue is for him the knowledge of the Good, and the Good is not the realization of a universal and absolute end, but of the true conceptions or ends of individual objects or acts. The Good, in other words, is the useful. Upon being asked by one of his disciples if he knew anything good, Socrates replied, "Do you ask, Aristippus, if I know anything good for a fever?"[1] The Socratic ethics is unscientific, and, in consequence, utilitarian and eudæmonistic. Notwithstanding the abstract and radical character of its first principle—All virtue is knowledge—it remains, for lack of development of that principle, nearly on the level of mere custom and utility. The principal virtues are *assumed* to be *temperance, friendship, courage, right citizenship*, (which, in its highest form, is) *justice, piety;* the *root* and *sum* of them all being *wisdom*.

Temperance. — Temperance, the fundamental (though not the crowning) virtue, is the keeping of the bodily impulses in subjection to the desires of the mind. "I consider it," says Socrates, "as a mark of perfection in the gods that they want nothing; he, therefore, approaches nearest the divine nature who wants the fewest things." This must be construed, however, not as an argument for asceticism, but for self-control merely. "To continue master of himself in the midst of the allurements of the senses by the unruffled dignity of his own

[1] *Memorabilia*, Bk. III. ch. 8.

inner life — that was the aim," says Zeller, "which his moderation proposed to itself." Without temperance, thought Socrates, men can be nothing in themselves or to their fellows; the good general, the good guardian, the good neighbor, the good herdsman, the good slave, is temperate.[1]

Friendship. — Of friendship and love, Socrates, as we learn from both Xenophon and Plato, made much. Although, he said, the majority of mankind are more diligent in acquiring houses, lands, slaves, flocks, and household goods than in gaining friends, the firm and virtuous friend is the most valuable of all possessions. But the Socratic theory of friendship is not rose-colored: friends are good because they are useful. True friendship, however, can exist only between the intelligent, virtuous, and disinterested. Socrates adopted the common Greek notion that the end of conjugal love was the begetting of a numerous and healthy progeny. The force of the Socratic doctrines of friendship must have been enhanced for his associates by his spirit and manner in conversation; he would "frequently assume the character and language of a lover"[2] for the purpose of winning the confidence of others and getting them enamored of the truth. It is the doctrine of Socrates set forth in the light of his spirit that Plato has presented in his *Symposium*, where Socrates is discoursing in an inspired manner on spiritual love. In the Socratic conception of friendship and love, there was, it seems, an element not usually present in the Greek conception, namely, that of the duty of love to enemies as well as to friends.[3]

[1] *Memorabilia*, Bk. I. ch. 5.
[2] *Ibid.*, Bk. IV. ch. 1; Bk. II. chs. 6, 28.
[3] Plato's *Crito*, p. 49.

Right Citizenship and Justice.—Socrates never allowed to escape him any opportunity, on the one hand, to encourage those whom he thought competent, to engage in the active service of the state, and, on the other, to discourage those who were incompetent and overambitious. Charmides, who was competent, he urged to acquaint himself with his own powers and to lose no occasion for exerting them in his country's service;[1] but Euthydemus he checked, in the following satiric manner: "I never learned anything, O men of Athens," he feigns Euthydemus as saying, "from any one. On hearing that certain persons were skilled in speaking and in the conduct of practical affairs, I never sought to associate myself with them; nor did I ever seek an instructor among those competent to give instruction. On the contrary, I have persistently avoided not only seeking instruction but even seeming to do so. Nevertheless, I propose to offer such advice as may happen to occur to me."[2] Socrates then likens him to a man who should complacently announce that he never thought of making a study of medicine and had never received any instruction in it, and yet should solicit others to offer themselves as subjects for him to experiment upon. Socrates was, doubtless, one of the most ardent, one of the wisest, of all the apostles of political education and intelligent citizenship the world has ever seen. The highest privilege, the most commanding duty, the noblest function of the individual man are, he declared, those connected with citizenship in an intelligent, well-ordered state,—a state in which "not

---

[1] *Memorabilia*, Bk. III. ch. 7. [2] *Ibid.*, Bk. IV. ch. 2.

the possession of power nor the fortune of the lot, nor popular election, but knowledge alone, . . . confers a claim to rule."[1] If he did not seek a conspicuous part in the affairs of state,[2] that was because he saw the imperative need of checking ignorant ambition and demagoguism by steadfastly doing what he could to make knowledge and virtue prevail. As a subject, though he saw fit to criticise existing institutions and rulers, and to encourage independence of judgment everywhere, he rendered strict obedience;[3] as one of the governors, he was perfect in firmness and fidelity. Socrates was, in short, both in theory and practice, one of the comparatively few completely sane and whole-minded among men, — men who are able to preserve the balance between what is and what "ought" to be; he was a just man in the larger, Greek sense of the term. And, in the Greek view, justice, in which right citizenship culminates, is the crowning virtue, the virtue that harmonizes individual independence with friendship, the relation of the individual to himself with his relation to others.

Piety. — The days of Socrates, if ever those of any man were, were "bound each to each"; if not by a "natural piety" in exactly the Wordsworthian sense,[4] yet by a piety as pure, deep, and simple, — as natural, — as that, and more distinctively human. Though he discarded

---

[1] *Zeller's Socrates and the Socratic Schools*, ch. 7.
[2] *Memorabilia*, Bk. IV. ch. 1.
[3] *Ibid.*, Bk. IV. ch. 4.
[4] See, for example, Wordsworth's stanza beginning —
   "My heart leaps up when I behold
   A rainbow in the sky."

physical speculation as barren and impious, he believed that the order of the world was cognizable by the power of moral insight. He held that human wisdom, the knowledge that conduces most to human welfare, was but an image of the divine wisdom that ruled the world. He enjoined piety for the double reason that it was due to the gods (God) because of their (His) care for men, and because of the wisdom apparent in the order of the world, and that to the pious alone are communicated some of the divine secrets that may not be penetrated into by the unaided mind of man. He enjoined the customary sacrifices merely as symbols of a pure heart, and his prayer was simply that the gods would give him those things that were good. In his belief and teaching the Supreme Being was invisible, all-wise, all-powerful, all-good, exercising dominion over the world as the mind does over the body.[1]

Wisdom. — Wisdom, which was sometimes enumerated among the particular virtues by Greek teachers of ethics, was, as we have seen, regarded by Socrates as the root and the substance of all the virtues. "Socrates would often say that justice and every other virtue is wisdom."[2] This is, indeed, just what he meant by the dictum, All virtue is knowledge. And by knowledge he undoubtedly meant self-knowledge especially, — a clear, correct conception, on the part of the individual, of his own powers and limitations as well as of his divine nature. As we have already seen, Socrates constantly strove to cause those with whom he conversed to "examine into the nature of things and class them properly," *i.e.*, to form

---

[1] *Memorabilia*, Bk. I. chs. 4 and 8. [2] *Ibid.*, Bk. III. ch. 9.

the habit of framing correct conceptions, and he held it to be of the highest moment that they should apply the art of framing conceptions to the getting of a knowledge of themselves. Wisdom, then, was to Socrates the science of human nature; and since the end of this science is virtue, wisdom is simply ethical or moral science. Socrates did not construct such a science, but pointed the way to it. Further, Socrates, as we know, held that the scientific knowledge of self was sufficient to constitute virtue: he who *knows* how he ought to serve the gods is pious; he who *knows* the laws that men ought to observe is just:[1] "justice and every other virtue is wisdom": true conceptions rightly apprehended have an inherent and necessary power to make men good.

Beauty. — To the Socratic doctrine of the Good may be appended, as in some sort a corollary, his doctrine of Beauty. The term *beauty* is scarcely more with Socrates than another name for what is also called goodness. Beautiful is whatever is adapted to the purpose for which it was intended, *i.e.*, whatever realizes its conception; a dung-cart is beautiful if so made that it answers its purpose.[2] The work of the true painter or sculptor — the artist — is not a medley of individually beautiful elements having no connection with each other for thought; it is the embodiment of a conception.[3]

General Result. — The general character of the Socratic philosophizing may be stated as follows: Socrates was by natural temperament, by deliberate choice, and by circumstances given the task of introducing the

---

[1] *Memorabilia*, Bk. IV. ch. 6.   [2] *Ibid.*, Bk. III. ch. 8.
[3] *Ibid.*, Bk. III. ch. 10.

problem of self-knowledge and of instituting a tendency which should result in the substitution for the (to a large extent) unscientific and unfruitful speculations of the early Greek philosophers about nature, and for the superficial subjectivism and humanism of the Sophists, scientific — or at least definite — and fruitful conceptions about man, and, later, about universal reason and nature. "All beyond him lies in the region of unsophisticated use and wont, or prescriptive ethics, like that of the Chinese or other Oriental civilizations; on the hither side, the chief interest is the ever-widening influence of the individual consciousness of moral necessity, the long and gradual discipline of mankind into independent responsible wills, endowed with 'rights of conscience.' In the ante-Socratic principle the individual takes the impulse from without — from auspices or auguries — nothing being undertaken without them. Individual conscience and personal decision date from the epoch of Socrates, and their growth from that time is the progress of the world's history."[1] Socrates instituted the science of man; he did so by instituting in the world's consciousness true manhood. And it is very largely as a *personal force* that he holds his place, a very high one, in the history of the world's abstract thought. Hence, we may repeat in conclusion, the necessity of presenting, in any account of the philosophy of Socrates, so much, relatively, that is personal and concrete in connection with what, in agreement with the nature of the subject, must be impersonal and abstract.

[1] "Socrates" (art. by W. T. Harris in Johnson's Cyclopædia).

GREEK PHILOSOPHY.   65

§ 9.

The Followers of Socrates. — It would be too much to expect that more than a very few of those who came under the influence of Socrates could understand experientially his personality or interpret the thought that lay underneath it; and, in fact, the immediate disciples and successors of Socrates may be divided into three classes: first, those who (like Xenophon) reproduced with little or no modification the Socratic doctrines but only incompletely the Socratic spirit and method; second, those who, according to their several personal temperaments and predilections, attributed special importance to some one feature of Socrates's teaching or personality; and third, those, or, rather, that one who, combining the principles and doctrines of Socrates with principles and doctrines of other thinkers, and interpreting freely the personality of Socrates, was the first to give to philosophy, on a Socratic basis, something like completeness of content and form — namely Plato. Of the second class were the so-called *Lesser Socratics*, whom we have next to consider.

§ 10.

The Lesser Socratics.[1] — Of the Lesser Socratics there were three schools, representing three very distinct tendencies in the Socratic philosophizing: the Megarians or Megarics, the Cynics, and the Cyrenaics.

[1] The following account is in matters of detail based largely upon Zeller's account in the *Socrates and the Socratic Schools*. Assistance has been derived from Hegel's interpretation (which is the best) in his *Geschichte der Philosophie*, Vol. II.

The Megarians, or Megarics. — The Megarians took their name from the place Megara (not very far from Athens), in which the school flourished. These thinkers — children of the intellectual subtlety of Socrates (see p. 46) — occupied themselves with dialectics and conceived reality, which they termed the Good, not as ethical Being but as a purely abstract ontological entity, Being in the Eleatic sense. The Good, they declared, and *only* the Good is. Their method was similar to that of Zeno, and so tenaciously did Euclid, the founder of the school, cling, theoretically at least, to the principle of identity, the logical counterpart of pure Being, that he rejected the Socratic reasoning by analogy, affirming that to explain things by means of others unlike them is impossible and to explain them by means of things like them is superfluous. The principal Megarians besides *Euclid* were *Eubulides*, *Diodorus*, and, unless he belongs rather with the Cynics, *Stilpo*, said to have been the most brilliant of them all. The method of the Megarics, it appears, degenerated into logical hair-splitting and fell into disrepute under the name "eristic." From one point of view, indeed, it seems idle to affirm, as did Stilpo, that only "identical proppositions" (*e.g.* A man is a man) are valid; but Stilpo was consistent: simple, abstract identity is, as we shall find Plato demonstrating, no principle of synthesis. This, however, was not the most disagreeable phase of the "eristic"; it became, to use words[1] applied by Plato to the corrupt Sophist in general, "disputatious, controversial, pugnacious, combative," and if it served

---

[1] *Sophist*, p. 226.

any good purpose whatever, served only to stimulate minds more profound than the Megarian to a discovery of a serious, straightforward, logical method: the Megarians, bad as well as good, must share the credit of having incited both Plato and Aristotle to logical and metaphysical investigation deeper than their predecessors had undertaken. One of the most celebrated pieces of dialectic employed by the Megarians is that of Diodorus on possibility and actuality, which "is still admired after centuries as a masterpiece of subtle criticism": — "From anything possible nothing impossible can result. But it is impossible that the past can be different from what it is; for had it been possible at a past moment, something impossible would have resulted from something possible. It was therefore never possible, and generally speaking it is impossible that anything should happen differently from what has happened."[1]

The Cynics. — Nearest in method and spirit to the Megarians were the Cynics, who also declared that only "identical propositions" are valid, and who conceived the Good, if not as the abstract, universal, sole metaphysical entity, the One, yet as the equally abstract particular, individual One. The Cynics took their name either from a place near Athens, — a gymnasium called the Cynosarges, — where *Antisthenes* (born 444 B.C.), their leader, taught, or else from their unsociableness, churlish (*doggish* = κυνικός = *cynical*) manners and mode of life. Antisthenes — a pupil of Gorgias — was an intimate associate of Socrates and considered himself the genuine

[1] *Zeller's Socrates and the Socratic Schools*, p. 232.

Socratic. Superficially speaking, such he was. He affected a preference to ethics over logic and physics (philosophy of nature), holding logic to be entirely subsidiary to ethics, and physics to be valueless; and adopted the narrowest view of ethics, the view, namely, that treats the individual as merely such, as merely a particular, isolated, empty self. He inverted, or technically speaking, converted, Socrates's dictum, All virtue is knowledge (making it All knowledge is virtue) and then took as the ideal of virtue a strained conception of the Socratic self-control and superiority to appetite. The Cynic doctrine of virtue is *practically*, therefore, in a word this: The Good is the realization, to the fullest possible extent, of the conception of the abstract individual self. In conduct, — for the Cynics were conscientious and attempted to live up to their ideal, — this doctrine had for its result shabbiness of dress, indecency of manner and life, mendicancy, vagrant "citizenship of the world," almost complete abandonment of all concrete relation to family, state, and religion. This, obviously, was pure asceticism, unlovely, unhuman; but it was the asceticism not of "supernaturalism" but of naked "naturalism," abstract "positivism." Antisthenes was himself a true exemplar of the Cynic virtue: "He wore no garment except a cloak; allowed his beard to grow; carried a wallet and staff; renounced all diet but the simplest; . . . [was] stern, reproachful, and bitter in his language; careless and indecent in his gestures."[1] The most cynical and famous of the Cyn-

---

[1] Lewes's *Biographical History of Philosophy*, p. 178; also Diogenes Laertius, *Life of Antisthenes*.

ics, however, was Diogenes of Sinope, who was conceited, scurrilous, witty, more than half wise, a caricature of Socrates, — sleeping in porticos, coarsely and scantily clad, living on the rudest fare, drinking water from the palm of his hand, violating all rules of decency, railing at whatever and whomever he whimsically conceived a dislike to, an admired, privileged "Dog" indeed![1] At their best, however, the Cynics undertook to be moral benefactors : to teach and enforce by moral suasion the doctrines of simplicity in living, sincerity and candor in speech, the paramount value of the inner life. But they were extremists, and their doctrines passed into and gave rise to those diametrically opposed to them.

The Cyrenaics.— From particular, individual will it is but a step to particular, individual pleasure, and the next form to be considered of that peculiar mode of abstraction which characterizes the Lesser Socratics is found in the Cyrenaic doctrine of the good as happiness, or pleasure. The founder of the Cyrenaic school was Aristippus of Cyrene (born 435 B.C.), who, notwithstanding his appetite for luxury in living, and the abundance of his means for gratifying it (for he was wealthy), was strongly attracted by Socrates and his teachings, and became an enthusiastic disciple of his. The point of greatest attractiveness to Aristippus was, doubtless, Socrates's practice and theory of self-control, not in the form of self-denial but of easy mastership of self in the midst of free indulgence. The doctrine of the Cyrenaics appears to have been in its origin and development substantially as follows : happiness and virtue, or the good,

[1] Diog. Laert.

coincide. Whatever does not conduce to that, the sole end of human existence, is worthless (logic and physics are completely subsidiary to ethics). The only objects of knowledge are feelings, which are the sole end of action. Each individual knows only his own feelings, which, therefore, constitute the sole end of his actions. The only feelings of absolute worth are pleasurable feelings. Hence virtue, the good, is the pleasure,—and primarily the bodily pleasure,—of the individual. This view underwent a development which is substantially as follows:—The discovery was made that there is a difference among pleasures in degree and kind, and that the idea of pleasure *as such* is untenable. Pleasures must sometimes be purchased by pain, and a balancing of pleasures with pains is necessary to a determination of the value of pleasures. Again, it was discovered that pleasures, to be most fully desirable, must at least be *accompanied* by thought or wisdom, and hence that mere bodily pleasures are inferior in kind. The Cyrenaics thus arrived at a theory of happiness which, as we shall see, differed from those of Plato and Aristotle, which had from the beginning a thought-basis, only as regards basis, and consequently as regards value for a life that is *radically* determined by thought. There is here the same weakness that appears in the theories of the other Lesser Socratics, and in the philosophizing even of Socrates himself: namely, the want of a thought-basis, and hence of essential synthesis and wholeness. The lives of the Cyrenaics, it appears, conformed fairly well with their doctrines. Aristippus was a brilliant pleasure-seeker, but he was more than that; he understood something of true nobility of mind—*that* he had felt in Socrates, and he appears to have possessed it so far as to know "how to preserve calmness and composure in the midst of the perpetual change of human affairs, how to govern his passions and inclinations, and how to make the best of all the events of life."[1] Nearly a century later the Cyrenaic doctrine underwent still further development. This began with Theodorus (near the close of the fourth century B.C.), who affirmed the self-sufficiency of private intellectual satisfaction, for the attainment of which he renounced, theoretically at least, family, country, the popular religion, and all else. Hegesias, advancing a step, affirmed happiness to consist in resignation, a struggle to avoid or endure pain rather than an effort to find positive pleasure, which he regarded as beyond human attainment. According to him, indifference, not positive desire, was the philosophic attitude of mind. He is said to have committed suicide. Anniceris, finally, retreated towards the earlier Cyrenaic doctrine, advocating the active pursuit of pleasure and a due attention to all possible sources of enjoyment. He even recognized self-sacrifice as a means to true happiness. To intelligence or mental culture he seems to have assigned only a secondary position in the scale of desirable things.

Result. — The general character of the doctrines of the Lesser Socratics need not be dwelt upon here. It has already been pretty fully indicated, and will receive further elucidation in the accounts that are to follow of the doctrines of Plato, Aristotle, and the post-Aristotelian schools of philosophy, with which last they will be seen to have very close connection. We there-

---

[1] See above, p. 58, for a similar statement concerning Socrates.

fore pass at once to Plato, who was the truest continuator of the philosophy of Socrates.

§ 11.

Life of Plato. — Plato was born either at Athens, or at Ægina, on the island of the same name, probably in the year 427 B.C. He was of a wealthy and aristocratic family, and doubtless received the highest educational advantages the brilliant age in which he lived afforded. He assimilated the best parts and elements of the good poets, himself possessed unquestionable poetical talent, having written some dithyrambics, lyrics, and tragedies, and had a clear eye for universal truth; he was, in short, one of those youths of fine gifts, spirit, and education who were the delight of the great teachers in Greece. "By Heracles!" exclaims Socrates, speaking of the beautiful youth Charmides, in Plato's dialogue of that name, "there never was such a paragon, if only he has one other slight addition." "What is that?" asks Critias. "If he has a noble soul," says Socrates. From all accounts, one of which represents him as a son of Apollo, it would appear that Plato was, in the eyes of his master, Socrates, just such a paragon. Before he came under the influence of Socrates he may have been possessed by the then ordinary ambition of Athenian youths, to shine among politicians. It is difficult to conceive, however, that a youth of poetical and meditative temperament, and of very decidedly aristocratic predilections, could find anything congenial in the corrupt politics of a degenerated and degenerating democracy such as ruled Athens in Plato's early manhood. At all events, his mind was, by his intercourse with Socrates, permanently fixed upon philosophy — he had already studied Heraclitus, if not others of the earlier philosophers — and he chose for himself a life of comparative seclusion and contemplation rather than one of active intercourse with the world at large. Coming to Socrates at the age of nineteen or twenty, he remained a modest and devoted disciple until the death of the master, a period of eight or nine years. His intercourse with Socrates must have had as consequences an intensification of already existing intellectual appetites, and awakening of new ones, and the implanting of an ideal of manhood — in brief, a drawing out and strengthening of all his faculties. After the death of Socrates, Plato, to escape the hostility of the persecutors of Socrates, went to Megara, and there became a pupil, or at least a companion, of Euclid. How long he remained there is not known. It is certain that before many years he travelled to Cyrene, in Africa, to Italy, and to Sicily. Probably he visited Egypt also. At Syracuse, Sicily, the tyrant Dionysius, who thought his doctrines impracticable, "senile," and was anxious to get rid of him, treated him as a prisoner of war, and delivered him to a Spartan ambassador, "who exposed him for sale in the slave market of Ægina. Ransomed by Anniceris, a Cyrenian, he thence returned to his native city." Through his travels his views of life and society were expanded, and he acquired a fuller knowledge of mathematics and of the Pythagorean philosophy and ethical régime — facts that must be taken into account in any view of the development of his philosophical theories. By the year 387 or 384 B.C., if not earlier, he was teaching and writing at Athens, where he had founded a school in a gymnasium called the Academy. His devotion to his school — avowedly a place of scientific, in contradiction to sophistic, instruction and culture — seems to have been complete. The instruction given, which was free, was mostly oral in form, because of his fear that written discourse would be misinterpreted, and of the value he set upon personal contact and the living word. In his preference for this method he was a true Socratic; he was also not un-Socratic in combining with instruction, social intercourse and the enjoyment with his pupils of an occasional feast. But the purely scholastic life did not afford him the opportunity he desired for the practical application of his theories, and about the year 367 B.C. we find him in Syracuse, Sicily, instructing the younger Dionysius, who, by the death of his father, had become ruler of that city, in ethical and political philosophy. But whatever hopes Plato may have had in common with other ancient philosophers of seeing philosophy successfully applied to government, failed. Even had the Platonic theories been truly "practicable," Dionysius, it seems, was far from being the man to appreciate and apply them. Plato returned to Athens, and, with the exception of an interval (about 361 B.C.) during which he went on a third journey to Sicily to reconcile Dionysius with his brother-in-law, Dion, an earnest disciple of Plato, devoted the remainder of his life exclusively to teaching philosophy in the Academy. He died in 347 B.C. at the age of eighty, with powers undiminished, and reverenced both by fellow-countrymen and by foreigners for the exceeding brilliancy of his intellect and the loftiness and beauty of his character. No philosopher, either of ancient or of modern times, save, perhaps, his master Socrates, and his pupil Aristotle, has so won and retained the esteem of thoughtful men. "Plato," says Hegel, "is one of the world-historical individuals; his philosophy is one of the world-historical facts which, from their beginning to all subsequent times, have exercised the most important influence upon the formation and development of mind."[1]

Plato's Works. — Regarding the Platonic writings — their authenticity, the order (or approximate order) of their production, the growth of ideas and theories in them, and their style — there are a few points which it seems indispensable that even the general student of the history of Greek philosophy should be aware of. For a full account of these, however, the reader must, of course, be referred to the accessible learned authorities, particularly Zeller, Ueberweg, and Grote. As to the authenticity of the Platonic dialogues the student has simply to accept, as Plato's own, all (or nearly all, the exceptions being unimportant) the dialogues that appear in the collection known as Professor Jowett's translation. The doubts of Ueberweg and certain others as to the authenticity of the important dialogues *Meno, Parmenides, Statesman,* and *Sophist* are not concurred in by authorities generally.[2] As to the order of the writings and the growth of Plato's ideas and theories there are two (three) leading hypotheses; one (Schleiermacher's) is, that the dialogues were produced according to a more or less fully preconceived philosophical scheme; the other (Hermann's) is that they appeared in a succession

[1] "Geschichte der Philosophie," Bd. II. p. 147.
[2] See *Zeller's Plato and the Older Academy* (a translation from Zeller's *Geschichte der Philosophie der Griechen*), p. 82.

determined by the "natural growth of Plato's mind." The most recent authorities see fit to adopt a mean between these two hypotheses, inclining, it would seem, rather toward the latter. According to the theory of Hermann, the dialogues may be divided into three classes. Those of one class are "Socratic, or elementary, of another dialectic or mediatizing, of the third, expository or constructive." The first, "written, in part, before the death of Socrates, in part, immediately after, have a fragmentary, more exclusively elenchtic and protreptic character, confine themselves almost entirely to the Socratic manner, and as yet go no deeper into the fundamental questions of philosophy. The second class is distinguished by greater dryness, less liveliness, less cheerfulness of form, and by that searching criticism (sometimes approving, sometimes polemical) of the Megaro-Eleatic philosophy which occupied the time of Plato's sojourn in Megara. In the third period, there is, on the one hand, as to style, a return to the freshness and fulness of the first; while on the other, Plato's horizon has been enlarged by the inquiries of the Megarian period, by residence in foreign countries, and especially by the knowledge he acquired of the Pythagorean philosophy, and from the fusion of all the elements we get the most perfect exposition of his system, in which the Socratic form receives the deepest content and thus attains its highest ideal."[1] Combining the two theories with certain minor considerations and certain indications noted in

---

[1] *Plato and the Older Academy*, pp. 103, 104; also pp. 117-119. Schwegler agrees with Hermann; see his *Handbook of the History of Philosophy*, pp. 62-67 (Stirling's translation). Practically the difference between Zeller and Schwegler here is of little consequence to any but the specialist.

the study of the dialogues themselves, Zeller arrives at substantially the following groups: 1. *Lesser Hippias, Lysis, Charmides, Laches, Protagoras, Euthyphro, Apology, Crito;* 2. *Phædrus, Gorgias, Meno, Theætetus, Sophist, Statesman, Parmenides, Symposium, Phædo, Philebus* (transitional); 3. *Republic, Timæus, Critias, Laws.* The places of *Euthydemus* and *Cratylus* are uncertain. *First Alcibiades, Menexenus* are by Zeller considered spurious.[1] In the first group, then, — to expand a little what is contained in the foregoing, — we must look for the purely Socratic doctrines wrought out in the Socratic manner, and for the historical Socrates, the substance of these dialogues being ethical; in the second group is to be found principally the Platonic theory of Ideas, — of conceptions and the corresponding archetypal entities; in the third group are contained, besides the theory of a dialectic as a science, the theories of virtue, of the state and of nature. The general student will find all that he requires in the *Apology* (for a picture of Socrates), *Protagoras* (for Socratic dialectic applied to ethics), *Theætetus* (for the theory of knowledge), *Phædrus* and *Phædo* (for the theory of the soul and of Ideas), *Republic* (for the theory of Ideas, of virtue, and of the state), *Philebus* (for the theory of the finite and infinite, of Ideas and the good), *Timæus* (for the theory of nature and the soul). The student will be disappointed if he expect to

[1] It should be noted that certain English authorities at the present moment, chief among them Henry Jackson and R. D. Archer-Hind, regard the *Parmenides* and the *Philebus* as among the very latest of Plato's works and as containing, therefore, the latest form of Plato's leading thought, the Theory of Ideas. See below, p. 112. (See *Journal of Philology*, Cambridge, 1882.)

find dogmatic conclusions at every step in Plato. Plato believed thoroughly in keeping the mind open and trying questions in every possible way. One may read several dialogues — go through, so to say, several movements of the Platonic symphony — without finding a real pause. As to the external style of the dialogues, the wise reader will guard against treating the myths and metaphors in which the dialogues abound in a temper too prosaic. Plato's philosophy is, in many places, steeped in poetry, but, if rightly read, is not *un*philosophical on account of that. The force of these remarks will receive pointed illustration when we reach Aristotle and his criticisms upon Plato.

Plato's General Conception of Philosophy. — Philosophy, says Plato, speaking half-allegorically, springs from a certain "divine madness" caused by the recollection, at the sight of the "beauty of earth," of that "true beauty" of which the soul had a vision in a pre-existent state.[1] And this "madness" is no superficial thing: it springs from the very essence of the soul as an immortal being: it is a prophecy of the soul's return to the knowledge and enjoyment of eternal reality. This return is brought about by philosophy. By philosophy alone can the Idea of the Good be represented among men and they become like God, "in whom is no unrighteousness at all."[2] Not, indeed, that any philosopher has perfect wisdom, for God alone is wise, and the Idea of the Good is with difficulty discerned.[3] Men are, as it were, confined in a dark den, where they can scarcely tell shadows from realities. The ascent to the

---

[1] *Phædrus*, p. 249. [2] *Theætetus*, p. 176; *Phædo*, p. 82. [3] *Phædrus*, p. 278.

upper world is slow and difficult, and the Idea of the Good is seen last. In this ascent there are four stages, in the last of which, only, is the real truth apprehended.[1] The first is mere opinion; the second, right opinion, or true belief, which, however, is "without reason," *i.e.*, is unscientific; the third is understanding, or what is commonly termed science, though it is in reality only *quasi*-scientific, because it rests on certain unproved presuppositions; the fourth is science, or completely reasoned knowledge, knowledge in which there are no unexamined or unfounded presuppositions or hypotheses.[2] Now the last stage is reached only through a course of discipline which may be described as follows. The "divine madness" being presupposed to exist, in germ, at least, in all minds, but especially in certain ones who are, therefore, embryo philosophers, there must, in the first place, be "right opinion" "engrafted" on it. This must be done by training in gymnastics and music,—gymnastics for the body and music for the soul. (Music is to be understood here as including poetry.) "He who has received this true education of the inner being will most shrewdly perceive omissions or faults in art and nature, and with a true taste, while he praises and rejoices over and receives into his soul the good, becomes noble and good, he will justly blame and hate the bad, now in the days of his youth even before he is able to know the reason of the thing: when reason comes, he will recognize and salute her as a friend with whom his education has made him long familiar." The gymnastic education[3] supplements the

---

[1] *Republic*, p. 517.   [2] *Ibid.*, pp. 511 and 533.   [3] *Ibid.*, p. 402.

musical with strength and firmness, courage and spirit, both animal and mental. But, in the second place, there must be mathematical training to enable the soul to "rise out of the sea of change and lay hold of true being." Such training gives measure, harmony, unity to thought, and tends in its results towards the "vision of the Idea of the Good"; it furnishes the mind with a method and enables it to give something like scientific form and validity to its "right opinion." Such training, however, is but the "prelude" to the "actual strain of philosophy."[1] Philosophically speaking, the defect of mathematics (*i.e.*, arithmetic and geometry) is that it is but a half step from sense. It reasons correctly, but it reasons about that which is, as compared with being, semi-sensuous, and its first principles are mere hypotheses: "as to the mathematical arts, which, as we were saying, have some apprehension of true being — geometry and the like — they only dream about being, but never can they behold the waking reality so long as they leave the hypotheses which they use, undisturbed, and are unable to give any account of them."[2] It is "dialectic and dialectic alone which does away with hypotheses in order to establish them; the eye of the soul, which is literally buried in some outlandish slough, is by her taught to look upward; and she uses as hand-maids in the work of conversion the sciences we have been discussing. Custom terms them sciences, but they ought to have some other name, implying greater clearness than opinion and less clearness than science; and this in our previous sketch was called

[1] *Republic*, p. 525.   [2] *Ibid.*, p. 533.

understanding."[1] Dialectic, then, is the highest science, the "coping-stone" of the sciences. The preparation required for it is of the severest kind, and demands the strongest and steadiest minds. Only the "unwearied, solid man," who loves labor, has a good memory, is morally whole and sound, should undertake it; dialectic, in fact, cannot be undertaken without risk of intellectual and moral disintegration (such as the Sophistic culture fosters) until the age of thirty, and even then only by the best minds in the best bodies. Five years must be given to the theoretical mastery of it before any attempt to make practical application of it to the affairs of state (for the state is to be ruled by philosophy); the remaining years of a man's life after fifty are to be given to the pursuit of it.[1] Such is Plato's general notion of philosophy.

The Divisions of Philosophy and their General Relations. — Plato nowhere formally makes a division of philosophy into distinct parts. Circumstances had made his task one of synthesis rather than of analysis. He had gathered together what he saw to be the strands of philosophy which earlier thinkers had held in separation, and in his hands philosophy became for the first time something like a complete whole. But such a division or analysis was virtually contained in his synthesis, and was made actual by a pupil of his, Xenocrates. The parts recognizable in Plato's philosophy, are, then, Dialectic, the theory of thought and being, as such, Physics, the theory of nature, and Ethics, the theory of the Good. Now of these parts dialectic is highest, the

---

[1] *Republic*, p. 533.   [2] *Ibid.*, pp. 535-540.

"coping-stone"; as regards both method and content it furnishes to the other parts the *ideal* of truth. In its purest form it is the science of absolute knowledge and being, whereas all other sciences are sciences of being that is derivative and has cognoscibility and reality only in so far as it "participates" in that true supreme being.

Dialectic as a Twofold Science. — The dialectic of Plato may be described as the natural result of the Socratic conception developed under the influence, in Plato's mind, of the negative, or repelling, force of the Heraclitic doctrine of the eternal flux of things of sense, and the positive, or attracting, force of the Eleatic doctrine of being as one and unchangeable. Plato, in other words, held with Socrates that knowledge exists only in the form of the conception, a definite, unchanging notion, and, with the Eleatics, that that of which there is knowledge is not the world of sense as Heraclitus had characterized it, but being, one and universal. Knowledge and being are thus correlative, and dialectic is hence a twofold science, the science of knowledge and of being. It is also the application of the science of knowledge in the getting of knowledge, and hence is a method; and, we may say also, of the science of being in action, though Plato does not use the term frequently, if at all, in this sense.

Dialectic as a Theory of Knowledge and as Method. — As a science of knowledge it is a true account of the way in which true conceptions are formed and of conceptions in their relations. But this way is dialectic as method. In its lowest form dialectic is simply the art of speech, the art of developing and expressing clearly and effectively our ideas concerning the "essence of each thing."[1] This, it will be seen, is but a description of the Socratic practice in its outward aspect, which Plato seems always to have regarded as of vital importance. To him philosophy was an energizing of the whole soul, a matter of life as well as of thought, pre-eminently a personal thing. Hence that preference of his, already mentioned, for the spoken over the written word. Inwardly the dialectic method was with Plato the Socratic induction supplemented by division and classification and the comparing of the consequences of opposite hypotheses.[2] This is the method of thought (not of sense) and is based on the hypothesis that real knowledge is contained in conceptions, not in sensations. The sensational theory of knowledge, the theory first propounded by Protagoras, Plato condemned with arguments among the principal of which are the following. If the sensational theory be true, "I wonder that he [Protagoras] did not begin his great work on Truth with the declaration that a pig or a baboon or some other stranger monster which has sensation is the measure of all things;" again, that theory fails to account for the permanent character of knowledge, since on the supposition that both "object" and "percipient" are in constant flux there can be no permanence anywhere; and, finally, the theory is self-contradictory, since by its own terms it may be just as well false as true. No, the

---

[1] *Republic*, p. 534; *Phædrus*, pp. 277, 278.
[2] *Phædrus*, pp. 265, 266; *Parmenides*, pp. 128 and 136; *Republic*, pp. 427, 428. In the passage last mentioned, Plato refers to, by name, the method termed by Mill the "Method of Residues." "Modern Inductive Philosophy" was largely "anticipated" by Plato and Aristotle.

truth is that knowledge is given in conceptions and conceptions only. The method of knowledge is the method of thought; the seeing of "unity and plurality in nature." "If I find any man" who can do that, "him I follow and walk in his footsteps as if he were a God." Now induction, the "upward way" of knowledge, is to Plato but tentative, suggestive, not final and conclusive; a begetter of insight but not of science; and must be supplemented by division, the "downward way" of knowledge. Induction suggests a hypothesis or possible definition of some whole; division verifies or overthrows the hypothesis by exhibiting distinctly and in their relations the parts of the whole defined. With regard to division Plato says, "you should not clip off too small a piece . . . the safe way is to cut through the middle, and this is the more likely way of finding classes. Attention to this principle makes all the difference in a process of inquiry."[1] This method of division is known as dichotomy. The method of investigation which consists in following out opposite hypotheses and comparing their consequences is, of course, Eleatic in origin. That hypothesis whose consequences are the most probable is the truer hypothesis. The dialectic method as just described is, as we shall see, the precursor of the Aristotelian logic.

Dialectic as a System.

Thought and Being. — In the conceptions arrived at by the dialectic method, then, we have knowledge, *i.e.*, we have the real thought of being, and the only real or permanent conviction possible for us. That this is true appeared to Plato, not only as a consequence of the

[1] *Statesman*, 262; *Sophist*, throughout.

synthesis of the Eleatic and Socratic doctrines of being and knowledge but from such considerations as the following : The "divine madness" that seizes upon "ingenuous natures" and impels them to philosophy, can be but the working of the soul's innate knowledge of a higher state than the present, a state in which thought and being are more immediately one. Again, the source of knowledge even in the present existence is not the organs of sense, but the soul working through them, and our cognitions, which must be cognitions of something, are cognitions, not of the world of sense as such, but of being. Finally, we cannot suppose that there is anything absolutely out of relation to us, for in such a case, God who, if anything, would be out of relation to us, since he is absolute, could not know us and our world : we should constitute an absolute being by ourselves, — all of which is absurd, "monstrous."[1] But if this be true, being is intelligent, since thought as the thought of being is (by virtue of the unity of thought and being) being so far as it (being) is capable of being thought. Being, therefore, thinks or is intelligent.

The World of Ideas. — To determine, then, the nature of being as an object of thought (and it is only as such that we can know it) we must determine what are the absolute conceptions. These, in number and nature, correspond with the types or classes of phenomenal existence. Now as thought and being are one, and as the absolute conceptions have each a separate character and place in thought, it follows that being is not merely one in nature but many also. Being as one in many is

[1] *Phædrus*, p. 245; *Theætetus*, pp. 184, 185, 203-209; *Phædo*, pp. 74, 75; *Parmenides*, 132-135.

termed by Plato the Idea or World of Ideas (εἴδη). So far as we can speak of beings, there are, then, corresponding to the types or classes of phenomenal existences, certain entities, which are noumenal: Ideas. As objects of definite knowledge, the Ideas are distinct, fixed, independent:[1] in this they are in sharp contrast with sense-natures, which as Heraclitus held, are fleeting and pass into their opposites, "admit generation into or out of one another." But the Ideas "participate" in, or "commune" with, each other. Not, however, promiscuously, but in certain cognizable ways. The ideas of rest and motion, for example, do not participate in each other except indirectly, through participation in being.[2] The communion of being and not-being is explained as follows. Being is all-inclusive, embracing even not-being, unless, indeed, being is "pure and fixed emptiness." But being is not such: we cannot conceive it "to be devoid of life and mind, and to remain in awful unmeaningness and fixture."[3] In speaking, therefore, of not-being, *i.e.*, generation, motion, variety, etc., we speak not of something opposed to being but different merely. In general, then, not-being is the element of otherness or difference inherent in being.[4] The Ideas together constitute an organism which is governed by the Idea of the Good (the end of all things). The Idea of the Good embraces

[1] *Phædo*, pp. 78–103.
[2] The communion of Ideas is treated especially in the dialogues, *Sophist, Parmenides*, and *Philebus*.
[3] *Sophist*, pp. 247–250, 257, 259.
[4] Translated into modern phraseology, this means that all motion, all change, is but the self-affirmation, the self-identification of the Eternal.

within itself a "mixture"[1] of "mind" (which is definite and knowable) and "pleasure" (which is relatively indefinite and unknowable) together with the cause of the "mixture," or soul. The Good is thus not abstract but concrete; and as the only causal principle in the universe is soul, the Idea of the Good is a concrete, intelligent (and intelligible) power. The Good is further described by Plato as including measure, beauty, symmetry, as well as "mind," "pleasure," and "causality."[2] Of the Good as the supreme Idea he says: "Whether I am right or not God only knows; but, whether true or false, my opinion is that in all the world of knowledge the Idea of the Good appears last of all and is seen only with effort, and when seen, is inferred to be the universal author of all things beautiful and right, parent of light and lord of light in this world, and the source of truth and reason in the other: this is the first great cause which he who would act rationally either in public or in private life must behold."[3] Again, "the Good is not only the author of knowledge in all things known [as the sun is of "visibility in all things visible"] but of their being and essence, yet the Good is not essence [mere being?] but exceeds essence in dignity and power."[4] As the supreme Idea is an intelligent and intelligible power, those below it must, as partaking in it, also be intelligent and intelligible powers. (Being, indeed, is simply power.[5]) The realm of Ideas is, then, a spiritual kingdom: an independent, self-existent, eternal community of intelligent beings.[6]

[1] *Philebus*, p. 27.   [2] *Ibid.*, pp. 61, 63, 65, 67.   [3] *Republic*, p. 517.
[4] *Republic*, pp. 508, 509. See p. 506.   [5] *Sophist*, pp. 247, 248.
[6] There seems to be no real warrant for affirming (as some do) that to Plato the Ideas are merely thoughts in the "mind" of God.

Relation of the Ideal, to the Phenomenal, World. — In the foregoing is virtually contained Plato's answer to a question that now naturally arises, What is the relation of the world of Ideas to the phenomenal world? to knowledge and objects of knowledge in the world given to us? The answer is, in general terms, as follows: "That which imparts truth to the object and knowledge to the subject is what I would have you term the Idea of the Good, and that you will regard as the cause of science and truth as known by us." But to speak particularly, *first*, of *Ideas as related to human knowledge.* It is by virtue of the presence of the Idea in us that we are self-moving, self-identifying, and so, capable of knowledge, whether it be scientific comprehension or common understanding. The idea as the source and synthesis of cognition and being, makes possible for us by its working in us the true thought of reality. For Plato, consequently, knowledge possessed certain elements not recognized by earlier philosophers. The Eleatics failed to find in our cognition of phenomena anything but "opinion"; Plato declaring things themselves, and our cognition of them to be of the Idea, posited philosophically (and was the first who did so) the knowledge of the real in the phenomenal. Again, the Lesser Socratics affirmed that only "identical propositions" are valid. Plato discovered a principle of synthesis, and thus showed the possibility and the necessity of real *judgments*. Thirdly, Socrates did not entirely rise above the notion of merely correct conceptions to that of ontologically true conceptions, was sceptical as to the possibility of absolute science, hence did not attain to a pure metaphysics. Plato did this in positing the Idea as the fountain of knowledge and being. In so doing, he gave a new content and a new method to philosophy. The content of philosophy is not the abstract entity termed by the Eleatics Being, nor the purely phenomenal world, which the Sophists declared knowable only in individual sensation, and Socrates only in individual conception, but the concretion of these, the world of Ideas, in itself and as having effect and manifestation in the phenomenal world, and the phenomenal world as having its source and cognoscibility in the Ideal world. Again, from the fact that the Idea is the source of knowledge and being, it follows that the true method or "way" of knowledge is the "downward way," induction being but an eye-opener, merely a condition of nascent or incipient insight. Dialectic, then, is in the last analysis, not merely the method of our thinking and our theory of the Idea, but is also the method of the Idea and the Ideal theory of the Idea. And as the "downward way," it is not *mere* division, but, since the Idea is universal and not to be *absolutely* divided — also synthesis; it makes place for the "unity of opposites." But, *secondly*, as to the *relation* of *the Ideas to the world of objective, sensible phenomena*, the Ideas are conceived by Plato, not only as causes,[1] but as archetypes of things, the eternal patterns to which the artificer of the world looks in framing the world.[2] The world of Ideas is self-existent and independent; phenomenal objects "participate" in Ideas or are "imitations" of them.

[1] *Phædo*, p. 75; *Phædrus*, p. 95; *Zeller's Plato and the Older Academy*, pp. 262, 268. Schwegler's *Handbook of the Hist. of Philos.* (Stirling's trans.), p. 79.
[2] *Parmenides*, p. 132; *Timæus*, p. 28.

The exact nature of this participation, or imitation, seems not to have been explained by Plato quite satisfactorily to himself (or to those coming after him). In fact, Plato recognized at this point certain unsolved difficulties in his theory of Ideas, and was impelled towards a modification of the theory.[1] For example, if the Ideas are entirely independent of the phenomenal world, *how* can they be the source of existence to other things or of knowledge in us? These difficulties were afterwards pointed out and used against the theory by Aristotle.[2] Though participating in Ideas, phenomenal objects are but imperfect representations of Ideas. Why this is so, is explained in the theory of nature, or of that which, instead of being uncreated, fixed, and scientifically cognoscible, is created, changing, and an object of "opinion" and "sense."

Physics, or the Theory of Nature.

The Method of Physical Speculation. — In the philosophical study of nature it is necessary, first of all, Plato reminds us, to remember that, owing to the contingency pertaining to things created and changing, we cannot, in speculating upon such things, proceed with dialectic exactness and certainty of method, but must "observe the rule of probability."[3] Plato shared, to some extent, Socrates's distrust of physical speculation, (as well as Heraclitus's view of the mutability of all phenomenal things), regarding it, however, as a kind of pardonable and perhaps praiseworthy indulgence, though far from

---

[1] See below, p. 112.
[2] *Parmenides*, pp. 132–135; Aristotle's *Metaphysics*, Bk. XIII. chs. 4 and 5.
[3] *Timæus*, pp. 28, 29, 48.

possessing the dignity and value of dialectic, or true science. "A man may sometimes set aside arguments about eternal things, and for recreation turn to consider the truths of generation which are only probable; thus he attains pleasure not to be repented of, and makes for himself during his life a wise and moderate pastime."[1]

The Cosmos. — The created world is as perfect an imitation and manifestation of the Idea as was practicable : it is a living, intelligible being, a "blessed god." God formed the world because he is good and "desired that all things be as like himself as possible." The world is not an absolutely perfect manifestation of the Idea because there was, when the world was created, a certain element of necessity which reason had to "persuade" or "get the better of," though it could not completely overcome it.[2] This element of necessity and obstacle to the complete manifestation of the Idea is "matter." God (Idea as power working towards an end) formed, first, the world-soul, by uniting as perfectly as possible, according to certain numerical relations, an unchangeable, indivisible essence (Idea as fixed, intelligent and intelligible nature) and a divisible, corporeal, movable nature, thus creating an intermediate essence partaking of the nature of the "same and other" and possessing the power to declare the "sameness and diversity of things." This mediating, mathematical intelligence (the world-soul) — mathematics, we have seen, is, with Plato, intermediate between science and opinion — God diffused throughout, and united perfectly with, a perfect body made of the four elements, fire, air, water, earth — "in the harmony

[1] *Timæus*, p. 59.   [2] *Ibid.*, pp. 30, 33, 48.

of proportions " — and smooth, even, perfectly spherical. The soul he formed prior in time and excellence to the body to be the "ruler and mistress of it."[1] The world is, accordingly, a "blessed god," not eternal, indeed, but an image of eternity and a perfect whole, indissoluble except by the hand of the Creator. Time and the world, created together, are without end. The world is divided according to the "sameness and diversity" of "motion" into two spheres, that of the fixed stars and that of the planets, all these having souls and being gods. The latter revolve about the earth (which is fixed and spherical and is pierced by the spindle or axis of the universe) in spiral courses from west to east. The four elements are not eternal but were created out of an eternal indestructible somewhat, the "receptacle and in a manner the nurse of all generation," an "invisible, formless being which receives all things and attains in an extraordinary way a portion of the intelligible, and is most incomprehensible." Plato seems to identify it with space, a "third nature" — the indivisible essence and the corporeal, divisible essence being the first and second — which is "eternal and perceived without the help of sense and by a spurious reason."[2] It is not a corporeal substance for it is not that *out* of which but that *in* which phenomena have become, and it is in its very essence negation or not-being (passive, however, rather than active), and the occasion of the relative not-being, or the mutability, of phenomena. It may be likened to a mother, phenomena to a child, and the source of phenomena to a father.[3] It is the mean, or middle term, between phe-

---

[1] *Timæus*, pp. 32, 34, 35, 38.   [2] *Ibid.*, pp. 51, 52.   [3] *Ibid.*, p. 50.

nomena and the Idea.[1] It is that element of "necessity" — "matter" — which hinders, while it makes possible, the manifestation of the Idea. Fire, air, water, and earth are, consequently, not corporeal but merely geometrical bodies, fire being four-faced, air eight-faced, water twenty-faced, earth six-faced (cubical). All this (and much more of similar character), it must be remembered, is, to Plato, only "probable" or conjectural — not science.

Body and Soul. — Thus much for that portion of the work of creation which God himself performed. The rest was given into the hands of the created gods. These, "imitating the power" of God, formed man and animals, the latter being but a lower type of the former.[2] The "seed" of the immortal part of the soul of man was provided by God himself. It is, of course, by this part, which is simple, self-identical, self-moving, and indestructible, that the soul participates in the Idea and is rational. The mortal part has two portions, the "spirited" (courage) and the appetitive (desire). The former is naturally inclined to obey the immortal, or rational, part of the soul, but is too often dragged down by the appetitive part, which is animal, and even vegetable, in its tendencies. The rational part of the soul is located in the head, courage in the heart, and desire in the lower portion of the trunk, particularly the liver, which is the seat also of inspiration and prophecy, these being but a very low order of knowledge. To Plato the so-called parts of the soul are not parts but faculties. Of their inter-connection he

[1] See Jowett's Introduction to the *Timæus*, section 3.
[2] Plato not an "evolutionist."

offers no explanation. Perception is of like by like (as with Empedocles). In sight, for example, the fire from the eye meets the external fire, and vision is the result. Sight and hearing are the noblest of the senses. "Thus much let us say: that God invented and gave sight to this end, — that we might behold the courses of intelligence which are akin to them, the unperturbed to the perturbed; and that we, learning them and being partakers of the true computations of nature, might imitate the absolutely unerring courses of God and regulate our own vagaries. The same [*mutatis mutandis*] may be affirmed of speech and hearing."[1] The soul was "implanted in the body by necessity": entered into it in consequence of a fall from a nobler, preëxistent state. There is not between the two that perfect harmony which exists between the world-soul and its body ("the perfect animal"). On the contrary, there is a certain antagonism[2] between body and soul, the influence of the former upon the latter being evil and degrading, the cause of ignorance and spiritual disease. The body, indeed, is the soul's prison. The relation between the two is represented as follows in the well-known allegory of the Charioteer and Winged Horses, in which are symbolized, on the one hand, reason, on the other, "courage," or passion, and appetite.[3] "Now the winged horses and the charioteer of the gods are all of them noble, and of noble breed, while ours are mixed; and

---

[1] *Timæus*, pp. 45, 47.

[2] There is a certain discrepancy between the accounts of the *Phædrus* and the *Timæus* on this point. The *Phædrus* has been followed in what is now given.

[3] *Phædrus*, pp. 246-255.

we have a charioteer who drives them in a pair; and one of them is noble and of noble origin, and, as might be expected, there is a great deal of trouble in managing them. . . . Now the chariots of the gods, self-balanced, upward glide in obedience to the rein; but the others have a difficulty, for the steed who has evil in him, if he has not been properly trained by the charioteer, gravitates and inclines and sinks towards the earth, and this is the hour of extremest agony and conflict of the soul. For the immortal souls, when they are at the end of their course, go out and stand upon the back of heaven [the sphere of the fixed stars], and the revolution of the spheres carries them around and they behold the world beyond." When, through the unruliness of the steeds, the soul becomes unable to rise sufficiently high to "behold the vision of truth, and through some mishap sinks beneath the double load of forgetfulness and vice, her feathers fall from her and she drops to the earth, then the law ordains that this soul shall in the first generation pass not into that of any other animal but only of man, and the soul which has seen the most of truth shall come to the birth as a philosopher, or artist, or musician, or lover; that which has seen the truth in the second degree shall be a righteous king, or warrior, or lord; the soul, which is of the third class, shall be a politician, or economist, or trader; the fourth shall be a lover of gymnastic toils or a physician; the fifth, a prophet or hierophant; to the sixth, a poet or imitator will be appropriate; to the seventh, the life of an artisan or husbandman; to the eighth, that of a sophist or a demagogue; to the ninth, that of a tyrant: all these are states of probation, in which he who lives righteously improves, and he who lives unrighteously deteriorates his lot." The soul's chief inspiration to righteousness is the recollection of the eternal beauty of which it had heard or caught a glimpse. This "wingless probation" continues for the soul of the philosopher or the lover who is faithful to his insight, three thousand years, the soul then returning to the place whence it came. Others are judged "when they have completed their first life," and, at the end of the first thousand years, they have a new choice of life, the good and the bad souls alike taking what they prefer, *i.e.*, what their natures prompt them to take. "And the soul of the man may pass into the life of a beast, or from the beast again to the man;" but the souls of those who have not seen the truth will not pass into human forms, but into those of animals. After death souls are classified as holy, moderately good, curably wicked, and incurably wicked. The last are punished eternally.—From the foregoing may be gathered several essential points in the Platonic psychology: the mixed nature of the soul, its participation in the Idea, and the necessity that the Idea be in a manner realized in it, the preëxistent state, and the recollection of that state, the immortality of the soul, future retribution, and the transmigration of souls. The logical connection between these may be briefly, though imperfectly, indicated as follows: the soul as participating in the Idea must be prior to the body; it must, even though immersed in the slough of sense, retain some recollection of that preëxistent state, for the Idea *is* and cannot be obliterated by sense; but the Idea as the Good cannot be completely attained to in the world of sense; hence there must be a future state and future retribution; and finally, the character of the retribution must vary with the bodies or immediate environment of the souls of men. The doctrines of preëxistence and of recollection, or reminiscence, demand special notice. They seemed to Plato to follow not only from the theory of the soul as an offshoot of the Idea, but also from the nature of knowledge as such. A certain boy, Meno, knows nothing of geometry, and yet Socrates succeeds in getting him to understand a geometrical demonstration and in drawing from him certain principles of demonstration; which would be impossible, thinks Plato, if the principles of demonstration had not lain already in the boy's mind.[1] Again, though we say that pieces of wood or stone are equal, we yet perceive that they are not absolutely equal, and the conclusion must be that the soul possesses, by a sort of recollection implying preëxistence, the conception of absolute equality.[2] The argument for the immortality of the soul may be summarized as follows:[3] The soul is "ever in motion" and self-moving; it cannot be destroyed by immorality, the only thing that could destroy it, if anything could; the soul is immortal because God is good, and cannot allow so beautiful a creation to perish; the thirst for absolute knowledge and for a future life, implies immortality; opposites pass into each other, sleeping into waking, death into life, etc.; preëxistence implies immortality; the soul is an invisible essence, and so possesses the

---

[1] *Meno*, pp. 81–83.
[2] *Phædo*, pp. 74 and fol.
[3] See Ueberweg's *History of Philosophy*, Vol. I. p. 127; also *Phædrus*, p. 245; *Republic*, p. 609; *Timæus*, p. 41; *Phædo*, pp. 62–107.

imperishable, indestructible character of the Idea; the soul is not a "harmony" of bodily activities, but is itself, the rather a principle of harmony; it participates in the Idea of life, is immortal by virtue of the fact that it *lives*. In the *Phædo* (p. 79) Plato conceives immortality as synonymous in essence, not with everlastingness, but with wisdom, *i.e.*, perfect self-knowledge and self-determination.

Plato's Ethics.

General Basis. — The conception of the soul as participating in the Idea and as immortal, is the basis of Plato's ethical doctrines. The life of the soul is one life; it is, by reason of the very nature of the soul as an original indissoluble harmony and principle of harmony, the union of the individual with himself and others, not only in the present existence, but in a future state also; it is the life of justice with its necessary concomitant happiness. The state, therefore, in which alone the individual soul is furnished with the conditions necessary for the realization by the soul of harmony in itself and with others in this present existence, is but an instrument of the Ideal, eternal life, the life of the Idea of the Good.[1]

The Method of Ethics. — From the immediately preceding statements it appears that Ethics and Politics, the sciences of individual and of statal good and virtue, are to Plato one. And it is an essential characteristic of the method of Plato in the *Republic* that he begins with a consideration of the state as being the "individual written larger and on a larger scale,"[2] and having given a merely tentative theory of that, passes to the

[1] *Republic*, pp. 611, 612.   [2] *Ibid.*, p. 368.

individual, then back to the state, and so on. This characteristic as well as the content of his theory has its source in Plato's ever-present anxiety about the true ideal totality of things, his never-ceasing quest after a true and comprehensive principle of synthesis among things. By the use of this method he diminishes, if he does not obviate altogether, the appearance of arbitrarily applying to one sphere principles discovered in another. To him there is no abstract individual: the individual is the state in miniature.

Nature and End of the State. — Historically considered, the state, Plato agrees with the Sophists in holding, arises out of natural, human necessity: physical need, self-interest, lead to division of labor and to association for common and mutual benefit. But the state is not *merely* an association for the better supplying of natural or animal wants, the realization of the nature of the individual as such; government is not merely a police force having its only use in the prevention of the clashing of individual wills and interests. The state is an organism, a vital totality, whose essence lies in its being an instrument and manifestation of the Idea; the individuals constituting it consciously coöperate in the realization of the absolute conception of the whole. The state exists for the special benefit of no particular individual or class of individuals.

The "Parts" of the State and the Virtue pertaining to Each. — The members of the state are divided into three classes: the husbandmen, who supply the natural needs of the state; the fighters or military class, who defend the state against encroachment from without, or make conquests for the enlargement of the territory of the state; and the rulers, or counsellors, who determine the plans by which the state subsists as an instrument of the Idea, the embodiment of the conception of justice. The two last-named classes Plato designates as the guardians of the state. Each of these classes has its peculiar virtue: the virtue of the husbandmen being temperance, that of the fighters courage, that of the rulers wisdom. A careful and long-continued training is necessary to the making of the guardians: they are to be tried "more thoroughly than gold is tried in the fire." They are not only to be given that education in music, gymnastics, and the sciences which is requisite as a preparation for the study of philosophy, but they are to be tried with tests of memory, with "toils and pains and conflicts," and "with enchantments and terrors." If they retain under all circumstances, "a rhythmical, harmonious nature, such as will be most serviceable to the man himself and to the state," they are worthy to become guardians of the state.[1] They are to have no property beyond what is absolutely necessary, to have no private houses, to be allowed only a "living" salary, to have common meals, and to reside together. — But what are the virtues in themselves, and where is justice? To answer this latter question, we must, says Plato, by the "method of residues" carefully eliminate the known virtues, one after another, until we arrive at justice. First, then, is wisdom, the virtue of the counsellors, which is knowledge that advises "not about any particular thing in the state [*e.g.*, carpentering, brazen implements, agriculture] but about the whole state, and considers what may be regarded

[1] *Republic*, Bks. II. and III.

as the best policy both internal and external."[1] Next may be eliminated courage, the virtue of the fighters, or auxiliaries of the counsellors, which is the "preservation in the soldiers of the opinion which the law ordains about the true nature of dangers." Temperance, the virtue of the husbandmen, may be best described as the "natural harmony of master and slaves, both in states and individuals, in which the subjects are as willing to obey as the governors are to rule."[2] Now justice, also, would appear to be a harmony, and is not with perfect ease to be distinguished from temperance. It is, however, that harmony wherein each individual minds his own business and is not a "busy-body," and each class in the state preserves its own sphere. Justice is the all-pervading spirit of harmony, the union of the many in one, of whole and part in the state.

Virtue in the Individual. — According, now, to the method proposed at the beginning, we are to apply what has been found to be true of the state to the individual. The individual, then, has in him the three principles of wisdom, courage, and temperance; wisdom being the virtue of reason, courage of spirit or passion, and temperance of appetite. The individual, therefore, "whose several principles do their own work will be just, and will do his own work." "Assuming the threefold division of the soul, must not injustice be a kind of quarrel between these three — a meddlesomeness and interference, and rising up of a part of the soul against the whole soul, an assertion of unlawful authority, which is made by a rebellious subject against a true prince, of whom he is the natural vassal — that is the sort of

[1] *Republic*, p. 428.   [2] *Ibid.*, pp. 428-434.

thing: the confusion and error of these parts is injustice, and intemperance, and ignorance, and in general all vice."[1] Further, the qualities that make a state, make a man: the good citizen is the good man. — As a corollary to this theory of virtue, it follows that the Sophistic notion of virtue as the whim or pleasure of the individual, and of justice as the will or pleasure of the strongest,[2] is false. And (it may not improperly be added at this point) to Plato the Socratic idea that virtue is knowledge is not quite the correct one. Virtue, as we learn from the dialogue *Philebus*, is a union of "mind," or knowledge, and pleasure, and there is a kind of natural virtue consisting in a disposition, unconsciously acquired, to do right deeds. The great benefit of education to the young is the creation in them by it of this tendency (unconscious though it may be) to take pleasure in good things, to have good instincts, to entertain right feelings generally.[3]

State Administration.[4] — But how shall the state be managed, and, in particular, what is to be done with the women and children? Is not the state to be conducted on the principle that "friends will have all things in common"? It is, in the first place, hardly possible to refuse to the women the same education that is given to men, ridiculous as such a plan may appear at first sight. The mere difference as regards the begetting and bearing of children is unessential. The education that makes a *man* a good guardian will make a woman, also, a good guardian. In the second place, there must be not only sameness of education and pursuits but also community,

[1] *Republic*, p. 444.
[2] *Ibid.*, Bk. I.
[3] *Ibid.*, p. 402.
[4] *Ibid.*, Bk. V.

or the holding in common, of women and children — "no one is to know his own child, nor any child his parent." The union of the sexes must be made as "holy" as possible, and, to this end, must be under the strict and scientific supervision of the wise men of the state. The best of either sex must be "united with the best as often as possible, and the inferior with the inferior, and they are to rear the offspring of the one sort of union, but not of the other." The union is to be managed secretly and by proper officers, who will also take charge of the offspring. There must, of course, be no irregular or illegitimate unions. But, in the third place, there must be community of property. The public spirit of the guardians must not be allowed to suffer a check from any such distinction as *meum* and *tuum*. As to the practicability of a state in which there is community of women, children, and property, there is, indeed, some doubt. In times of war there would be no difficulty; the women and children would accompany the men. The children should become accustomed to the sight of such dangers as they themselves may have to face when they become adults. Acts of bravery must be recompensed by increased liberty to beget children; acts of cowardice by degradation to the rank of husbandmen or artisans. Love for the state must be kept pure and strong. It remains true, however, that only "when philosophers rule, or the kings and princes of this world have the spirit and power of philosophy, will this ideal state, as has been said, have a possibility of life and behold the light of day." But the theory is, nevertheless, none the worse as a theory "because we are unable to prove the possibility of a city being ordered in the manner described."[1]

The False Forms of State and their Genesis. — Having constructed the pattern state, which he designates as the *Aristocracy*, Plato gives, with a view to showing still more pointedly the nature of justice and injustice and the relation between them and happiness and misery, an analysis of the false forms of the state, together with the kinds of individuals corresponding to them, and of the genesis of these forms and the classes of individuals corresponding to them. The false forms of the state are four in number; the *timocracy*, or government of honor; the *oligarchy*, or government of the few and the rich; the *democracy*, or government of the (uneducated) multitude; and *tyranny*. There are, of course, four sorts of individuals to correspond with these. The false forms of the state, taken in the order in which they have just been named, are regarded by Plato as successive degenerations of the true form, or aristocracy, *i.e.*, the government of the wisest and best. "All political changes originate in divisions of the actual governing power," that is, in strife. Now the strife by which aristocracy degenerates into timocracy arises in the following way. The guardians losing, through ignorance and mismanagement, the control of marriages and births, there springs up a weaker race, which undervalues knowledge and culture, and, lacking thus the principle of harmony, falls into inequality, irregularity, and, finally, strife. The courageous, or "spirited," element gets the advantage of the knowledge-loving and, although the guardian class remains the honored class and does not fall back into

[1] *Republic*, Bks. VIII. and IX.

the place of the husbandmen or artisans, philosophers are excluded from power, the military class predominates, and the state is better fitted for war than for peace: one thing, and one thing only, is predominantly seen, — the spirit of contention and ambition. Such is the timocratical state and its genesis. The timocratical individual and *his* genesis are like unto them. The son of a "brave" but "easy-going" father, he comes to lack "single-mindedness towards virtue," and to be a lover of power and honor; he is no longer wise and morally sound and whole, but ambitious and contentious. Oligarchy arises when the desire of power and honor, which characterizes the timocracy, grows into a thirst for gold and exclusive possession. For the realization of this desire, force and intimidation are resorted to. The evils of such a form of government are manifestly these: riches hold the place of knowledge; the state is divided against itself, the rich on the one side, the poor on the other; war cannot be carried on because the rich rulers are more afraid of the poor subjects than of the external enemy of the state; there is no longer a systematic division of pursuits; there is in the state a large floating element that has no vital interest in it: in short, oligarchy is a government of the wildest extremes. The oligarchical individual is of the same pattern; avaricious, selfish, arbitrarily coercing his better impulses and bending all his energies to the hoarding of wealth. Instead of rationalizing and ennobling his passions, he keeps them in slavish subjection to his one desire, and they are ready to turn against him at the earliest opportunity. Democracy and the "democratical man" originate as follows: the rich come to rule arbitrarily and exasperate the poor; war comes, from within or without, and then the rich must fight against or by the side of the poor, and there is a general redistribution of power and privileges. Then follow false freedom, irreconcilable differences of opinion, a throwing off of responsibility to the State, entire abandonment of principle, an altogether "charming form of government, full of variety and diversity, and dispensing equality to equals and unequals alike." As for the democratical individual, he grows out of the oligarchical in the most natural manner possible. He just gets a taste of the honey of dissipation and the unrestrained gratification of desire, and away fly the old, miserly habits, the passions grow fierce and numberless, and "insolence and anarchy and waste and impudence," under the lead of vain conceit, come trooping into his soul in "bright array" called by the sweet names of "breeding," "liberty," "magnificence," "courage"! If he attemps to reform, he assumes one virtue, then another and another, and finally "shakes his head and says they are all alike, and that one is as honorable as another." He is a rare being, full of "liberty, equality, and fraternity," an epitome of all mankind, is emulated by all — men and women alike — but he knows nothing about order and law. "And now comes the most beautiful of all, man and state alike, tyranny and the tyrant." Tyranny springs from democracy by excess of liberty. In the anarchy that follows "when all things are ready to burst with liberty," the people "always have some champion whom they nurse into greatness" and make "protector," and he, with the mob at his back, accuses, condemns, and banishes or kills whomsoever he pleases. If he is driven out he gets back again, for he is the "people's friend"; then he is more of a "wolf" than ever. Happy man! he flatters and is flattered, hates and is hated, suspects and is suspected, plots and is plotted against, and the state over which he tyrannizes is in a most "blessed" condition. The tyrannical individual is like unto him. Giving his appetites full liberty he is obliged to deceive, to coerce, and to perform deeds of violence in order to maintain himself and his rabble. He has in him the essence of the highwayman, the robber of temples, the man-stealer; is just the sort of creature the rabble choose for their leader when anarchy comes. No man is meaner and more unhappy than he; none more of a slave, more of a coward — except the tyrant in *public* station. Unquestionably the tyrannical man and the tyrannical state are the worst — the most unjust and the most miserable — of all. — The upshot of Plato's masterly analysis of the false forms of state and the individuals like unto them is this: justice and happiness, whether in the individual or the state, are inseparable. "Must we hire a herald or shall I proclaim the result — that the best and justest man is also the happiest, and that this is he who is the most royal master of himself; and that the worst and most unjust man is also the most miserable and that this is he who is the greatest tyrant of himself and of his state."[1]

The Eternal Life. — Plato's account of justice does not end with his analysis of the state. With him justice is a matter of the soul as an immortal being, and of the Idea; and ethics, in the broad sense of the term, is more than politics. The paramount thought with Plato is that of the Eternal Life, the life of the Idea, or God.

[1] *Republic*, p. 80.

Justice, instead of being merely the proper performance of duties incident to membership in a social order, is the perception, enjoyment, and application of absolute truth and beauty; the being like God, and the living as a member of an eternal order. The just man is the child of the gods as well as the state. In all this is to be found further proof of the union of justice with happiness: for the enjoyment of that which, as the pleasure of the just man must be, is essential and permanent, is itself essential and permanent, and the "gods have a care of any one whose desire is to become just and to be like God, as far as man can attain his likeness by the pursuit of virtue." The true life is therefore a blessed life; the crown of victory in the immortal race belongs to the just alone.[1]

Beauty and Art. — To the foregoing account of the Good we may append a word on Beauty, which is inseparable from goodness. Beauty is the symmetry pervading that mixture of "mind" and "pleasure" which constitutes the Good; and the business of art is to reproduce, or imitate, ideal reality, or the symmetry of the ideal truth and goodness that are reflected in phenomena. Plato cares nothing for "art for art's sake": he cares only for the Idea, — a faithful "imitation," or representation, of that is respectable, but an "imitation" of an "imitation" of it is abominable. The good man "imitates" the Idea, and is beautiful; but the tragic poet who "imitates" bad men, even perfectly, is a monster, "thrice removed from the king and from truth."[2] "We must remain firm in our conviction that hymns to the gods, and praises of famous men are the only poetry

---

[1] *Republic*, pp. 612, 613.   [2] *Ibid.*, p. 597.

which ought to be admitted into our state."[1] Homer and his followers must therefore be expurgated or else must be driven out. As for rhetoricians and orators, let them learn the nature of the soul and speak accordingly. The Idea, whether in men's minds or the outward universe, is sufficient unto itself. Rhetoric as practised by the Sophists and professional rhetoricians is on a level with the art of cooking; it is a mere "knack," gotten by a kind of accident and having nothing in common with a science of the soul or with dialectic, which is the true and only science and art of thinking and speaking.

The Later Form of Plato's Philosophy. — The foregoing is a sketch of the philosophy of Plato in that form which is most conspicuous in his writings, and has been historically the more celebrated and, perhaps, more influential. There are certain other doctrines of Plato, later, apparently, in origin than those already considered. From Aristotle[2] we learn that Plato, who, as we have seen, was not completely satisfied with the doctrine of Ideas in its earlier form, came, under the influence of Pythagoreanism, to hold that Ideas, instead of being original, were derivative, having for their elements, on the one hand, the One, and on the other, the Great and the Small; the One being the principle of definiteness in the Ideas, and the Great and Small, which are elements of "duas" or duality, being the principle of diversity and indefiniteness, *i.e.*, the material principle. "Plato," says Aristotle, "conceived that, since the Ideas are causes of all things else, the elements of them are the

---

[1] *Republic*, p. 607. See also Bks. II. and III.
[2] *Metaphysics*, Bk. I. ch. 6, and other passages.

elements of all existences. The Great and the Small, therefore, are causes as matter (*i.e.*, material causes) and the One and Numbers as substance (*i.e.*, formal causes). From the Great and the Small Ideas arise by participation in the One." Plato held with the Pythagoreans that the One is an entity, not a predicate of something else; also that numbers are the causes of existence to all other things (than Ideas). But though the Pythagoreans identified numbers and phenomenal existences, Plato regarded them as separate, having been determined so to do by his method. In the later theory of Plato, then, Ideas and numbers constitute, as distinguished from phenomenal existences, a class by themselves. Aristotle expressly says, however, that Plato held the Ideal numbers to be intermediate between Ideas proper and sensible things. Ideal numbers differ from ordinary numbers in being qualitatively different from one another. This theory of Ideas and Ideal numbers has affinity, it will be observed, with the doctrine of the *Timæus*, already stated, that the world-soul is mathematical in nature. — In the *Laws* Plato gives a theory of the "second best" (not an Ideal) state; "the first and highest form of the state, and of the government, and of the law," being "that in which there prevails most widely the ancient saying that friends have all things in common"[1] (the form described in the *Republic*). In the *Laws*, as in the *Republic*, it is declared that the state has as end the good of all, not of any person or party merely.[2] But the good is conceived not so much as the Ideal good (the rule of the Idea in the lives of men) as the good of man as

---

[1] *Laws*, p. 739. [2] *Ibid.*, p. 715. (See *Republic*, p. 420.)

such. The rulers of the "second best" state need not be dialecticians, but only morally and religiously wise and prudent men. Instead of philosophy, they have, as their guide, religion and the science of number.[1] The supreme power in the government is a council of twenty persons, ten old and ten young, — priests, " guardians of the law," and " the general superintendent of education."[2] Community of property, and of women and children, does not obtain in the "second best" state. There are, however, certain regulations as to the maximum and minimum amounts of property that may be held by any person, and as to the disposition of property by purchase, sale, marriage, inheritance, etc.; regulations, also, regarding marriage, the number of families (5040), the disposal of children not heirs.[3] Education is strictly a state affair, and men and women are to be educated alike. The citizens, of whom there are four classes (the class distinction being based on a property distinction), devote themselves to the state and their mental and bodily development; agriculture, commerce, and the industrial arts generally, being carried on by slaves or resident foreigners. The "second best" state is (as, indeed, the title of the work expounding it should suggest) a state based upon the idea of government by *law* instead of by the decisions of wise men, or philosophers, merely. It has no immediate relation to the Idea, the theory of Ideas playing *no* part in the *Laws*.

Result. — The philosophy of Plato is in its genesis a synthesis of elements drawn from earlier thinkers, a

[1] *Laws*, pp. 738, 747, 884, 885, 909.
[2] *Ibid.*, pp. 951, 961.   [3] *Ibid.*, pp. 740–745.

conservation of most, if not all, of the truth, with much of the error (as from a modern point of view it must be deemed) contained in the earlier systems. In its idea and end it is an attempt to discover a complete and true universal of thought and being: no thinker could have been more anxious to do full justice to all the elements of experience in the effort to comprehend the universe in a single mental grasp. But, as has already been suggested, and as Plato himself saw, there is a certain lacuna, or gap, in the system: its first principle, the Idea, does not stand in a perfectly concrete relation with the terms that require to be united. As *the Idea* is merely Plato's name for perfect intelligence, and will, and power, and is the only possible philosophical first principle, the system of Plato is not at fault in its first principle; it is at fault, rather, in the want of complete development of that. Plato has not fully shown why and how the Idea is the source of being, of knowledge, and of goodness. The "ascent to the Idea," which Plato describes as so difficult, is made by Plato with sufficient truth and reality: it is the "downward way" that is imperfectly pointed out and traversed. Plato's thought in this part of his system seems, however, to have undergone a steady development. At first he held that there must be Ideas for all groups of "individuals having a common name,"[1] artificial as well as natural; then, that there are ideas for actual natural classes only (not, as he had formerly held, of relations and negations); and, again, that Ideas may perhaps be merely "patterns [or types] fixed in nature."[2] This last thought, it was left for Aristotle to develop. Finally, in

[1] *Republic*, p. 596.   [2] *Parmenides*, p. 132.

the *Laws* the theory of Ideas found no place.[1] Again, as to the nearness of Ideas to phenomena, the Ideal numbers of the later theory above-described were evidently adopted by Plato as a means of rendering the abstract concrete, or of making the "rational real," and the "real rational." The mathematical nature of the world-soul was assumed for the same purpose. Finally, the notion of "participation" was explained as equivalent to "assimilation," or the bearing a *likeness*, to the Idea. Further critical comment on Plato at this point is rendered superfluous by the fact that we shall have to consider, later, criticisms passed upon him by Aristotle, his truest interpreter and the noblest continuator of his philosophy.

§ 12.

The Disciples of Plato. — The disciples of Plato were numerous.[2] But the difficulties that have just been pointed out in Plato's doctrines, made it impossible that any of them, even Aristotle, should be complete followers of Plato. In fact, it has to be said that just what was most characteristic in Plato's technical doctrines — the theory of Ideas and of the state founded thereon — was *not* adopted without modification and developed, by any of his disciples. But there was a marked difference in the ways in which the ideas of Plato were taken up

---

[1] Not given up completely by Plato himself, however; only held in abeyance.
[2] See the list given by Zeller in *Plato and the Older Academy*, pp. 553–555, note.

and developed by his followers, and on the basis of this we may divide them into two classes, into which fall, on the one hand, Aristotle, who had mastered all of Plato's teaching, and had adopted and developed in natural sequence a larger portion of it than any other of Plato's disciples, and, on the other, certain persons who became leaders in the school of Plato, the Academy, after his death, and who gave adherence only to comparatively limited portions of the Platonic theory, particularly, what has above been given as the Later Theory of Plato. We take up first these incomplete disciples, the members of the Academy.

§ 13.

The Old Academy. — To the Academy in various periods of its existence various names have been applied. As it was in the period immediately after Plato's death, it is known as the Old Academy. The names *Middle Academy* and *New Academy* apply to it in later periods of its existence. At the present moment we are concerned only with the the Old Academy, and have to speak particularly of *Speusippus, Xenocrates, Heraclides of Pontus, Polemo, Crates, Philip of Opus,* and *Crantor.*

Speusippus. — Speusippus, Plato's nephew and successor at the head of the Academy (347–339 B.C.), discarded the Theory of Ideas, and posited many principles instead of one, reducing the Idea of Plato to three distinct "causes," or "principles," viz., the One, Reason, and the Good. He adopted the Pythagorean theory of numbers, separating, however, numbers from things.

He slighted physics; and in ethics advanced the theory that the highest good, or happiness, is virtue *plus* certain external goods needed to make life agreeable, in other words, is "life according to nature."

Xenocrates. — Xenocrates of Chalcedon, the successor of Speusippus at the head of the Academy, and the most distinguished member of the Old Academy, modified the Theory of Ideas, identifying Ideas with mathematical entities. Following Plato, he held all things to be derived from Unity and Duality. He distinguished three media of knowledge and three corresponding classes of existence: thought (which affords pure knowledge), perception (which gives knowledge, though not pure), and opinion (in which truth and knowledge are mixed in equal proportions); intelligible objects (beyond the heavens), sensible objects (within the heavens), and objects intermediate between these (the heavens themselves). The soul, which like all things else springs from the two primary causes, Unity and Duality, is a self-moved number; souls differ by virtue of the difference in the manner in which Unity and Duality unite in forming them. The soul is a spiritual essence, may exist apart from the body, and is, in its irrational as well as its rational part, immortal. The world is a system of graduated existences, is permeated by soul, is ruled by gods and dæmons, and is eternal. The five elements, ether, fire, air, water, earth, originated from atoms. Goods are goods of the soul, of the body, and of the outer life. Virtue is the highest good. Happiness is virtue, or the proper development of natural faculties, *plus* the external goods conducing to it. Wisdom and science are related to prudence as the theoretical to the practical.

Other Members of the Old Academy. — Heraclides of Pontus, who is said to have been "entrusted with the direction of the Academy during Plato's last journey to Sicily," Polemo, who succeeded Xenocrates as head of the Academy, Crates, successor to Polemo, Philip of Opus, editor of Plato's *Laws* and supposed author of *Epinomis*, a supplement to the *Laws*, and Crantor, "the earliest expounder of Platonic writings," deserve mention. Heraclides followed Plato in ethics, and the Pythagoreans in cosmology, in general, but assumed as material principles atomic bodies having the power to affect each other not mechanically but by a kind of affinity, and affirmed the soul to be an ethereal essence. Polemo is said to have devoted himself exclusively to ethics, particularly discountenancing dialectical speculation.

§ 14.

Aristotle.

Life of Aristotle. — Aristotle was born at Stagira, in Thrace, in the year 384 B.C. He was the son of Nicomachus, friend and physician to Amyntas, king of Macedonia. Early left an orphan, he came under the charge of a guardian, named Proxenus, a native of Atarneus, in Asia Minor. In his eighteenth year (367 B.C.), he went to Athens, and for about twenty years was associated with Plato, a considerable portion of the time, no doubt, as pupil, directly and indirectly. Diogenes Laertius says[1] that Aristotle "seceded" from Plato, and that there was a tradition that Plato once declared, "Aristotle has kicked us off as chick-

---

[1] *Lives of the Philosophers* (Bohn's Class. Lib.), p. 151

ens do their mother after they have been hatched"; but modern critics[1] are unwilling to believe that there was any serious breach between master and pupil. Every reader of Aristotle knows, however, that Plato receives a full share of the criticism that it was Aristotle's habit to mete out to all his predecessors in philosophy. Aristotle's ability, intellectual independence, and disposition to criticise, were doubtless early felt by his teacher. Not long after the death of Plato, and perhaps because of that, Aristotle left Athens. He resided at Atarneus, the native place of his guardian, Proxenus, and of Hermeias, a fellow-pupil and governor of Atarneus and Assos. Here he married Pythias, a near relative or friend of Hermeias, and remained until, three years afterwards, Hermeias was betrayed to the Persian king to be put to death; thence he went to Mytelene, and from that place, two or three years later (342 or 341 B.C.), to the court of Philip of Macedon to become the tutor of his son Alexander, afterwards surnamed "The Great." What the effect of this relationship between Aristotle and his pupil was upon the mind and future career of Alexander we cannot exactly say. By it Aristotle gained a royal friend and patron, who rendered him large pecuniary aid towards the prosecution of scientific and philosophical research. At this time he obtained King Philip's consent to the rebuilding of his native city, Stagira, which had a few years previously been destroyed in war, and he himself directed the rebuilding. In 335 B.C., he returned to Athens and there established a philosophical school (a rival to the Academy) in a gymnasium "attached to

[1] See Ueberweg, Zeller, and Grant.

the temple of Apollo Lyceius," whence the school was called the Lyceum. To this school, which became flourishing, and to the composition of scientific and speculative treatises, the next twelve years of Aristotle's life were exclusively devoted. From the fact that instruction was given while the teacher, or teacher and pupils, were walking, or was given in a place called "The Walk" (ὁ περίπατος), the school received the name of the *Peripatetic School.* As between Plato and his pupils, so between Aristotle and his, the friendliest personal relations were cultivated. In 323 B.C., because of his friendship with Alexander and other members of the Macedonian Court, and his supposed sympathy with the Macedonian power, and because of popular, democratic animosity towards philosophers, and of religious bigotry among the Athenians (for he was formally accused of impiety by the chief priest), Aristotle felt compelled to leave Athens. He died the next year, on the island of Eubœa, at the age of sixty-three. From the events of his life, from his will, a copy of which may be found in the "Life" of him by Diogenes Laertius, and from his ethical and political writings, it may be inferred that he was a man of probity and good feeling, and deserved and won the respect and kindly regard of his fellows.

General Character of Aristotle's System, and his Chief Philosophical Works. — To understand the general character of Aristotle's philosophy, not only, but even the outward character of his chief philosophical works, it is necessary to bear in mind the status of philosophical thinking when he began to frame his system. The personal element which Socrates by his character and method had made prominent in philosophy, had been, in large measure, preserved by Plato. Definite and penetrating as was Plato's conception of philosophy, there is, manifestly, in his writings a large mixture, as regards both matter and method, of purely philosophical elements with elements not purely philosophical but *personal;* though in a larger sense of the term than is applicable to the Socratic philosophizing, for the personal element of the Platonic Dialogues is not merely individual and realistic (as is that in Xenophon's *Memorabilia*, for example), but largely dramatic and poetic. From one point of view, though perhaps not the highest and truest, there is an essential duality in the Platonic philosophy, in that it is a compound of philosophical and in a sort non-philosophical elements. Now it happened that (as must be perfectly evident to any one upon even a superficial acquaintance with any of Aristotle's extant writings) Aristotle was, by mental temperament, just of a nature to observe and feel this duality, and to take up and prosecute the inquiry, What *is* and what is *not* pure philosophy, as regards both matter and method? His *earliest* works, written probably when he was under the immediate influence of Plato, were, it is known, dialogues, and were praised by Cicero in such terms that we may properly infer that they were in part imitations — and not unworthy ones — of Plato himself. But his late works, those from which we have to draw our knowledge of his philosophy, are evidently based on a full consciousness of what is, technically speaking, philosophy and what is *not*, and of the grand-divisions of philosophy itself. There had been practised from the time of the Sophists a certain art, or method, of handling ideas as such. This art, which he found in considerable degree of perfection, Aristotle investigated thoroughly, — and was the first who did so, — discovering that there was one branch of it that, if developed, was adequate to real, or scientific, truth, and another that was adequate to probable truth only. This art, or method, and particularly the first-named branch of it, he thought to be an essential feature in philosophical thought (though not a branch of philosophy proper) as distinguished from that which is not philosophical. He expounded it in certain works, which, taken collectively, are now known as his *Organon*, the name originating not with Aristotle himself but with certain of his followers. The name was adopted because of a remark dropped by Aristotle that the thing treated of in the works was a means to, or instrument (ὄργανον) of, philosophy rather than a part of philosophy itself. The works are, therefore, in large measure merely introductory to the strictly philosophical works, though an account of his philosophy has to borrow much from them. One of the six works constituting the *Organon* is on categories of thought, its title, *The Categories;* one on terms and propositions, viz., *On Interpretation;* two on scientific proof, or demonstration, *The Prior Analytics* and *The Posterior Analytics;* and two on probable proof, *The Topics* and *The Sophistical Refutations*. But now, philosophy, as a system, has certain parts or branches, distinguished by the having of different ends, or objects. According to Aristotle, one branch has for its end pure truth as such, another truth in conduct, and a third truth in art.[1] The first of these is termed *Theoretical, or Speculative, Philosophy*, the second, *Prac-*

---

[1] Aristotle's *Metaphysics*, Bk. V. ch. 1; Bk. I. ch. 1, *De Caelo;* Bk. III. ch. 7.

tical Philosophy, the third, *Poetical*, or if, for distinction's sake, we transfer the Greek term (ποιητική) without alteration, *Poietical Philosophy*. Speculative Philosophy has three branches : *First Philosophy* (πρωτὴ φιλοσοφία) or *Theology, Mathematics*, and *Physics*. The parts of Practical Philosophy are *Ethics, Œconomics* (there is no complete genuine Aristotelian treatise extant on this subject [1]), and *Politics*.[2] First philosophy, or theology, is treated particularly in the so-called *Metaphysics* (= μετὰ τὰ φυσικά = "after or beyond the physics," a name given by editors of Aristotle's writings to certain books, either because they followed *The Physics* in the manuscript or were regarded as treating subjects logically subsequent to "physical subjects"). Physical subjects (*i.e.*, subjects relating to nature) are treated in several works, the chief of which are *The Physics, On the Heavens, On the History of Animals, De Anima*, or *Psychology*. No extant work of Aristotle is devoted to mathematical topics. The chief works in Practical Philosophy are *The Nicomachean Ethics*,[3] and *The Politics*. The *Poetic* is the only work exclusively devoted to Poietical Philosophy ; certain chapters (Bk. V. [VIII.]) in the Politics, however, treat important topics in this branch of philosophy. Aristotle's *Rhetoric* stands alone as a kind of appendix to the logical and ethical works.— As to the time and order of the production of the works above-mentioned, it has been conjectured that they were written during Aristotle's last residence in Athens,

[1] See Ueberweg, V. l. I. p. 148.
[2] *Metaphysics*, Bk. V. ch. 1; Bk. X. ch. 7; *Nic. Ethics*, Bk. VI. ch. 8.
[3] The *Eudemian Ethics* and The Great Ethics (Magna Moralia) are "Aristotelian," but not Aristotle's own. Certain books (V.-VII.) of the *Nicomachean Ethics*, however, are probably Eudemian in authorship.

while he was at the head of the Lyceum, and probably in nearly the following order:[1] 1st, *The Organon;* 2d, *The Nicomachean Ethics* and *The Politics;* 3d, *The Poetic* and *The Rhetoric;* 4th, *The Physics, On the Heavens, On the History of Animals, The De Anima,* or *Psychology;* 5th, *The Metaphysics.* It seems certain that they were all produced after the general idea of his system had matured in Aristotle's mind. In this regard, as in others, Aristotle's method, we may note in passing, was quite different from Plato's. In fact, growth is not particularly characteristic of the philosophy of Aristotle as exhibited in his works.

Aristotle's Theory of Knowledge. — We begin the exposition of Aristotle's philosophy with an account of what Aristotle himself regarded as introductory to philosophy proper, viz., his theory of knowledge, of its sources and method.

Kinds of Knowledge. — There are in knowledge three fundamental differences that Aristotle takes cognizance of in his theory of knowledge: differences as regards the object, method, and source of knowledge. Knowledge may have for its object causes (or first principles) or phenomena. Its method may be apodictic (demonstrative) or dialectic ("probable"). Its source may be sense or reason.

Scientific, or Philosophical Knowledge. — Scientific, or philosophical, knowledge ($\epsilon\pi\iota\sigma\tau\acute{\eta}\mu\eta$) is knowledge, the subject of which is causes ($\dot{\alpha}\rho\chi\alpha\acute{\iota}$), the method, demonstration ($\dot{\alpha}\pi\acute{o}\delta\epsilon\iota\xi\iota\varsigma$), and the source, reason ($\nu o\hat{v}\varsigma$). In the knowledge of causes is involved the knowledge of whatever else can be shown demonstratively to flow

---

[1] Compare the statements of Ueberweg, Zeller, Grant, and Wallace.

GREEK PHILOSOPHY. 123

from them; and a theory of scientific knowledge is an account of the source from, or faculty by, which we get the knowledge of causes, and of the method of demonstration. Now it was natural, both from the previous history of speculation and the character of the problem itself, that Aristotle should consider the latter part of the problem of scientific knowledge first, which he does, particularly in the *Prior Analytics.*

Demonstration. — Considered as regards method, knowledge is scientific, or demonstrative, when it is derived from certain, or necessary, premises by a certain, or necessary, process of reasoning.

The Syllogism (Deductive). — Now the process in which, certain things being assumed as true, a certain other thing obtains, necessarily and because of the things assumed, is called by Aristotle the *Syllogism.*[1] The syllogism is, therefore, the central point in the method of demonstration expounded by Aristotle; it was regarded, and rightly so, as his own discovery.[2] The syllogism (συλλογισμός) consists of three propositions: two premises (προτάσεις) and a conclusion (συμπέρασμα); and has three terms (ὅροι), the major or larger term (μεῖζον ἄκρον), the minor or smaller term (ἔλαττον ἄκρον), and the middle (μέσον), which may be larger in compass than either of the others or between them. The middle term is so called because it is the mean, or uniting term, in the syllogism.[3] — The members

---

[1] *Prior Analytics*, I. 1. The reader cannot do better here than to follow the account of Aristotle's logic given in Wallace's *Outlines of the Philosophy of Aristotle.*   [2] *Soph. Elench*, ch. 33.

[3] *Prior Analytics*, Bk. I. chs. 25, 1, 4, 5, 32, 26, 6 (see Wallace's *Outlines*, pp. 37-39).

of the syllogism are *propositions*. Propositions may be either affirmative or negative, universal, particular, or indefinite. There are four sorts of propositions that may enter into the syllogism: the universal affirmative, the universal negative, the particular affirmative, the particular negative. As regards the relations of these, — the universal affirmative and particular negative are opposed as contradictories (ἀντιφατικῶς ἀντικεῖσθαι); so are the universal negative and particular affirmative. The universal affirmative and the universal negative are contrarily opposed (ἐναντίως ἀντικεῖσθαι). Of contradictory opposites, if one be true, the other is false: contraries may both be false.[1] — Now the *rules of the syllogism* given by Aristotle are, that in every syllogism there must be one affirmative premise, there must be one universal premise, and terms must not be treated as universal in the conclusion which are not so in the premises.[3] — Syllogisms *differ in kind* and *scientific value* according to the relative compass and the position of the middle term. A syllogism in which the minor term is "in the whole middle" (*i.e.*, is the subject of a proposition of which the middle is predicate) and the middle term is "in the whole major" (*i.e.*, is the subject of a proposition in which the major is predicate) is termed a syllogism of the "first figure" (πρῶτον σχῆμα). In a syllogism of this figure the middle term lies "between" the extremes. A syllogism in which both major and minor terms are "in [less than] the whole middle" (*i.e.*, are subjects of propositions in each of which the middle term is a predicate), is a syllogism of

---

[1] *On Interp.* 6; *Cat.* 10; *Pr. Analyt.* I. ch. 2, etc. (Wallace, pp. 29-31).
[2] *Prior Analytics*, Bk. I. ch. 24 (Wallace, p. 40).
[3] *Pr. Analyt.* Bk. I. ch. 24 (Wallace, p. 40).

the second figure (δεύτερον σχῆμα). A syllogism in which the major and minor terms are each greater than the middle (*i.e.*, are predicates of propositions in each of which the middle term is subject) is a syllogism of the third figure (τρίτον σχῆμα).[1] (The "fourth figure" of modern text-books was not recognized by Aristotle; it did not spring out of his conception of the syllogism.) Now the first figure is the only one that gives universal conclusions; the second figure giving only negative conclusions, and the third only "particular" conclusions. It is also the only figure that yields naturally and directly in the conclusion all that is contained in the premises and no more. We can sometimes derive a universal conclusion from the premises of a syllogism of the second and third figures, but this can be done only indirectly; hence these figures are "imperfect," the first alone being "perfect."[2] — The hypothetical syllogism (συλλογισμὸς ἐξ ὑποθέσεως) is a syllogism in which, there being a certain *condition*, a certain proposition obtains. The latter, however, may obtain when the former does not; but if the latter does *not* obtain, the former does not.[3]

Definition and the Predicables. — Now the conclusion of a syllogism the premises of which are true, states, if the conclusion be a universal affirmative and is correctly drawn, a scientific truth, and is virtually the expression of the essence (οὐσία), or nature, of some real existence; hence is a definition. The knowledge of the essence of a thing embraces a knowledge of the common and

[1] *Prior Analytics*, Bk. I. chs. 5, 24, 26, 32, 56 (Wallace, pp. 37-39).
[2] *Ibid.*, Bk. I. chs. 1, 5, 7, 23, 24, etc. (Wallace, pp. 39-41).
[3] *Ibid.*, Bk. II. 4 (Wallace, pp. 41-42).

characteristic attributes of the class, or genus, to which it belongs and of the specific attribute that renders the thing an individual representative of the class. In other words, the definition (ὅρος) contains the expression of the union of the genus (γένος) and the differentia (διάφορα) of the thing defined. Other attributes (not necessary to definition, however) are the property (ἴδιον), which, though essential, is not a mark of distinction, and the accident (συμβεβηκός), which may or may not belong to the subject defined.

The Categories.[1] — Essence, or substance (οὐσία), is one of the ten aspects, according to Aristotle, under which things in general must be viewed. Substance is whatever is the subject of attributes, *e.g.*, man, Socrates; and it is either an individual, a species, or a genus. Substance in the primary sense is the individual, species and genus being only secondary substance.[2] The remaining nine aspects are quantity (πόσος = how many?), quality (ποιός = of what kind?), relation (πρός τι), place (ποῦ), time (ποτέ), position (κεῖσθαι), condition (ἔχειν), action (ποιεῖν), passivity (πάσχειν). Of these ten — termed categories — substance is principal; all others imply it. These are everywhere employed by Aristotle. (The idea of a table of categories may have been suggested to him by the Pythagorean table (see p. 7).) These categories were not "deduced" in any manner from a higher conception by Aristotle, but were

---

[1] *Categories,* 4, 7, 8; *Topics,* Bk. I. 9; *Metaphysics,* Bk. VI. 1, 7 (Wallace, pp. 25-27).

[2] Aristotle's doctrine of substance, as we shall see in what follows, appears inconsistent or at least undeveloped (see *Metaphysics,* Bk. VII. ch. 7). The above view is the earliest, and the one that seems to harmonize best with the theory of categories, in which it occurs.

taken empirically, as suggested, perhaps, by the fundamental forms, or "parts," of speech in the Greek language.

Syllogism (Inductive). — Now causes (in the knowledge of which or of what can be syllogistically shown to flow from them scientific knowledge consists), though visible to the eye of reason, are not known to us immediately. Knowable things are of two kinds: those which are prior for us (πρὸς ὑμᾶς πρότερον) and those which are prior by nature (φύσει πρότερον). Of the latter-named kind are causes, or first principles.[1] Our knowledge of causes, or what is prior by nature, has its beginning in our knowledge of things as they are for us. The (syllogistic) process by which we reach those firm universal propositions which state the essence, or are the definitions, of causes is *induction* (ἐπαγωγή), which is the "passing from particulars to universals," and is the inverse of deduction, which is the passing from universals to particulars.[2] Induction, like deduction, is syllogistic: for in induction we unite by inference the middle term to one of the extremes (major and minor terms) by means of the other. Thus, if B is a "middle" to A and C, we can prove by means of C that A may be predicated of B. For example, let the deductive syllogism be, "B is A, C is B, therefore C is A"; then the inductive syllogism is, "C is A, C is B, therefore B is A." The conclusion of the inductive syllogism corresponds to the major premise of the deductive. The inductive syllogism is a syllogism of the third figure, and strictly speaking, its conclusion is not universal

[1] *Posterior Analytics*, Bk. I. ch. 2.
[2] *Topics*, Bk. I. 12, 18; *Prior Analytics*, Bk. II. 23 (Wallace, pp. 42–44).

but particular. We may, however, assume it to be universal if we know that C and B are inter-convertible and that "B is C" holds. (The syllogism is then practically a syllogism of the first figure.) A real induction presupposes a knowledge of all the individuals of a class. "No particular kinds of Induction are formulated by Aristotle, but he has noticed incidentally the *principle* of most of the 'Experimental Methods,' and in particular that of the method of concomitant variations."[1] The premises of the inductive syllogism are not truths of reason, corresponding to first principles, but perceptions of sense. But sense as such gives knowledge only of the particular, and we can by induction reach universals only on the hypothesis that there is a common and permanent nature in the many. The idea of a common permanent nature originates in a higher faculty than sense. Animals have the faculty of sense-perception, but not all animals have the power of "retaining one certain thing in the soul" and of forming universal notions. Permanency and universality presuppose reason. Aristotle, however, allows himself to say that sense-perception introduces, or "informs" (ἐμποιεῖ), the universal.[2] (He compares the manner in which the universal unconsciously grows out of the particular of sense to the way in which soldiers in battle are caused to fly by the perception of one, and then another, and so on, fleeing.) In so far, however, as there results from the inductive syllogism something that is not given in sense-perception as such (and it is by induction only that we reach the first universals that

[1] Wallace, p. 43; see *Prior Analytics*, Bk. II. ch. 23.
[2] See below, pp. 144-146.

are the foundation of science), induction does not *prove* (ἀποδείκνυσιν) anything (it is *not* ἀπόδειξις) though it does *show* (δηλοῖ) something.

Probable Proof ; Dialectical and Rhetorical Method. — The foregoing is, in outline, Aristotle's account of *scientific* method as employed particularly in speculative, or theoretical, philosophy. He recognizes and gives a full analysis of another sort of method, which is only *quasi*-scientific and finds place especially in Practical Philosophy, — ethics, politics, etc. Here "dialectical," or probable, reasoning is employed. In practical affairs it generally suffices if we have premises that possess only a high degree of probability, and if our conclusions have, not absolute validity, but a fair warrant in the premises. In such matters it is not always easy or even possible to arrive at absolutely correct definitions, and it is not always necessary that all steps in our processes of reasoning should be stated, that everything should be *proved*, even plausibly; indeed, it is better that many things be taken for granted, that many things be left to the natural bent of mankind towards truth and justice. This is the case particularly in rhetorical argumentation; in dialectical reasoning logical method prevails though the premises may be only plausible.[1] In rhetorical reasonings the enthymeme, a *quasi*-syllogism, having but one premise, and example, by which we argue from a particular to a particular (through an

---

[1] It is a part of Aristotle's catholicity of temper that he shows some fondness for this *quasi*-scientific method. Absolute truth, he repeatedly says, is not in all cases within the reach of human powers, and it is oftentimes necessary and best to be content with less than that. If we deny that this is in any sense a philosophical view, we must throw away his works on Ethics and Rhetoric. See below, pp. 148 and 181.

assumed universal), may be employed instead of the complete syllogism and induction.

"*First Philosophy*," *or Metaphysics.* — We come now to Aristotle's theory of Being (τὸ ὄν) which at the very outset we shall find to be in close agreement with his theory of knowledge. Being is fixed or changeable. That there is fixed being appears from a consideration of the doctrines of Heraclitus and Protagoras. If all things are in a continual flux, we have to say that a thing is and is not the same at the same moment and in the same regard. If we say that contradictory propositions are equally true, we practically affirm that all propositions and terms mean the same thing, and may affirm, for example, that a man is a wall. And if being is not in any regard fixed and definite, what becomes of affirmation, and demonstration, and rational action?[1] Being is, then, in one aspect fixed, and in this aspect it is being *per se* (τὸ ὄν ᾗ ὄν), being in the highest sense; it is being that answers to scientific knowledge, and is known by us last in order of time, though (and because) first in the order of nature. Now the science of being *per se*, being as being (τὸ ὄν ᾗ ὄν) Aristotle deems to be the highest part of philosophy and terms it "First Philosophy" (πρώτη φιλοσοφία). It is what we, following the example of the early editors of Aristotle's works, term metaphysics. "First Philosophy," then, does not treat, as does mathematics, for example, of some phase or department of being, but of being taken universally, or as such. And just as the "science of health" treats of the preservation, the production, the symptoms or signs of it, and the capacity for it, so the science of

[1] *Metaphysics*, Bks. III and IV.

being treats of whatever has reference to it, whatever is primarily or derivatively being.

Being; Plato's "Ideas." — But what is being, *i.e.*, under which of the categories must we conceive it? Evidently under that which is highest and first, which denotes not anything that can be predicated, but is itself the subject of all predicates. Being, in other words, is substance, οὐσία ; and in the highest sense it is individual in nature, since primary substance is the individual.[1] Being, or substance, therefore, is not identical with those "universals" which Plato held to be being. Plato's theory of Ideas is untenable ; because, if the Ideas are transcendent and perfectly independent of the world of individual phenomenal existences, they are not in any explicable manner causes of the existence, or of the character of things, or of our knowledge of them. If substance is primarily individual, the substances of things must be in and with things themselves, and it is only on the hypothesis that they are, that we can conceive them as having anything to do with the existence or changes in things or can attain a knowledge of them by the process of induction. Universal notions are indeed necessary for demonstration's sake, but demonstration does not necessarily presuppose the existence of the Platonic universals, because it is necessary, and sufficient, for scientific knowledge, if there be a One in or among the many instead of being separate from and in addition to the many. The supposed participation of things in Ideas is therefore a mere fancy, to be allowed only in metaphorical speech ; and the Ideas, if

---

[1] For a different view, see *Metaphysics*, Bk. VII. ch. 7.

there were such things, would be only idle copies of the things of the sensible world or mere barren entities, of which nothing could be known or said.[1]

Matter and Form; Potentiality and Actuality. — Every finite substance is the result of the becoming actual of that which already was in possibility. As it actually is for us, it is a definite cognizable being; as only possible, it was, relatively at least, indefinite, incognizable. That by virtue of which it is definite and cognizable — relatively or absolutely — is termed its form. As it existed in possibility, it was but matter. As its actual being is but the realization of its being in possibility, every substance contains, or is the union, in some manner, of matter and form. The stone out of which the statue is made is in possibility a statue — is "matter" for a statue. When form (*i.e.*, a particular character) is given to it there results the actuality, *i.e.*, the statue, which is the union of a certain matter and a certain form, and is an individual substance. Matter ($\ddot{v}\lambda\eta$) and form ($\mu o \rho \phi \acute{\eta}$), it must be observed, are, like possibility, or potentiality ($\delta \acute{v} \nu a \mu \iota \varsigma$), and actuality ($\dot{\epsilon} v \acute{\epsilon} \rho \gamma \epsilon \iota a$), generally speaking, correlative terms, because it is the *same thing* which in one aspect is form and in another matter. Not *every* possibility becomes actuality, and there is one form which is pure form (God). In the union of matter and form there are, in different substances, different degrees of preponderance of form over matter. Those substances that have stability, universality, or, at least, generality, as a characteristic, owe this to the largeness of the element of form in

---

[1] *Metaphysics*, Bk. I. ch. 9; Bk. VI. chs. 14, 15, 16. *Posterior Analytics*, Bk. I. chs. 11, 8, etc. (See Wallace's *Outlines*, and Ueberweg.)

them, contingency in things being due to the influence of matter.[1] A thing is in a state of imperfection as long as it is in the process of becoming; it attains perfection, or is an entelechy (ἐντελέχεια), only as actuality.[2] In this respect, then, actuality is "prior" to potentiality. But it is also "prior" in another respect: we know the potentiality only (as we reason by the principle of analogy) from the actuality. The actual is partly prior in time to the potential, partly not. The child is prior to the man, and yet the existence of the child presupposes the existence of a man prior to that of the child. The actual is prior to the potential because the actual is that which *is* what it is, whereas the potential may or may not be, is therefore not self-identical, but self-contradictory.[3]

Causes, or First Principles (ἀρχαί). — If, now, we inquire why matter assumes form, why the possible becomes actual, the answer is, that "there must be an efficient cause imparting motion from potentiality into actuality." Every substance, therefore, involves in its existence and nature, matter, form, and efficient power.[4] These three are consequently principles, or causes. To them must be added a fourth, the end (τέλος), or final cause; for every thing that becomes, not only is "produced from something, by something, and is something," but has an end. These four causes — to take an illustrative example — would be, in the case of a house, as follows: The end, τέλος, or final cause, οὖ ἕνεκα, is comfort and protection; the matter, ὕλη, or material cause, is earth and stones; the form, or formal

[1] *Metaphysics*, Bk. V. ch. 2. [3] *Metaphysics*, Bk. VIII. ch. 8.
[2] *Ibid.*, Bk. VIII. ch. 6.   [4] *Ibid.*, Bk. VI. ch. 7; Bk. I. ch. 3.

cause, τὸ τί ἦν εἶναι, is the mental pattern or idea in the builder's mind according to which it is made; the efficient cause, ὅθεν ἡ ἀρχὴ τῆς μεταβολῆς, is the builder and his art.[1] But the four causes are not always so widely distinct as here. The child is the end of a certain process of which the material, formal, and efficient causes are in the parent.[2] Again, the end and the process may be the same; the end of sight is the act of seeing, of speculation, speculation.[3] In these two cases there is also a certain degree of identity between the formal and the final cause, on the one hand, and the efficient cause, on the other; *i.e.*, seeing and speculation are "inherent" in him who sees and him who speculates. Speaking generally, since the final cause of a thing is only its form, or ideal nature, *plus* existence, the formal cause and the final cause may, without logical inconsistency, often or, perhaps, generally, be regarded as one, viz., the formal cause, τὸ τί ἦν εἶναι. Again, in beings that have souls the efficient cause is in a manner identical with the formal and final cause. Thus the name *formal cause* often implies more than its definition really contains. Further, form being necessary to the actuality of a thing, it is natural to think and speak of things as "forms," although they involve matter. It is owing to this importance of form that Aristotle comes to speak of form or essence, instead of the individual, as substance.[4] The forms of absolute, or infinite, substances necessarily imply the existence of the actuality of those substances.

---

[1] *Metaphysics*, Bk. II. ch. 2.
[2] *Ibid.*, Bk. VII. ch. 4.
[3] *Metaphysics*, Bk. VIII. ch. 6.
[4] *Ibid.*, Bk. VII. ch. 7. See above, p. 126.

Kinds of Real Substance: Immovable Substance, God. — Logically regarded, substance is, we have seen, of two (three) kinds: substance as individual, as species, and as genus, the first-named being primary, the others secondary, substance. Ontologically speaking, substance is of two (three) kinds: sensible substances, of which one part is mere body and subject to decay, and the other is soul and eternal; and super-sensible, " immovable substance."[1] Of the existence of sensible substance we need no proof; the existence of the immovable substance is proved partly, as we have seen,[2] from the very idea of demonstration, and partly, from the known nature of sensible substances. These substances change and pass out of being ceaselessly and forever. The causes of sensible beings as sensible, are other sensible beings, and the causes of these are also other sensible beings and so on *in infinitum*. No such being, or substance, has in itself the principle of change, or motion: they move or change, produce motion, or change, only as moved or changed by some other being. We must, then, look for an original source, or cause, of motion, or change, which must lie in that which produces change, or motion, without itself being subject to these. This, then, must be the immovable substance. It exists purely as energy and as actuality, and hence is separate from the world of change, or motion.[3] If it is asked how the immovable substance causes change, or motion, the reply must be that it does so as a thing that is known and desired, *i.e.*, as a thing that is loved, does. It is the source of order in the world, as the general is

[1] *Metaphysics*, Bk. XI. ch. 1. [2] See p. 130.
[3] *Metaphysics*, Bk. XI. chs. 6, 8.

of order in the army. From it is "suspended the whole Heavens." The life of the Prime Mover is excellent and blessed. That perception and that enjoyment are the most excellent which are of that which is most excellent. It is characteristic of the human mind to find its highest satisfaction in the contemplation of itself, the most excellent of the things it has power immediately to know: much more so is it of the Divine Mind, and the life of the Divine Being is therefore, a life of blessed self-contemplation. God is just the "energy," *i.e.*, the activity and complete realization, of the ideal essence of mind, — he is the Thought of Thought. His life is eternally what our life is only for short periods of time. God is the highest substance, the individual that is (in form and efficiency at least) also universal: the absolute and eternal, alone of all things sufficient unto himself. He is the absolute Good, the supreme ideal end of all things else.

Physics, or the Philosophy of Nature. — We have just seen that substance is immovable and movable, and that the science of immovable substance, or of substance as immovable, is First Philosophy or Metaphysics. The science of immovable substance, or of substance as movable, is Physics, or the Philosophy of Nature. Movable substance is of two kinds: that which has, in a manner, the principle of motion in itself, and that which has not. But the principle of motion in this is the soul; hence Physics discusses, and is primarily the philosophy of, the soul.[1]

Essential Character of Nature. — Nature, as having the principle of motion within itself, is possessed of a soul,

---

[1] *Metaphysics*, Bk. V. ch. 1; Bk. X. ch. 3, etc.

is a living being, and its works are in all respects like those of an artist, except that the latter have their efficient cause outside themselves, whereas the efficient cause of the works of nature is immanent. Nature is governed by the principle of the end and does nothing in vain.[1] The end is an immanent end: the end of the plant or the animal is to be just the plant or the animal. Nature is both matter and form, but the form prevails to such an extent that nature works *generally*, if not always, in the same way and towards cognizable ends. There is, indeed, a certain mechanical necessity in nature: but it is secondary, not primary, a condition merely, not a cause,—just as "heavy" and "light" are conditions but not causes with reference to the house made by the builder.[2] There is, also, a certain element of contingency in nature: there are in the animal kingdom monstrosities, which are examples of nature's failure to attain to form, or reason. Such failures are inherent in matter, which is the contingent cause of what is accidental.[3] But in spite of necessity and chance, or contingency, nature is governed by form, or inherent end.

Method of the Philosophy of Nature. — As governed by the end, or reason, nature is an object of science; and yet owing to the contingency inherent in matter, the science of nature, or Physics, is not so purely a demonstrative science as is that of being. Careful and comprehensive observation and induction are requisite as a basis from which to rise to principles; truth is not to be attained by those who, preoccupied with theories, neglect

---

[1] *De Anima*, Bk. III. ch. 12.   [2] *Physics*, Bk. II. 9.
[3] *Metaphysics*, Bk. V. ch. 7.

facts.[1] But observations and deductions from facts are to be governed by the idea of the end: the highest of the "causes" of knowledge as of being is in Physics, as in Metaphysics, the final cause.

Motion, Space, and Time. — Motion ($κίνησις$) is the entelechy or natural state of the potential as potential. In other words the world of matter is inherently a world of movement — matter has reality (form) for us only as in motion. Motion is distinguished by Aristotle from change ($μεταβολή$), which embraces origin and decay, increase and diminution, alteration (in kind or quality), and change in place. Motion is merely a kind of change, and includes only the six last-mentioned kinds of change, all (six) of which are or involve change in place. The six kinds of motion referred to may be grouped into three: changes in quality (alteration), in quantity (increase and diminution), and in "place." "Place" ($τόπος$) is not (as we understand it) position, nor the space occupied by a body, but the limit presented to a body by a surrounding body or by surrounding bodies; it may be compared to a vessel in which water or any other material substance is held. No "place" is empty (there is no empty space); the world is a plenum. The movement of bodies is therefore merely an exchanging of "places." Space is not infinite but ends with the sphere of the fixed stars. The world as a whole is not in any "place." The perfect motion is circular; for only such a motion, a motion the path of which is without beginning or end, answers to the eternal nature of the Prime Mover. Such is the motion of the sphere of the fixed

---

[1] *Posterior Analytics*, Bk. I. ch. 33; *De Generatione et Corruptione*, Bk. I. ch. 2.

stars, upon which God acts, though without touching it. Motion is eternal, since every motion of a real thing implies, on the one hand, an antecedent motion which, again, implies another and so on *in infinitum* and, on the other hand, a subsequent one, which, in turn, implies another and so on *in infinitum*. The eternity of motion implies an eternal cause of motion,[1] — a corollary to the theorem of the eternity of motion is that of the eternity of time. Time is the "number of motion with reference to earlier and later." We should have no conception of time merely from the idea of a "now." Consciousness of succession (arising from the perception of motion) is also necessary. Practically, however, every "now" is a union of "before" and "after," and so time is in itself potentially infinite. Time as a numbering presupposes a "numberer," infinite time an infinite mind.[2] The universe has always been, and always will be the same.

The Visible Universe. — The visible universe was conceived by Aristotle as a living sphere. Exterior to the sphere is the abode of the Prime Mover. That part of the sphere nearest the abode of the Prime Mover — the region of the fixed stars — partakes of the perfection of the Prime Mover, or Deity, dwelling in felicity and realizing the highest end of existence; the centre of the sphere, the region of our earth, is the place of imperfection. The region of the planets is intermediate in character as in place between the other two. The material elements are five in number, — earth, water, air, fire, ether. Ether, the most perfect of them, exists only in the upper heaven, is not subject

---

[1] *Physics*, Bk. VIII. ch. 1.   [2] *Ibid.*, Bk. VIII. ch. 1; Bk. VI. ch. 6, etc.

to changes either in quality or in quantity, but to change in place only, and has only a circular (perfect) motion. Of the other elements, earth is lowest, fire highest, in place and nature. They easily pass into one another, being active and passive in nature, and are, as compared with ether, the fifth element, or quintessence, imperfect and the cause of imperfection in the lower world. Their motions are not circular: earth moves downwards, fire upwards, air and water having intermediate motions. Of fire, air, water, and earth all living beings are composed, homogeneous parts, *e.g.*, flesh or bones, being formed of like parts, and heterogeneous of the homogeneous.

Graduated Scale of Being in Nature. — There is throughout nature a gradation of being, and at certain points it is with difficulty that beings of one kind can be distinguished from those of another.[1] Certain plants (*e.g.*, the sponge) very closely resemble animals, and the attributes possessed by animals are possessed by man in a higher degree of perfection. Life pervades even the elements.

Psychology: Its General Character and Place among the Sciences. — Aristotle's work on the soul is the earliest of the distinct systematic treatises on the subject, and is based on a careful review of all previous theories as well as a profound special knowledge of the subject. He takes the general position that psychology is a part of the science of physical nature, because the "feelings of the soul are inseparable from the physical substratum of animal life"; and yet, also, that it is of a transcendental character, since there are clear cases of "states" that

---

[1] *On the Parts of Animals*, Bk. IV. ch. 5.

"are peculiar to the soul alone," *c.g.*, thought. Both the purely materialistic and the purely transcendental theories of the soul are therefore treated by him as one-sided; and his investigations are both empirical and speculative in character. Regarding the place of psychology among the sciences he says: "The acquisition of knowledge is, we conceive, always something high and honorable: but one form of knowledge is superior to another either in virtue of the self-contained simplicity of its truths or by the greater dignity and wondrousness of its contents; and on both these grounds the investigation of the soul might with justice claim a foremost place, and, besides, the knowledge of it is thought to have important bearings on truth generally and especially on nature: for soul is, as it were, a prime factor in animal existence."[1]

Body and Soul. — Life is a process of nutrition, growth, and decay.[2] Where this process goes on, there is organic being; and where there is organic being, there is soul. Soul (the principle of motion) may be defined as the entelechy, or perfection, of organic bodily existence. It is not itself, however, bodily, or material; it has not magnitude nor parts; nor is it subject to motion. If it possessed magnitude, there would be no thought, for thought is a unit and may be exercised once for all, whereas the parts of a thing are repetitions of one another.[2] Since the soul is not a magnitude, is not spatial except only "incidentally," *i.e.*, as related to body, it does not move itself (topically, or in place), and

[1] *De Anima,* Bk. I. ch. 1. (See *Aristotle's Psychology in Greek and English, with Introd. and Notes by Edwin Wallace,* etc.)
[2] *Ibid.,* Bk. II. ch. 1.

is not capable of being moved by anything outside itself.[1] It is even better not to say that the soul sympathizes or thinks or learns, but that man does so by means of the soul.[2] But the soul, though not "movable," is the cause of motion, and operates in and through the body as a whole and in its parts, developing it and using it as an instrument. Just by virtue of the unity of the soul, and of its power over the body, is the body an organism, the soul being the entelechy of the body, the form that gives intelligible existence to the body, which is "matter." Body and soul are, then, one, as form and matter are one. The soul is, indeed, dependent upon the body, but only in so far as the body is a condition to its activity, and a condition, too, to which the soul, as being form, is prior.[3] The soul, in short, is the efficient, formal, and final cause of the body.[4] But the soul is more than the mere entelechy of the body. One part of it, we shall see, is separable from the body, and has no single and separate correlative in the body.

Parts, or Faculties, of the Soul. — The faculties (δυνάμεις) of the soul are those of nutrition (θρεπτικόν), which includes generation, or reproduction,[5] of sense-perception (αἰσθητικόν), of desire, or volition (ὀρετικόν), of locomotion (κινητικόν), and of intellect (διανοητικόν),

---

[1] *De Anima*, Bk. I. chs. 2 and 3. (See also ch. 5.)
[2] *Ibid.*, Bk. I. ch. 4.
[3] The existence of the soul in the body is, in other words, a stage in its process of self-realization. We can as well say that the body is in the soul.
[4] *De Anima*, Bk. II. ch. 4.
[5] *Ibid.*, Bk. II. ch. 3. That the nutrition is a function of the soul follows from the principle that whatever exhibits an idea or an end belongs not to matter but to form. *De Anima*, Bk. II. ch. 4.

which embraces understanding and reason. The last-named faculty is separable from the body, and is peculiar to the soul of man. (Animals have all the other faculties except, in some cases, that of locomotion. Plants have only the nutritive soul.) These faculties are related one to another as successive stages in a developing life, the higher involving the lower (man contains within himself the life of the plant and the animal[1]). By means of the nutritive (reproductive) function the (universal) soul gives itself outward permanence, *i.e.*, though the individual dies, the species survives. Thus the form has actuality. In sense-perception, the form (not the matter) of objects is preserved, to be transmuted by the higher faculties of the soul.[2] Desire and locomotion give external reality to conceptions. Reason is the faculty of form purified of all sensuous or *quasi*-sensuous matter. The primary seat and organ of *sensation* is the heart, the brain acting merely as a regulator of the heart's action. But perceptions of sense are gained through five special organs (the organs of the five well-known senses), a general faculty of sense through which such impressions (*e.g.*, number, figure, size) as are not given through any one particular organ alone but by all in common, are received, and the power of inference.[3] The sense of touch underlies the other four, contact through a medium being necessary to render the *possible* object of sensation *really* such.[4] Of the five senses hearing has the most of reason in it. In perception by inference, or "inci-

[1] See what was said above on the Socratic Natural Theology, p. 55.
[2] *De Anima*, Bk. II. ch. 12.   [3] *Ibid.*, Bk. II. ch. 6.
[4] *Ibid.*, Bk. II. ch. 7.

dental perception," we learn of sensuous attributes by reasoning from concomitant, or accompanying, attributes. In sense-perception is apprehended not the mere individual but what is universal,[1] since sense receives the form of objects without the matter of them. Springing immediately out of the sense-faculty are phantasy (φαντασία), or imagination, and simple memory (μνήμη). Phantasy is perception sublated and given a *quasi*-permanence and independence but weakened. Memory, also, is a permanent, or relatively permanent state of the soul, resulting from the lodging of impressions produced in sense and the imagination : it is consequently an image of previous states of the soul.[2] Necessary to memory is the idea or reflection (involving the presence of the purely active faculty of the mind, reason) that the idea before the mind has previously been before it. Repetition of an impression may be spontaneous or volitional : in the former case it is an act of pure memory ; in the latter, of recollection so-called (ἀνάμνησις). In this act the mind moves from one idea to another connected with it through the implicit idea of similarity, contrast, or contiguity, so recalling the idea sought.[3] Such an act has in it a larger degree of spontaneity than simple memory, imagination, or sense-perception, though even sense is not mere receptivity. The activity of soul as primarily spontaneous is *reason*. That there is such a faculty appears from the fact that there must be a distinct power that perceives the essential nature

---

[1] *Posterior Analytics*, Bk. II. ch. 19. Hence the possibility of induction. See above, p. 128. See below, p. 146.
[2] *Ibid.*, Bk. II. ch. 19, and *De Memoria*, 1.
[3] *De Memoria*, 2.

of things, a power different from that which perceives things themselves, a power, *e.g.*, that perceives the essential nature of flesh different from that which perceives flesh itself : in short, a power that perceives and judges of form apart from matter. Now this faculty is no doubt "unmixed" (as Anaxagoras asserted) with the body or with things ; it must, however, if it be anything more than a bare potentiality, be capable of having an object, and must, therefore, have in it, or be related to, an element of passivity like sense, though different in degree and somewhat in kind. There must, in other words, be a kind of passive reason, related to the active as matter is related to creative mind in the external world. The ideas of reason are potentially in the passive reason and are brought into actuality by the power of active reason, just as potential color is made into actual color by the power of light. Now that the ideas thus made actual by active reason are ideas of objects is manifest from the fact of the unity of reason in man with the reason in the external world, and from the fact, also, that in sense-perception there must be a unity of subject and object as a condition of there being any communication between subject and object, — receptivity presupposing community of nature.[1] In regard, further, to the nature of the relations of the active and passive reason, Aristotle says that the passive reason (which it would seem can be nothing more nor less than the *ensemble* of all the powers of the mind beneath pure eternal reason) is perishable and can "think nothing without the support of the creative intellect," whereas the active is immortal and eternal. and eternally thinks.[2] Now the ideas of

[1] *De Anima*, Bk. III. chs. 4 and 5.   [2] *Ibid.*, Bk. III. ch. 5.

active reason viewed merely as *possible objects* of reason, or *possible forms* of its functioning, constitute science (ἐπιστήμη). The actual employment of these, or functioning with them, is speculation (θεωρεῖν).[1] As the perfection, or entelechy, of the soul's activities, reason presupposes the activities of sense, imagination, simple memory, and recollection, and is immanent and implicit in these. (Passive memory is thus the middle term between reason and the phenomenal real world.) This explains why it is that the special senses, and the common, or general, sense, still more, apprehend not mere individuals but qualities in individuals, and that imagination, simple memory, and recollection have a permanent element in them : that, in short, no operation of the mind is purely passive and relative (irrational), but all partake more or less of the spontaneity and absoluteness of pure reason. The mind has *knowledge* even in sense-perception. The reason that is in the world is perceived by the reason in the soul. The essences of things it knows absolutely, for they are the objects, as they are the creations only of reason. Active reason, however, is, according to Aristotle, entirely separable from the body, and eternal. Immortality for the finite individual, consequently, is not a necessary postulate of the Aristotelian psychology. The *appetitive and locomotive faculties of the soul* are related to the others through the feelings of pleasure and pain. Every perception, conception, or thought awakens a feeling of pleasure or of pain which involves the "judgment" that the object of the perception, thought, or conception is good or evil, and to be

[1] *De Anima*, Bk. II. ch. I.

desired or avoided accordingly. (This "judgment" is entirely analogous to the judgment in the purely intellectual sphere, that a thing is true or false.) The desire or aversion thus aroused produces in the heart, which is the seat of sensation, feeling, and motion, a certain degree of warmth, which, if sufficient, is followed by bodily motion, external action. In animals the stimulating cause of desire or aversion may be only a dull perception; in man it is also, and most characteristically, an idea of reason.[1]

Practical Philosophy. — Man as a being that is subject to desire limited by reason and leading to choice and action, is termed practical. The philosophy of man as such a being is Practical Philosophy, to which we now naturally come.

Method of Practical Philosophy. — In accordance with his idea that the highest activity of the soul is that of reason, or the theoretic faculty, Aristotle affirms that the highest and best life for man is a life of contemplation, the life of the speculative philosopher. But this proposition, instead of being assumed at the beginning as a starting-point for a deductive and scientific treatment of the subject of man's practical activity, appears as the conclusion, or, rather, as a conclusion, of an investigation that is only *quasi*-scientific. Aristotle, in other words, after stating in very general terms[2] what the end (for every art and every methodical procedure must be governed by the conception of the final cause) of the science dealing with man as a practical being is, premises that different subjects require to be differently

[1] *De Anima*, Bk. III. chs. 10, 11, etc.
[2] *Nicomachean Ethics*, Bk. I. ch. 2.

treated, some, *e.g.*, mathematics, with strictness of method, others with greater freedom of method. Political science (for such is the name given by Aristotle to the science in question) is of the latter class ; human affairs are especially uncertain, and here especially we must proceed from things better known to us to things better known (or knowable) in themselves, *i.e.*, from facts to principles. Hence, also, the student in political science should have been "well and morally educated": the inexperienced, ill-educated, or morally deficient (whether old or young) are unprepared for the study of this science because they have not the completeness and excellence of character and information that afford to the student the materials that must form the content of the science.[1]

End of Practical Philosophy, or "Political Science."— Now the end of Political Science is the (conception of the) good of man, and the good of man may be considered as the good of the individual and that of the state, though these are in essence the same. Political Science has, then, two natural branches : Ethics, treating of the good of the individual man, and Politics, treating of the good of the state.[2] But what is the "good of man"? Following a practice common with him, Aristotle dis-

---

[1] *Nicomachean Ethics*, Bk. I. chs. 2 and 3. We hear much of Empirical Psychology at the present day. But this must be of little value if the souls empirically studied are poor in quality and attainment.

[2] Perhaps Economics should be included among the Political Sciences. "Eudemus (*Ethics*, I. 8, 12, 18, b. 1·3) distinguishes between πολιτική-οἰκονομική, and φρόνησις as the three parts of a philosophy of action; but Aristotle himself nowhere puts the matter so definitely. Cf. however, *Nic. Eth.*, VI. 8. 1141, b. 30, where a similar distinction is implied" (Wallace, p. 23).

cusses current opinions on the subject of the good, and pays particular attention to Plato's doctrine of the Good as Idea. This doctrine he rejects as being false, chiefly on the grounds that it presupposes a real unity among things that are one in name only, and that it is too abstract for application to the matters in hand (since human good is found only in what is practicable for man);[1] and limits the idea of the Good to that of the "good for man." Now the good generally, is that which is an end, and the good of man is simply the realized end of man as man. The end of man, his peculiar function, or work (ἔργον), is the energizing of the soul according to reason; or, since in reason lies man's characteristic quality, we may say an "energy of the soul according to virtue" (ἀρετή); or, if there be more than one virtue, the "best and most perfect virtue"; and, further, "in the most fortunate life since, as neither one swallow nor one day makes a spring, so neither does one day nor a short time make blessed and happy."[2] This realization of the soul's peculiar excellence we may call happiness. Complete happiness, however, does not exist without the presence of certain external conditions, such as the possession of friends and of wealth; nor without the element of pleasure, since no one can be called truly just who takes no pleasure in acting justly, or truly liberal, who takes no pleasure in being liberal.[2]

Psychological Basis of Ethics (and Politics). — The student of political science must, it is obvious, study the soul (though not necessarily with scientific exactness

---

[1] *Nicomachean Ethics*, Bk. I. ch. 6. [2] *Ibid.*, Bk. I. chs. 7 and 9.

and completeness); he must know what its functions, which are the virtues, are. Now the vegetative soul is not capable of any virtue or the want of any virtue that we need consider here. The appetitive soul, though rebellious, yet participates in and submits to reason, and has, therefore, a certain capacity for real virtue. For present purposes, then, the soul is two-fold, one part being reason itself, the other, obedient to reason; and virtues are accordingly of two kinds: ethical (ἠθικαί) and intellectual or dianoetic (διανοητικαί).[1]

Sources and Conditions of Virtue. — Virtue has two sources, the intellectual virtues, resulting chiefly from instruction, the ethical, from habitual action, or habit. Virtue is, then, not innate and necessary, not a natural phenomenon (like, for example, the falling of a stone), which is no result of habit but of natural necessity; nor is it, as Socrates thought, identical with knowledge; but the result of habit and teaching as affecting a natural capacity.[2] This natural capacity, however, is not such a capacity as is, *e.g.*, sight, which requires only to be exerted to be an "energy." This natural capacity for virtue is also a capacity for its opposite. Right instruction and right habit are required to render it a real capacity for virtue, *i.e.*, a capacity for virtue only. Men become just and temperate and brave by performing actions that are just and temperate and brave. In this case, Aristotle remarks, the "energy" *precedes* the "capacity" instead of following it. Virtue, being a result of habit, is by Aristotle termed a

[1] *Nicomachean Ethics*, Bk. I. ch. 13.
[2] This is Aristotle's answer to the question, argued by the Sophists and by Socrates, whether virtue could be taught. See above, p. 57.

habit.[1] That it is a habit and not a mere feeling nor a mere natural capacity is evident from the circumstance that men are not called good and bad merely because of their feelings or their capacities as such. Inherently, *i.e.*, without relation to deliberate intent or choice (which, as we are about to see, is a condition of virtuous action), the feelings are morally indifferent. Moreover, by our feelings we are said to be "moved," by our habits to be of a certain disposition. Again, our capacities are ours by nature, but men are not good and bad by nature.[2] Now the actions that give rise to habits constituting virtues are of a certain definite nature. Acts leading to (established) virtue must, in the first place, be distinguished from those resulting in works of art. The latter class have for their end the production of what is excellent in itself, without reference to the character or mental condition of the doer; but actions are just and temperate, not if they have a certain result, but if the doer does them in a certain condition of mind; viz., if, first, he does them wittingly; if, secondly, with deliberate choice, and choice of the things done for their own sakes; and if, thirdly, he does them from firm and settled purpose or principle. Just acts and temperate acts are such as a just or temperate man does or would do. The artist is an artist by virtue of the possession of a certain kind of knowledge and skill; the conditions just mentioned as conditions necessary to the rendering an act virtuous are not con-

---

[1] Habit (ἕξις is from ἔχειν, *to have*, and etymologically = *habit*) fairly means in Aristotle's usage, a fixed and definite power and tendency in the soul (*i.e.*, a faculty, almost), not merely a customary mode of action.
[2] *Nicomachean Ethics*, Bk. II. ch. 5.

ditions of his action. On the other hand, knowledge or skill is only of secondary importance among the conditions of virtuous action.[1] But it is necessary to show by what sort of habit virtue is constituted. Habits, regarded as quantities, may, as dependent upon the passions or emotions, be in the mean or may be in either extreme, and, this, either as regards other habits or ourselves. Virtue must be the habit that is in the mean, because virtue, like nature, is more "accurate" and excellent than any art, and every art as well as every science realizes its end by aiming at the mean. The *ethical mean*, however, is, of course, not identical with arithmetical, but is determined by an investigation involving the application of certain categories, — "the time when, the cases in which, the persons towards whom, the motive for which, the manner in which" actions are performed.[2] Certain convenient rules for hitting the mean as regards ourselves are the following: one must avoid the worse of two extremes; one must avoid especially that extreme to which he is more inclined; one must be on his guard in matters pertaining to pleasure and the pleasant.[3]

Definition of Virtue. — The foregoing discussion of virtue leads to the following definition of virtue: "Virtue is habit characterized by deliberate choice, in the mean relative to ourselves, which is fixed or determined by reason, and as the prudent man would determine it." There are involved in this definition two points that require elucidation, and are, accordingly, (by Aristotle

[1] *Nicomachean Ethics*, Bk. II. ch. 4.   [2] *Ibid.*, Bk. II. ch. 6.
[3] *Ibid.*, Bk. II. ch. 9; also Bk. VI. ch. 1.

or some faithful disciple of his[1]) further developed in later chapters of the *Nicomachean Ethics:*[2] viz., What, precisely, is deliberate choice? and What is reason as exercised by the prudent man (φρόνιμος)?

Deliberate Choice. — Deliberate choice must be distinguished from voluntary choice. That is voluntary choice or action which is made or done wittingly and willingly, the origin or cause of which, whether the consequence be or not, is in the person making the choice or doing the deed. (That is involuntary choice or action which is made or done through constraint, or through ignorance, not of general and commonly known facts or laws, but of certain particular circumstances.[3]) Deliberate choice is calculating choice exercised in regard to things contingent and within our power to do.[4] About that which is eternal, or necessary, or in the ordinary course of external nature, or irrational, or impossible, or purely accidental, there is no deliberate choice: it is beyond our sphere. We deliberate about means oftener than about ends, for they are more uncertain. Deliberate choice, as appears from the definition, is narrower in range than voluntary choice, which is not necessarily calculating, nor exercised with regard to things within our power. Children, fools, and madmen often exercise voluntary, but not deliberate choice. All deliberate choice is voluntary, but not all voluntary choice is deliberate. Now, by the definition, a virtu-

[1] It is a common opinion among critics that Bks. V.-VII. of the *Nicomachean Ethics* were not written by A. but by a close follower named Eudemus.
[2] *Nicomachean Ethics*, Bk. III. chs. 1-5; Bk. VI. chs. 1-13.
[3] *Ibid.*, Bk. III. ch. 1. See, also, *Rhet.*, Bk. I. ch. 4.
[4] *Ibid.*, Bk. III. chs. 2, 3.

ous act or habit is an act or a habit dependent upon deliberate choice, but Aristotle maintains, of course, that so far as acts are voluntary, they are of an ethical character and are classifiable as virtuous or the opposite.

The Ethical Virtues. — The determination of the nature of "right reason" as exercised by the prudent man requires an examination of the intellectual or dianoetic virtues. It is necessary, however, before undertaking that, to give an account of the ethical virtues. These, together with the corresponding extremes in "excess" and "defect," are assumed (not demonstrated) by Aristotle to be the following: Courage (the mean), rashness (the excess), cowardice (the defect); temperance, intemperance, want of susceptibility to feelings of bodily pleasure and pain; liberality, or moderateness in the ordinary giving and receiving of riches, prodigality, illiberality; munificence, or right measure in large expenditures of money, vulgar ostentation in expenditure of money, "smallness" in this regard; magnanimity or high-mindedness, vanity, excessive humbleness; moderate ambition, or love of honor, inordinate ambition, spiritlessness, or want of ambition; mildness of temper, irascibility, insusceptibility to anger; civility, obsequiousness, incivility; candor, arrogance, assumed self-depreciation; cleverness of wit, buffoonishness, clownishness; susceptibility to the feeling of shame, shamelessness, bashfulness; just indignation, envy, malice [!]; justice, equity, and injustice.[1]

---

[1] *Nicomachean Ethics*, Bk. II. ch. 6; Bk. III. ch. 6; Bk. V. Shame and indignation are not, A. says, strictly virtues and vices, but are mentioned as illustrations of the doctrine of the mean.

Special attention may, for illustration's sake, be paid here to courage (ἀνδρεία), high-mindedness (μεγαλοψυ-χία), and justice (δικαιοσύνη). *Courage* is the virtue possessed by any one who feels confidence with regard to what he ought to feel confidence with regard to, from the right motive, in the right manner, and at the right time; and fears in like manner. He whose seeming courage is a result of anxiety to appear worthy of distinction, of experience in matters demanding courage, of anger, of hope, or of ignorance, is not truly courageous. True courage springs only from the love of the honorable, and the suggestions of reason.[1] "*Magnanimity*" (high-mindedness) is the ornament of the virtues, making them greater and existing only where they exist. The "magnanimous" person is a person of conscious dignity and worth. He esteems honor, or the regard of good men, above all things else (though he does not "go in search of it"); he does not overrate worldly success, is courageous, liberal, independent, not resentful, above flattery, dignified in bearing.[2] *Justice* may be divided into universal justice and particular justice. *Universal justice* is the habit of obedience to law and of dealing with men fairly, *i.e.*, according to the principle of the mean. And since there are laws relating to all matters, universal justice in a manner comprehends all other virtues, and is therefore perfect virtue, — more admirable than "the evening or the morning star." It is greater in perfection than the other virtues also, because the exercise of it constitutes a reference of the individual to others as well as himself. It is not a kind, or division, of virtue; it is

[1] *Nicomachean Ethics*, Bk. III. chs. 7, 8.   [2] *Ibid.*, Bk. IV. ch. 3.

the whole of virtue.[1] *Particular justice*, which is one of the virtues and not the whole of virtue, is the mean relative to the distribution of wealth, honor, or whatever else can be distributed among the members of a political community, and to the correction of errors in transactions between men. The first-mentioned kind of particular justice is termed *distributive*, the second-mentioned, *corrective*, justice. Distributive justice takes account merely of the character and merits of individuals; corrective justice, of the equalities and inequalities of transactions. Distributive justice is based upon the geometrical mean, — as is a man's deserts so is that which he receives in the distribution: corrective justice is based upon the arithmetical mean, — the losses of one must be compensated for by the gains of another. Mere reciprocity is not justice.[2] Justice may be also divided into *natural* and *legal.* Natural justice is that which is "everywhere equally valid and depends not upon being or not being received." Legal justice is that which rests on enactments.[3] Supplementing and perfecting legal justice is *equity*, which is defined as the "correction of law wherever it is defective owing to its universality." Through inadvertence or through lack of knowledge, on the part of the legislator, the law may fail of being sufficiently specific. Its defect is supplied by the equitable man, who, feeling bound by the law of sympathy, and preferring arbitration to strict judicial procedure, takes due account of human failings, of the intention of the law-maker rather than the letter of the law, of the character and general conduct of

[1] *Nicomachean Ethics*, Bk. V. ch. 1. [2] *Ibid.*, Bk. V. chs. 2, 3, 4, 5.
[3] *Ibid.*, Bk. V. ch. 6.

the person accused, of the differences in faults and crimes.[1]

"*Right Reason*," *Prudence, and the Intellectual Virtues Generally.* — What, now, is the exact character of reason as exercised by the "prudent man" in determining the practical mean? The answer to this question will be brought out in the discussion of the intellectual virtues, which have now to be treated. The understanding has as object either that which is necessary and absolutely knowable or that which is contingent and only relatively knowable. Things of the first-mentioned kind are either principles or consequents of these; things of the second-mentioned class are particular objects of experience. Principles are known by intuition (νοῦς), their consequents by demonstration (ἐπιστήμη). Intuition and demonstrative thought, considered as habits, are virtues, and together constitute wisdom (σοφία), the highest of the intellectual virtues, — the highest because having reference to the noblest things.[2] The intellectual powers or habits the objects of which are contingent are art (τέχνη), and prudence, or practical wisdom (φρόνησις), which differ in that the principle of the one class (as related to persons) lies in the objects themselves, of the other in the doer.[3] Art is a certain "habit" of "making" governed by true reason; the absence of art, the "habit" of "making" governed by false reason. The nature of prudence, or practical wisdom, may be further explained by a consideration of the prudent, or practically wise, man. The mark of such a man is the ability to deliberate success-

[1] *Nicomachean Ethics*, Bk. V. ch. 10; *Rhetoric*, Bk. I. ch. 13.
[2] *Ibid.*, Bk. VI. chs. 3, 6, 7.   [3] *Ibid.*, Bk. VI. ch. 4.

fully respecting the good and expedient in relation to living well. Now, as we have seen, no one deliberates about things that cannot be otherwise than they are, nor about things that are beyond their power to do. Prudence, or practical wisdom, then, is not that wisdom in which intuition and demonstration are embraced, but a certain rational habit having practical reference to human good. Wisdom has to do with ends, prudence with means. But prudence is more than mere sagacity or shrewdness or fair-mindedness or intelligence, though these may be contained in it; it is the moral insight and the tendency to right action that are begotten of experience in acting justly, temperately, etc.[1] Until prudence is attained, virtue or, rather, what appears to be such, is but "natural" virtue, the virtue of those "who do what they ought and what a good man ought to do" only half-consciously and half-voluntarily. Virtue proper, as distinguished from natural virtue, is habit not merely in *accordance* with, but in *union* with, "right reason," or the perception of the true mean. Again, such are the unity and force of prudence that, whereas the natural virtues may exist separately, the true virtues exist in conjunction.

Self-Control and its Opposite. — With regard to the question, discussed and answered in the negative by Socrates,[2] whether knowledge is "dragged about," or overcome, by passion, Aristotle holds that when scientific knowledge is present to the mind, passion cannot arise, though it may do so "when that opinion which is the result of sensation" is present; and that one who virtually possesses knowledge may, nevertheless, do wrong

---

[1] *Nicomachean Ethics*, Bk. VI. chs. 10, 11, 13.   [2] See above, p. 57.

if he fails to use the knowledge he possesses.[1] The habit of yielding wrongly to feelings of pleasure and pain through the influence of passion is "incontinence," or want of self-control. It differs from intemperance in not being characterized by deliberate choice or preference. The "mean" habit corresponding to "incontinence" is self-control. The incontinent man is *less* blameworthy (not *more* blameworthy, as Socrates had held) than the intemperate man.

Friendship. — Closely related to virtue, if indeed it be not a kind of virtue, is friendship. It is certainly a condition to virtue and is, besides, most necessary, honorable, and pleasant. It unites individuals and states, and is a prime condition of the existence of society: it is eminently a subject for the consideration of the political philosopher.[2] Friendship exists when there is among men a common desire to do good one to another for that other's sake. It is "good-will mutually felt." No true friendship is based on a love of the merely expedient or agreeable; true friendship is consonant only with a love of the good, and exists among those who are themselves good. True friendship, however, is both expedient and pleasant. Perfect friendship is not merely a habit but an energy, and implies intercourse; it is active rather than passive, and consists more in conferring than in receiving benefits. Friendship as implying community (of interest) is closely related to justice as a bond of union among men.[3] By the good man friendship is greatly valued, because through it he acquires a second self (in others); he can contemplate virtue and the good in

[1] *Nicomachean Ethics*, Bk. VII. chs. 3 and 4.
[2] *Ibid.*, Bk. VIII. ch. 1.   [3] *Ibid.*, Bk. VIII. chs. 2, 3, 4, 5, 6.

others better than in himself alone, — and existence is desirable for the sake of the perception of the good.[1] Friendship, that is to say, is practically a species of self-contemplation.

Pleasure and Happiness. — Human good has been defined as happiness, which includes, besides virtue, a second ingredient, — pleasure; for pleasure is the agreeable consciousness that regularly attends the "energy," or perfect activity, of any power, an activity that is nothing more nor less than perfect virtue. Pleasure differs as "energies" differ, the highest pleasures attending the noblest energies. True pleasure is what appears such to the good man. Pleasure is not a good in itself; it is good only as a concomitant of virtue and a condition to absolute perfection.[2] Happiness, we have seen, is the energy of the soul according to the law of virtue, the highest happiness corresponding to the highest virtue. But the highest virtue is wisdom, the virtue of the speculative, or theoretic, faculty. The energy of this faculty is the noblest, most constant, most pleasant, the most self-sufficient, the most divine of all. It seems to be, in each man, his true self, the "ruling and the better part." In comparison with this, ethical energies are of secondary importance. Absurd, indeed, it would be were each man not to strive his utmost to live in accordance with the conception of this, — to be his true self!

Practical Ethics. — Theoretical ethics is not the whole of ethics; men must *be* virtuous, not merely theorize about virtue. Something more than theory is required,

[1] *Nicomachean Ethics*, Bk. IX. ch. 9.
[2] *Ibid.*, Bk. X. chs. 1, 4, 5.

for the making of men virtuous, for the majority of mankind are guided not by knowledge but by passion; they must be educated to virtue. And it is the business of the state so to legislate that its citizens may be provided with all necessary practical conditions to virtue. Even should the *state* neglect the education of its citizens, it is the duty of every individual to "contribute to the virtue of his children and friends." This he will best be able to do if he make himself fit to be a legislator.[1] This brings us to *Politics* proper, the second part of the general science of human good.

Origin of the State.[2] — The state is a growth the germ of which is the sexual relation, based on that desire of "leaving an offspring like oneself" which is "natural to man as to the whole animal and vegetable world," and those organic and inborn differences among human beings whereby some are naturally rulers, others subjects. Historically prior to the state are the individual, the family, or household, and the village, or community, the state being an association "composed of several villages," "the village" the simplest association of several households, etc. But the state is in idea prior to all these, for man is by nature a "political animal"; were he not, he would have to be a god or a brute. He is by nature fitted for the realization of the idea of law and justice, of which the state is but the embodiment and organ.[3]

[1] *Nicomachean Ethics*, Bk. X. ch. 9.
[2] The following outline follows the translation of the *Politics* made by J. E. C. Welldon, M.A. (1883).
[3] *Politics*, Bk. I. chs. 1 and 2.

The Family. — The elementary relations existing in the family, or household, are, according to Aristotle, those between husband and wife, parent and child, master and slave; and the science of the household has, therefore, three branches. Slavery is a natural and beneficent institution, owing to the natural differences in the intellectual and moral natures of men. The function of the slave is mere physical service; he is a tool, or instrument, of his master, the power of the latter over him being despotic. The slave is a kind of property. The head of the family rules wife and children not as a despot but as a constitutional ruler. Wife and children possess the same virtues as the head of the family, but possess some of those virtues in a lower degree than he. One part of the soul is natural ruler, the other natural subject; a corresponding difference exists among persons in society. In every part of the household and of the state there is a reference to the whole. In the household the whole is contained (ideally) in the head of the family; and the virtue of the child, the wife, the slave, has reference to that of the head of the family.[1] One branch of the science of the household is the art of acquisition, which has its foundation in the wealth realized from the products of the earth. This is natural finance; unnatural finance is the art of money-getting and trading in money. It is greatly subject to abuse.[2]

Criticism of Certain Theories and Forms of the State; Plato and Others. — The theory propounded by "Socrates" in Plato's *Republic* has, Aristotle thinks, three car-

[1] *Politics*, Bk. I. chs. 12 and 13.   [2] *Ibid.*, Bk. I. chs. 8–11.

dinal defects;[1] it aims at too great unity; the means proposed for the accomplishment of the end proposed are inadequate; the theory is vague, does not lay down proper limitations. (1) A state, as an organic whole, consists of a *number* of *different kinds* of individuals; the idea proposed in the *Republic* as the end to be realized is the idea of a household or an individual rather than of a state. The Platonic theory in its principle of rotation in office seems to assume that the actual personalities of the individuals who alternately rule and submit to authority are alternately changed, since different personalities naturally belong to those who are fitted to rule and those who should be ruled. The theory is thus false and self-contradictory. Again, the theory is false in the doctrine of unity, because independence is the object to be obtained by society, and a real state is more independent than a household or an individual.[2] (2) The proposition that all individuals in such a state can with equal right "call the same thing mine and thine" is a mere quibble. All *collectively*, not *distributively* "call the same thing mine." Again, people owning things in common care less for their possessions than those who individually have property. Community of wives and children would fail to conceal the parentage of children, and it would, besides, lead to endless mistakes, to crime and family pollution. Such community would be more appropriate among the husbandmen than among the guardians, because it diminishes, not increases, mutual affection, and so weakens the class in which it is practised. The greatest bless-

[1] *Politics*, Bk. II. chs. 2–6.   [1] *Ibid.*, Bk. II. ch. 1.
[2] *Ibid.*, Bk. II. ch. 2.

ing in the state is mutual affection : this is the only real source of the unity so eulogized by "Socrates." The transference of children from one class to another would be impossible, and, even if possible, would be an additional source of outrage, sensual love, and homicide. Community of property is also impossible, — at least in the Platonic sense, — as is evident from so simple a fact as that of the invariable quarrelling of persons keeping a common purse while travelling together. Community in the *use* of property is perhaps desirable, but not community in the *tenure* of it. The legislation proposed in the *Republic* has a "specious and philanthropic appearance," but is plainly impracticable. The only "community" practicable is that produceable by moral discipline, intellectual culture, and education.[1] (3) About the main body of the state — all, indeed, but the guardians — little or nothing is determined by the *Republic*. If there be community of wives and children and property among them, how will they differ from the guardians; and what will induce them to be ruled by the guardians ? There will be two mutually hostile states in one. If the husbandmen are given ownership of land on condition of their paying a fixed rent to the guardians, they will soon become arrogant and intractable. There are also certain minor defects in the *Republic*.[2] To the *Laws* of Plato nearly the same objections are applicable, since, with the exception of the community of wives, children, and property, the regulations are the same in the *Laws* as in the *Republic*.[3] Polities advocated by Phaleas, Hippodamus, Solon, and

[1] *Politics*, Bk. II. chs. 3-5. [2] *Ibid.*, Bk. II. chs. 5 and 6.
[3] *Ibid.*, Bk. II. ch. 6.

others, and the institutions of the Spartans, Cretans, and Carthaginians are also reviewed by Aristotle.

The End of the State. — Man, it has been affirmed, is a "political animal," and men would naturally unite in a social organization without the motive of a supposed or perceived common advantage to be realized in so doing. The true view of the state undoubtedly is that it is an association the real end of which is not the prevention of mutual injury or promotion of commercial exchange, though these are secondary objects of its being, but a "complete and independent existence, a life of felicity and nobleness" — not a life in *common* merely, but a *noble* life; the true state is devoted chiefly to virtue.[1]

The Nature of the Citizen. — As the state is a composite entity the elements of which are citizens, we have to determine the conception of the citizen. Not residence, nor the mere right to appear as plaintiff or defendant in a judicial action, nor the possession of freedom, nor the being indispensable to the existence of the state, as, for example, artisans and children are, nor all of these together, but a "participation in judicial power and public office" is the absolute mark of citizenship (in a democracy).[2] Now there is a question as to what is the virtue of a good citizen. Is it or is it not identical with that of the good man? The answer must be, in general terms, that the virtue of the citizen differs with different forms of government (for we may assume that there are several kinds of polity, or government), whereas the virtue of the good man is everywhere the same. And even in the same form of government, there

[1] *Politics*, Bk. III. chs. 6 and 8.   [2] *Ibid.*, Bk. III. chs. 1 and 5.

are different functions to be performed, and hence different virtues in the citizens as such. The good ruler possesses the virtue of prudence (*i.e.*, the virtue of the good man), which is not indispensable in the subject. Under a polity, however, in which the subject may become ruler, and ruler subject, there is doubtless an identity between the virtue of a good citizen and that of a good man; and "the virtue of a good citizen may be defined as a practical acquaintance both as ruler and subject with the rule characteristic of a free community." Virtue approximating that of the good man is, then, necessary to the citizen; and it is just because of this fact that artisans and children are not citizens.[1]

A Polity and its Kinds. — "A polity is an order of the state in respect of its offices generally, and especially of the supreme office." Polities are of two kinds, according as they have for their end public or private interest. "When the rule of the individual or the Few or the Many is exercised for the benefit of the community at large, the polities are normal, whereas polities which subserve the selfish "interest either of the individual or the Few or the Masses are perversions."[2] Polities may also be divided in accordance with differences as regards the governing power, which may be an individual or a few persons or many. A normal polity of the first sort is termed a Kingship, of the second, an Aristocracy (a government by the best, οἱ ἄριστοι, or else for the best interests of the community, τὸ ἄριστον), of the third, a Polity Proper. The corresponding corrupt polities are the Tyranny, Oligarchy, and Democ-

[1] *Politics*, Bk. III. chs. 4 and 5.   [2] *Ibid.*, Bk. III. ch. 7.

racy. The real difference between an oligarchy and a democracy is a difference as regards wealth, — wealth characterizing the former, poverty the latter.[1]

Who should be Rulers. — If it should be asked, Who ought to rule; one, few, or the many? the answer in general terms is, Whatever class embraces in itself the largest number of conditions to the good man, *i.e.*, virtues and external goods such as wealth, birth, etc. Collectively viewed, the masses or the many would, on this ground, generally have the supremacy; but if there are a few men, or if there is even one man sufficiently preeminent in virtue above the masses, to them or to him "all should render willing obedience."[2] From this it follows that the democratic form of polity (not, however, pure democracy but constitutional democracy) must generally be best, though there is a sufficient reason for the different kinds of polity in the fact that different kinds of populace demand different classes of rulers. "The populace which is suited to kingship is such as is naturally qualified to submit to a family whose superiority in virtue entitles them to political command; an aristocratical populace is one that is capable of yielding the obedience of free men to those whose virtue fits them for command as political rulers; and a constitutional populace, one that is capable of rule and subjection in conformity to a law which distributes the offices of state to the rich according to a principle of desert."[3] The kingship is unstable; for the king cannot, unsupported, rule the masses, and, if he have assistants, they may become his peers, and he is no longer king. In fact,

[1] *Politics*, Bk. III. chs 6–9.   [2] *Ibid.*, Bk. III. chs. 11–13.
[3] *Ibid.*, Bk. III. ch. 17.

the tendency of a polity not already constitutional is towards a constitutional polity, *i.e.*, a polity resting not on the *will* of one or a few, but on *law*. In the state as in the individual, the universal element rules the particular, the intellect (law is the creation of intellect) the passions.[1]

The Best Polity. — What, now, is the best polity? In general, it is that which furnishes the highest conditions to an independent and intelligent, *i.e.*, a virtuous, life for individuals and state alike. The state should comprise the largest number of persons consistent with a comprehensive knowledge, on the part of the citizens, of one another and the affairs of the state. The country should also be of such size and character in other respects that it can be "readily comprehended in a single view," *i.e.*, "allow of military succour being brought to any point at a short notice." The city should be so located with reference to land and sea that it will possess independence and security, and yet sufficient facilities for intercourse with other cities. It must have a suitable naval force. The citizens should be "spirited" and "independent." There must be food, mechanical arts, supply of money, religious ritual, means of administering justice. There must be a proper line of division between citizens and those who are not citizens, — the citizens comprising the soldiery and the deliberative class, those not citizens comprising the husbandmen, artisans, and hired laborers. The lands must be partly public, partly private, — public lands defraying the expenses of religious worship, and common meals,

---

[1] *Politics*, Bk. III. ch. 14-17. The state must have a true psychological basis.

and private lands being so divided that owners (who must be citizens) possess portions on the frontier as well as in the city. The cultivators of the soil should be slaves. The city must be favorably situated with regard to conditions for health and political and military action. The city should be walled and arranged, internally, with reference to the convenience of the citizens, buildings appropriated to religious services (with certain exceptions), common meals, "supreme magisterial boards" being in the same locality, etc. Education [1] must be the same for all citizens, and must be provided by the state, since training in the public business should be public, and every individual is but a subject member of the state. The education provided should be suited to leisure and peace rather than business and war, for the virtues relative to the former are higher than those relative to the latter. It should begin with the physical and ethical natures of the child and advance to the purely rational, since the natural order of development is from the "habits" to reason. Marriage and the begetting of children must be regulated by the state. Infancy and early youth must be carefully surrounded with the purest influences as regards speech and manners and scenes. Reading and writing should be taught, because of their general utility; the art of design or painting, for its usefulness as a means to forming right judgment of works of art; gymnastics, because it promotes health and vigor; music, because it is a source of rational enjoyment. Since the education of the body precedes that of the intellect, the first training of children must be in gym-

[1] *Politics*, Bks. IV. and V.

nastics. Before the age of puberty this should not be severe; for, as the experience of the Lacedemonians proves, severe gymnastics renders youths brutal in their feelings, and, besides, unfits them for intellectual occupations. Three years following puberty may be given to other studies, then severe gymnastics may be taken up. Music comes later, because its chief use is the purification of the passions or emotions and the affording enjoyment to the rational nature. The Dorian and Lydian airs, which are intellectual and emotional, may be employed, but not so frequently the Phrygian, which is largely physical in its effects. Flute-playing and "professional" musicians are hardly to be encouraged. The education provided by the state should, in a word, be not that which is indispensable or practically useful merely, but that which is, also, liberal and noble.

Characteristics of Different Polities.—The true statesman must possess a knowledge of all possible forms of polity and the laws appropriate to each. Differences in polities arise from differences in the combination of the elements or parts of a polity; the husbandmen or agricultural class, the mechanical class, the commercial class, the hired laborers, the military class, the rich, or the leisured, class, and the public officials, or the deliberative and judicial classes. Two or more of these may practically unite in one. Now there are two principal forms of polity, viz., Democracy and Oligarchy. "A democracy exists when the authority is in the hands of the free poor, who are in a majority; and an oligarchy when it is in the hands of the propertied, or noble, class who are in a minority." In a democracy either the laws or popular decrees may be supreme. If the laws are supreme, the democracy is constitutional. In a democracy in which popular decrees are supreme there is large scope for demagogues. When eligibility to office depends upon a property qualification or birth, or on the actual possession of citizenship, the democracy becomes practically constitutional, *i.e.*, is governed by fixed legislation, because, for want of means and of leisure for self-indulgence, the citizens are content with holding merely such meetings of the assembly as are indispensable. Constitutional democracy may then be of three kinds. Of oligarchy there are four species: one in which a moderate qualification for eligibility to office obtains, the poor being in the majority, and every one who has sufficient property enjoying full political privileges; another in which there is a *high* property qualification and "officers elect to the vacancies"; another in which office-holding is hereditary; a fourth, similar to the last-mentioned but placing the supreme authority in the executive and not in the law. In the first-mentioned form of oligarchy, naturally, the law is supreme; in the second, owing to the power of the rich, the law is "accommodated" to the "general principle of the polity"; the third form is ostensibly constitutional, but naturally verges towards the fourth, which is monarchical.[1] Other forms of polity are Aristocracy, Tyranny, and Polity Proper. Strictly speaking, an aristocracy is a polity in which the good man and the good citizen are identical. But any polity in which regard is had to wealth, virtue, and numbers, or to any two of these, is termed aristocratical. In a strict tyranny there is an

[1] *Politics*, Bk. VII. chs. 1-6.

"irresponsible rule over subjects, all of whom are equals or superiors of the rulers, for the personal advantage of the ruler and not of the subjects." A polity proper is, in general terms, a kind of mean between oligarchy and democracy — inclining, however, towards the latter. A "criterion of a good fusion is the possibility of calling the same polity a democracy or an oligarchy," and, further, the known existence in the state of no element anxious for a change of polity.[1] The best polity must be that which appears best when judged by the standard of a virtue not beyond the attainment of ordinary human beings, since the happy life is the mean life; and the best state will, accordingly, be that in which the middle classes (as regards wealth) are in the majority, or at least hold the balance of power, and laws are enacted that aim at the satisfaction of the middle classes. The reason why so many existing polities are either oligarchical or democratical is that the middle class is generally small in them.[2] Every good polity has three departments: the deliberative, the political, the executive. In democratical polities the function of deliberation is performed wholly or chiefly by the people, either collectively or by alternation; in oligarchical, by a few or comparatively few persons; in a polity proper, in some cases, by persons appointed partly by suffrage, and in others by persons appointed by lot, or in all cases by persons appointed partly by lot, partly by suffrage. "The deliberative body is supreme upon all questions of war and peace, the formation and dissolution of alliances, the enactment of laws, sentences of

---

[1] *Politics*, Bk. VI. chs. 7–10. [2] *Ibid.*, Bk. VI. chs. 11–13.

death, exile, and confiscation; to it belongs the election of officers of state, and to it they are responsible at the expiration of their term of office." As regards the executive department, some offices are common to the various forms of polity, others are peculiar: a council is a democratic institution, a preliminary council is oligarchical. The modes of appointment are different in different forms of polity. In a democratical polity "all" appoint "from all by suffrage, or by lot, or by a combination of the two"; in an oligarchical polity, appointment is made of some "from some by suffrage, or some from some by lot, or some from some by a combination of the two, though the appointment by suffrage is more strictly oligarchical than that by lot or by a combination of the two"; in a polity proper the "appointment is not vested in all the citizens collectively, but all are eligible, and the appointment is made either by lot, or by suffrage, or both, or in which the persons eligible are in some cases all the citizens, in others some of them, and the appointment is made either by lot or suffrage or both"; in a polity of the aristocratic sort the "appointment is made by some partly from all and partly from some, either by lot or suffrage, or partly by suffrage and partly by lot." The courts of law — constituting the judiciary — are eight in number: a court of scrutiny, a court to try offences committed against the state, a court to try constitutional questions, a court to try cases between officers and individuals respecting fines, a court to try important cases of private contract, a court of homicide, a court of aliens, a court for the trial of petty contracts. The forms of constitution of the courts in which universal eligibility and universal jurisdiction are combined are democratical; those in which limited eligibility and universal jurisdiction are combined are oligarchical; those in which there is a combination of universal and limited eligibility are "characteristic of aristocracy and a polity."[1]

Methods of Establishing and Maintaining the Various Forms of Government. — We have seen that differences in democracies arise from differences in the character of the population. Differences may also spring from differences in the *combination* of features that are peculiarly democratic. But there are two primary principles of all democracies: equality and the rule of the majority, and the liberty to live according to one's pleasure. Characteristic of popular government are the following-named features: "the eligibility of all citizens to the offices of state and their appointment by all; the rule of all over each individual and of each individual in his turn over all; the use of the lot in the appointment either to all the offices of state or to all that do not require experience or special skill; the absence of property qualification or the requirement of the lowest possible qualification for office; the regulation that the same person shall never hold any office twice, or shall not hold it much oftener than once, or shall do so only in a few cases, with the exception of military offices; a system of short tenure of offices either in all cases, or in all cases where it is possible; the power of all or of a body chosen from all to sit as judges in all or almost all, or at least the greatest and

[1] *Politics*, Bk. VI. chs. 14–16.

most important cases, such as cases arising out of the audit of the officer's accounts, constitutional cases, and cases of private contract; the supreme authority of the public assembly in all questions, or at least the most important, and of no individual office over any question, or only the smallest number possible." "The most characteristic feature is the council, except where all the citizens receive a large fee for attendance in the Assembly." Another characteristic feature is the payment of the members of the departments, as far as possible. Others are low birth, poverty, intellectual degradation, the not holding office for life, the decision of the majority of both rich and poor, if they agree, and if they disagree, of the absolute majority, or in other words of those whose collective property assessment is higher. There are four forms of democracy: the agricultural, the pastoral, the mechanical or commercial, and the extreme, in which "the popular leaders usually enroll the largest possible number of persons in the rank of the citizens, conferring political rights not only upon all the legitimate children of citizens, but upon their bastards, and upon children who are descended from citizens upon the side of one parent only, whether the fathers or the mothers." Of these, the first is the best, the last the worst.[1] It is the business of the legislator not only to establish democracies, but to provide for their security. Such laws should be enacted as will cause the poor to be satisfied with their condition. They should be subsidized, should be directed to industrial pursuits, given a share in the enjoyment of the

[1] *Politics*, Bk. VII. chs. 1-14.

property of the rich.[1] The best form of oligarchy, we have seen, approaches the polity, so-called. In it there are two degrees of property qualification, a higher and a lower: all persons admitted to citizenship are from the better elements of the commons. In an oligarchy the military class rules. This has four divisions: cavalry, heavy-armed troops, light-armed troops, marines. Only the rich can support cavalry and heavy-armed troops, and hence these are peculiarly oligarchical, the others being democratical. In a country suited to cavalry, that division of the military class may be supreme; in a country suited to heavy-armed troops that division may rule. Oligarchies are preserved by putting upon the rich the burden of heavy expenses for sacrifices, public buildings, etc., and relieving the poor of all such.[2] The offices of government must be properly constituted. Executive offices are: the superintendence of the market, the superintendence of all public and private property in the city, the superintendence of such property in the country and the suburbs of the city, the receiving and holding and distributing public revenues, the recording of public accounts, the levying and collecting of fines, the superintendence of military affairs, and marine affairs, the auditing of public accounts, the giving of preliminary consideration to bills to be presented to the public assembly, this last being the supreme office. Religious offices are the superintendencies of divine worship, and of the public sacrifices that are not assigned by the law to the priesthood, but are solemnly celebrated upon the hearth of the state.

[1] *Politics*, Bk. VII. ch. 5.   [2] *Ibid.*, Bk. VII. chs. 6, 7.

Other offices are the censorship of boys and women, presidencies of gymnastic exercises, and Dionysiac Contests. The Guardianship of the Laws is an aristocratical institution, the Preliminary Council oligarchical, and the Council democratical.

Causes of Political Revolutions, etc. — It remains to consider the "nature, number, and character of the circumstances which produce political revolutions, the agencies destructive of the several polities, the general sequence of polities in a revolutionary age, and, lastly, the preservatives of polities both generally and individually."[1] Generally speaking, the *cause of sedition* is "inequality." The common people are seditious when they think they have a smaller share of political advantages than others have, and the oligarchs when they think they have not a greater share than others have. In the one case it is from a position of inferiority that the people are encouraged to sedition by the hope of equality; and in the other, from the position of equality by a hope of predominance. The predisposing causes of sedition and revolution are: desire of gain and honor; envy and indignation at the gain and honors of others; the possession of too great power; fear of punishment or of becoming victims of crime; contempt of the oligarchs for the masses, or vice versa; the disproportionate increase of one class in the state; party-spirit; gradual change in government; diversity of race; the localities of states ("when the country is not naturally adapted to the existence of a single state"); the accession of persons of high repute or influence to some peculiar office or class

---

[1] *Politics*, Bk. VII. ch. 8.

in the state; an even balance of antagonistic classes in the state. Political disturbances may be brought about either by force or by fraud.[1] "The main *cause of revolution in Democracies* is the intemperate conduct of the demagogues, who force the propertied class to combine, partly by instituting malicious prosecutions against individuals, and partly by exciting the masses against them as a body." *Democracies* are transformed by revolution into democracies of a different type and into tyrannies. *Revolutions in oligarchies* are principally of two kinds: the oppression of the masses by the oligarchs, and sedition among the oligarchs themselves. Sometimes sedition in oligarchies is due to demagogues paying court to members of the oligarchical party or to the masses. Revolutions occur when the oligarchs, having wasted their means in riotous living, are eager for innovation and strive to establish a tyranny; and when some of the oligarchs suffer a repulse at the hands of others. Overdespotism in oligarchies, exciting indignation in members of the governing class, is a cause of sedition. Oligarchies are destroyed by the creation within them of oligarchies. Revolutions may be the result of accidental circumstances. In *aristocracies* one cause of revolution is the limitation of the number of persons admitted to honors of state. Another cause is the putting of a stigma upon persons of consequence. Another is the exclusion of an individual of strong character from honors of state. Another, the existence of excessive poverty on one side or excessive wealth on the other in the state. Finally, the existence already of a

---

[1] *Politics*, Bk. VIII. chs. 1–4.

sedition headed by a powerful individual able to extend his authority. The *main cause of sedition in polities and aristocracies* is a "deviation from their proper principle of justice in the constitution of the polity itself." Generally revolutions are from polities of a given kind into others of a similar kind, not into their opposites. Polities are liable to dissolution both from external and internal causes. *Polities are preserved* by watchfulness against illegality and gradual changes, against the beginnings of revolution, and artifices to impose upon the masses; by officials[1] keeping on good terms with citizens enjoying political privileges; by the limitation of the tenure of office to short periods; by proximity to destructive agencies which excite alarm and put the people on their guard; by legal regulations for restraining frauds and rivalries among the upper classes; by reduction of assessments at the proper time; by not investing any individual with disproportionate authority; by the creation of officers to exercise supervision over all whose life or conduct is detrimental in its influence upon the polity; by taking precautions with regard to those enjoying remarkable prosperity; by abstaining from confiscating the estates and profits of the rich, and chiefly by so ordering affairs that officers of the state find no opportunity for merely personal gain. "There are three qualifications requisite in all who are to hold the supreme office of state, viz. : firstly, loyalty to the established polity; secondly, the greatest capacity for the duties of their office; and, thirdly, the virtue and justice appropriate to the polity, whatever it may

[1] *Politics*, Bk. VIII. chs. 5–7.

be." All legislation beneficial to polities tends to preserve them in a fixed condition, but most especially that which is guided by *the principle of the mean.* The strongest preservative of polities is education in the spirit of those polities.[1] The *causes predisposing to insurrection in monarchies* are injustice, fear, and contempt, — the injustice consisting principally in insolence, sometimes in the spoliation of private property. "Insurrection may take the form of an attack either upon the person or upon the authority of the rulers." Attacks of the first form are occasioned by insolence, by personal affronts, by degrading corporal punishment. Ambition may cause insurrection. Tyrannies *are destroyed* by influences from without or within.[2] The *preservatives of monarchy* are, in general terms, the following: meanness of spirit in the subjects, distrust among them of one another, incapacity for affairs, affecting of good will on the part of the monarch towards his subjects, not exciting the indignation of the masses by lavish expenditures, the seeming to collect taxes and impose public burdens only for economical purposes, the preserving an address of dignity without sternness, the avoiding of insults to his subjects, moderation in sensual pleasure, enriching of the city by edifices and decorations in the assumed spirit of the guardian of the public interests, display of religious zeal, inflicting punishments through personal agents, the depriving officers of their places not suddenly and harshly, but gradually and mildly, avoiding oppression, — in short, "wearing the appearance not of a tyrant, but of a householder or

---

[1] *Politics,* Bk. VIII. chs. 8, 9. [2] *Ibid.,* Bk. VIII. chs. 8, 9.

king; not of a self-seeker, but of a guardian of public interests."[1]

The Most Permanent Polities. — The most permanent polities are the kingship and the polity proper; the least permanent, oligarchy and tyranny.

Plato's Theory of Revolution. — The theory of revolution advanced in the *Republic* is defective at many points.[2]

Rhetoric. — An offshoot of political science and of dialectic is Rhetoric, or the art, or "faculty," not of persuasion, but of discovering the possible means of persuasion (as medicine is the art, not of curing disease, but of finding and applying all possible remedies that cure or *tend* to cure); for it is the science or *quasi*-science of that kind of discourse, particularly, whose propositions are drawn from "political science" and whose method is borrowed from, or formed after, that of dialectic. It is not a science, because neither in theory nor in practice does it aim at exact truth but only probable truth of matter, or employ perfect rigidity of method. It adapts the truths of political science and the principles of dialectic to the ordinary life and mind. It differs, further, from dialectic in aiming at the production of conviction and not merely at the artistic and effective logical combination of propositions.[3] Persuasion may be the result of two classes of "proofs," or means of persuasion, designated as scientific and unscientific. In the former are comprised arguments, the character of the speaker, the disposition of the audience; in the latter, witnesses, tortures, properly

[1] *Politics*, Bk. VIII. ch. 2.   [2] *Ibid.*, Bk. VIII. ch. 12.
[3] *Rhetoric*, Bk. I. chs. 1, 2.

taking advantage of the state of the laws, deeds, and oaths. Arguments truly adapted for persuasion must possess at least a *quasi*-syllogistic character and must be composed of propositions that are, or seem to be, true or highly probable. The speaker must appear to be a person having ability, principle, and good-will towards his hearers. The only honorable and otherwise properly rhetorical means of controlling the feelings of an audience are to be found in the honesty and good-will of the speaker himself and the knowledge of the passions and dispositions of men. True rhetorical method does *not* consist in warping the mind by firing the passions.[1] There are three branches of Rhetoric: one treating of the "means of persuasion which address themselves to the understanding," another of style, and another of the arrangement of the parts of the discourse.[2] There are three kinds of oratory: that which finds place in the deliberative assembly, has for its end the expedient, and is termed Deliberative Oratory; that which finds place in irregular as well as regular public assemblies has for its object the honorable, is panegyrical or vituperative, and is termed Demonstrative (ἐπιδεικτική) Oratory; that which finds place in the courts of law, has justice for its object, and is termed Judicial Oratory.[3] Rhetoric is a useful and legitimate art, because it is in harmony with the general tendency in human nature towards truth and justice, and is better adapted than science to ordinary intelligence, trains the mind to look at both sides of a question, and is such a means

---

[1] *Rhetoric*, Bk. I. ch. 3; Bk. II. ch. 1; Bk. I. ch. 2.
[2] *Ibid.*, Bk. II. ch. 26 and Bk. III. ch. 1.
[3] *Ibid.*, Bk. I. ch. 3.

of defence for the mind as gymnastic skill is for the body.[1]

Poetical, or Poietical, Philosophy (see above, p. 121). — Poietical philosophy, or the philosophy of art, is the theory of the "habit of making joined with right reason." Art, together with conduct (or "doing"), has to do, we have seen, with the contingent, whereas wisdom, including intuition and science, is concerned with being. Art, as a form of knowledge, is superior to experience, and stands next in rank to wisdom. Under art as a whole is included house-building and other purely productive arts as well as the "imitative" arts, poetry, music, sculpture, etc. In art there are three processes: production, contrivance, and contemplation. The immediate end of works of art as such is in the works themselves[2] (not in the artist). Art either "imitates," or represents, or it perfects that which nature has left imperfect.[3] As "imitative," art makes prominent the universal element in things.[4] The "imitative" arts — poetry, music, painting, sculpture — may have for their effects amusement and relaxation, rational enjoyment and the purification of the feelings, and moral discipline. As a source of amusement and relaxation, art "heals" the pain of labor.[5] A rational enjoyment arises from the perception of the fact of resemblance between things "imitated" and their "imita-

---

[1] *Rhetoric*, Bk. I. ch. 1. Attention may here be called to the remarkable discussion of the passions and aspirations of men in the first seventeen chapters of Bk. II.
[2] *Nicomachean Ethics*, Bk. VI. ch. 4, and *Metaphysics*, Bk. I. ch. 2.
[3] *Physics*, Bk. II. ch. 8.   [4] *Poetic*, ch. 9.
[5] *Politics*, Bk. V. chs. 5 and 7.

tions," and the discovery that the imitations are representations or symbols of the objects imitated, a discovery that partakes of the character of an acquisition of new knowledge. ("All men have by nature a desire and impulse towards knowledge."[1]) Purification of the feelings takes place when, after an ecstasy of soul produced by works of art, we relapse into our normal state, experiencing "pleasurable feelings of relief."[2] Art affords moral discipline, and influences character by teaching men to "enjoy right pleasures and entertain right feelings of liking or dislike." This it does by "imitating," or representing, such pleasures and feelings, and producing effects similar to those produced by the original causes of them. In music, as has been stated, an ethical effect is produced by the Dorian melodies and harmonies, an emotional by the Lydian, and a physical by the Phrygian. Poetry consists in the imitation of actions, manners, and sentiments by means of rhythm, melody, and measure, — *i.e.*, by some or all of these, — in narrative or in action. The characters imitated may be better or worse, or neither better nor worse, than ordinary characters. In tragedy, better, in comedy, worse, than ordinary characters are "imitated." Tragedy is the representation in pleasing language by means of persons acting and not merely by means of narration, of an action having dignity, completeness, and magnitude; producing, by its effect upon the emotions of fear (or terror) and pity, a purification of the mind of such feelings.[3] The fear and pity (which must not be confounded here with horror and compassion) awakened

[1] *Metaphysics*, Bk. I. ch. 1; *Poetic*, ch. 4; *Rhetoric*, Bk. I. ch. 4.
[2] *Politics*, Bk. V. ch. 7.   [3] *Poetic*, ch. 6.

GREEK PHILOSOPHY. 185

by tragedy arise from the contemplation of a worthy character undergoing misfortune through some shortcoming incident to human nature.[1] Comedy is the imitation of only such worse than ordinary characters as are ridiculous merely. Epic poetry resembles tragedy in having for its subject an important action having beginning, middle, and end, but differs in requiring a more extended action, in admitting a larger degree of the wonderful, in being narrative and employing neither music nor the spectacle, and in requiring a nobler diction and more stable metre. Tragedy excels epic poetry for the following reason : it possesses every excellence of the latter and, besides, greater perspicuity and a greater degree of simplicity and unity.[2] The chief point to be attended to in both kinds of poetry is the fable, or story, of the action. As compared with history, poetry is the more philosophical, because it gives more truthfully the universal element of human life.[3]

Sources and Genesis of Aristotle's Philosophy. — We have now to consider (briefly) the sources and genesis of the philosophy of Aristotle, and its points of contact with earlier systems. And it is well to bear in mind here that Aristotle prepared a historico-critical sketch of Greek philosophy from its beginning down to Plato,[4] that frequently in various works he refers to and comments upon the doctrines of earlier thinkers, particularly, as we have seen, of his master, Plato, and that he was in mental temperament a natural, though not uncritical, conservative. It would, perhaps, be safe, then, to say, even without comparison of his doctrines

[1] *Poetic*, chs. 13 and 14.   [3] *Ibid.*, ch. 9.
[2] *Ibid.*, ch. 26.   [4] See *Metaphysics*, Bk. I. chs. 3–9.

with those of earlier thinkers, that there was no important doctrine of any earlier philosopher that had not passed under his critical notice, and that no leading principle of his own was discovered and adopted by him without reference, positive or negative, to the theories of those earlier speculators. A consideration of the sources and genesis of his philosophy and its point of contact with earlier systems involves, therefore, a glance at the principal features of the earlier Greek thought. Aristotle's *logical theories* appear to be, for the most part, new and original with him, and yet it is evident that they sprang out of the intellectual conditions of his age. The time was ripe for bringing out of the relative chaos of dialectic, false and legitimate, Sophistic and Socratico-Platonic, the formal order of logical system. In *metaphysics* Aristotle's Being and God are in a direct line with the Being of Parmenides, the Nous of Anaxagoras, and the highest Idea of Plato, and his attempt to unite being and phenomena through the doctrine of the four causes and the conceptions of possibility and actuality is an organic continuation of the effort of most of the thinkers before him, after Parmenides and Heraclitus, to reconcile the grand ideas of these two heroes in early Greek thought. The first suggestion of the doctrine of causes must, it would seem, have come to him from his teacher or his teacher's works, *e.g.*, the *Timæus*, but, judging from his point of view in his history of Greek philosophy,[1] it seems not improbable that Aristotle himself regarded his doctrine of causes as substantially his own,

---

[1] See above, p. 3.

and as the summing-up and flower of all previous Greek thought; and there seems to be no reason for denying that he was right in so doing. The theory of possibility and actuality is peculiarly Aristotelian. The first solid "putting" of the idea of a perfectly efficient, concrete, intelligent power, an actual immanent (as well as transcendent) mind must be credited to Aristotle. Possibility and actuality as organic unity is, virtually, Aristotle's formula for the universe as living, thought-determined being. In *physics* Aristotle deviated very widely, in one respect, from almost the whole previous course of Greek philosophy; he declared the world to be uncreated and always the same, whereas earlier thinkers, from Anaximander down, had held a doctrine either of physical evolution or of creation. This deviation finds its explanation, as we have seen, in the theory that motion, the characteristic of the phenomenal world as such, presupposes, in the last analysis, an eternal being which is the eternal cause of motion, — motion consequently having no temporal origin. The conception, also, of nature as a *self*-realizing *end*, or system of such ends, is peculiarly Aristotelian. In other respects Aristotle's theory of nature is, on the whole, that of Plato, and in minor points agrees with those of Parmenides, Heraclitus, Empedocles, Anaxagoras. To Plato and Aristotle alike the universe is spatially finite; it is a sphere, of which the outer portion is divine in nature, the central human and imperfect, the former through a descending series giving the law to the latter. Aristotle's definition of the elements has points in common with those of Parmenides, Heraclitus, Empedocles, and Plato. His theory of the soul, the first system of psychology, was framed after a thorough review[1] of all previous Greek theories on the subject; and it embodies and unites in a truly organic way the real *aperçus*, or true insights, of those theories. Here as almost everywhere else, he follows Plato more closely than he does any other thinker. Adopting substantially Plato's subdivision of the soul into parts and faculties, he yet by means of his original insight of the entelechy, or perfect realization, has made a true advance in thought, upon Plato, in the mode of viewing the soul as a substance, or real unitary being, though it must be confessed that in his negative attitude towards immortality he seems to fall far below the spirit of Plato's teaching. As regards his *ethical doctrines* we have already indicated sufficiently, perhaps, their relation to Socrates. (There are no ethical teachings prior to those of Socrates with which it is necessary here to compare Aristotle's.) In showing Aristotle's affinity in this respect with Plato, we cannot, perhaps, do better than borrow the words of Sir Alexander Grant. Aristotle plainly enough owes to Plato: "(1) The conception of moral science as a whole, — that it is a sort of politics, which is the science of human happiness. (2) The conception of the *practical* chief Good, — that it is τέλειον and αὐταρκές ['perfect' and 'self-sufficient'] and incapable of improvement or addition. (3) The conception that man has an ἔργον, or proper function, that man's ἀρετή perfects this, and that his well-being is inseparable from it. (4) The conception of Psychology as a basis for morals. (5) The doctrine of Μεσότης [the Mean], which is only

---

[1] Occupying nearly the whole of the first book of the *De Anima*.

a modification of the Μετριότης of Plato. (6) The doctrine of φρόνησις, which is an adaptation, with alterations, of the Socratico-Platonic view. (7) The theory of Pleasure, its various kinds, and the transcendency of mental pleasures. (8) The theory of Friendship, which is suggested by questions started but not answered, in the *Lysis* of Plato. (9) The Agnoiology, a theory of Ignorance, in Book XII., — to explain how men can act against what they know to be best, — which appears to have been considerably suggested by Platonic discussions. (10) The practical conclusion of the *Ethics*, — that philosophy is the highest good and the greatest happiness, being an approach to the nature of the Divine Being."[1] Aristotle's *theory of the state* has much less, relatively, in common with Plato's. The end of the state, as conceived by both philosophers, was, no doubt, the same, viz., the happiness or good of the whole, not of any part of the state; but Plato's preferred state was a state governed merely by wise *men*, Aristotle's a state governed by *law* (made and understood by the citizens). Each had in view a state that should have a true psychological basis, a state in which reason and not passion should rule; but Aristotle's, it would seem, is a theory which better accords with actual human nature and better provides for the *natural* rule of intellect over passion. Here, as elsewhere, Aristotle follows more closely than Plato the conception of the universal immanent in the particular. Aristotle's "best polity" has more kinship with Plato's "second best" state, expounded in the *Laws;* but Plato is as

---

[1] See Essay in Vol. I. of Grant's *Ethics of Aristotle.*

much an extremist in one way in the *Laws* as he is in another in the *Republic*.[1] Finally, Aristotle (it is easy to see) attained to his conception of the state largely through a struggle with Plato's, and his divergence from Plato here seems to be but a part of that general divergence which is the result of a natural development in metaphysical standpoint. Aristotle's *rhetoric*, or theory of persuasion, is the first systematic philosophical theory of the subject it treats, and is mostly original. He had thoroughly sifted the Sophistic rhetoric and, instead of adopting it or any part of it, condemned it as the false art of warping the judgment. Fundamental hints for his theory are to be found, however, in the *Phædrus* and *Gorgias* of Plato. The idea that men can be *really persuaded* only by instrumentalities capable of reaching their moral and logical faculties and habitudes is quite Platonic; but circumstances and Plato's hatred of the Sophists having made it *his* business to destroy false rhetoric rather than construct a theory of true rhetoric, it falls to Aristotle to construct such a theory, which, of course, as a thinker, if not as a stylist, he was qualified to do. To the *homeliness* (if we may apply the term here) of the Socratic conception of beauty and the austerity of the Platonic, there is little in Aristotle's that is akin. Aristotle would merely purify and elevate the inborn *play*-instinct in human nature; Plato would se-

---

[1] Aristotle has without doubt come nearer to the mean that is within reach of a race of beings that *naturally* tends towards truth and justice. The truth would seem to be that Aristotle had an abiding sense of the substantial rightness of his conception of *nature* as instinct with intelligence and hence *right* and *truth*, and could afford to rely on the *natural* positings of the human soul.

verely restrict feeling and imagination, which, in their union, constitute the art-instinct in human nature.

The Substantial Unity of Plato and Aristotle. — The divergences that have been pointed out between Aristotle and Plato need not blind us to the fact that they are, in spite of those divergences, in substantial harmony. This appears immediately if they be compared with one who is fundamentally opposed to either, *i.e.*, whose first principle is a purely material principle, whether water, air, fire, atom (ancient or modern), or all these, or any number of them together,— thus viewed, Plato and Aristotle are at one, for they are both completely committed to the view that spirit, and spirit only, is absolute. They do not, it is true, entirely get rid of "matter," but treat it as a kind of negative function of spirit, or form; to Aristotle matter is passive reason in the world; to Plato it is a kind of "spurious reason." The entire weight of Plato's teaching was, as we have already seen, thrown into the scale in support of the thesis that the real is rational and the rational is real, and Aristotle, with many criticisms and demurrings, it is true, in regard to secondary matters, simply added to Plato's thought the immense weight of his own. In fact, probably no other two of the world's master-thinkers are in such substantial agreement as these two. With such solidarity of thought throughout the whole history of human speculative thought, the philosophical mind of the world would be really one, as indeed it ideally is. Philosophy in itself and philosophy in its history would be all but identical.

Result. — We have now to attempt an estimate of the worth of the leading features of Aristotle's philosophy.

In general, it may be said that Aristotle carried the development of that conception of mind as absolute which Anaxagoras was the first to suggest, to the highest point possible under the circumstances of his age, and that he brought philosophy fully around to the opposite of the naïve naturalism with which it began. That he (together with Plato) established a consistent universalistic idealism has often been doubted. God, in the system of Aristotle, is, it has been held, a *deus ex machina*, has but an idle, shadowy being, and the system ends in dualism. The immovableness of being, the transcendence of the Deity, or Thought of Thought, the separableness of reason in the soul from the other faculties seem, perhaps, to warrant such an assertion. But, on the other hand, to make God merely the bond of union (even though organic) among the parts of nature is to ignore the fact of a separable reason, and is to be satisfied with the purely naturalistic view of the world, — with the naturalistic instead of the spiritualistic conception of organic unity. Somehow immanent in the world God must be, but he is, also, transcendent. Aristotle's category was that of spirit, not life merely, and his conception of God, or a transcendent divine reason, seems to be an excellence, not a defect in his system. A great feature in the system of Aristotle is its conception of nature, defective as that conception in some respect no doubt is. From the standpoint of modern physical speculation, Aristotle's theory of nature falls below that of most of his predecessors, — Anaximander and other "evolutionists," the Pythagoreans (the centre of whose universe was not the earth but the so-called "central fire"), the

Atomists (who discovered by speculation something very like the modern atom, the hypothesis of which is at least accounted as an indispensable "working hypothesis"). But in that it demonstratively put matter under the sway of reason and kept the "object" within the sphere of the "subject" and thus made it organic, Aristotle's theory far surpassed in *philosophic rightness* that of any of the early nature-philosophers, and has hardly been surpassed by that of any of those who have succeeded him. That his theory of the soul, the kernel of his theory of nature, has stood the test of centuries hardly need be said: his conception of reason and sense as organically one is far in advance of widely prevailing mechanistic psychological theories of this moment. In Aristotle's ethical and political theories there is wanting, no doubt, the clearness and decision of Socrates's "All virtue is knowledge," or Kant's "You ought, therefore, you can"; but there is a certain moral poise and health in the conception of a just synthesis of man's capacities in the right fulfilment of his function (ἔργον), and great strength and stability in the conception of virtue as a *habit* and *fixed tendency*, the foundation and moving force of which is eternal reason itself. There is, indeed, in the formula describing virtue a theoretical surd, or irrational "quantity," the idea of the "prudent man." But we may question whether, after all, moral activity is not such a surd, as involving something beside mere calculation, as being only semi-rational. Again, contemplation, the virtue of "the philosopher" in the *Ethics* has been felt to be *un*moral in character; but here again we may question whether Aristotle is not substantially correct. He practically admits that such a virtue is beyond the reach of most men; is there not, nevertheless, a certain *theoretical* justice in holding it to be the most perfect virtue? Is Aristotle so very far from Socrates and Kant in this? Were not the ethical requirements laid down by them more "theoretical" than "practical"? The doctrine that man is a "political animal" can, it might seem, never be entirely supplanted. But it must not be forgotten that even Aristotle, as did Plato, put man the philosopher above man the citizen, and that, practically, at least, the notion of man as a political animal must, so to say, recede and give larger place to that of man as a perfectly self-conscious and self-determining being. Society is an organism, not for life merely, but for spirit, and spirit is not to be shut up in outward institutions.

§ 15.

The Peripatetic School. — That, after the death of Aristotle, there should arise a thinker who should grasp and develop on all sides his philosophy as he had grasped and developed Plato's would appear strange indeed; and, as a matter of fact, there *was* no such thinker. The immediate followers of Aristotle comprehended and adopted only portions of his system, and those not of the highest importance in speculative thought. Of the school of Aristotle, the so-called Peripatetic School, there were very few thinkers even worthy of being remembered. We speak here of but three— *Theophrastus of Lesbos, Strato of Lampsacus*, and *Dicæarch of Messene*. Mention will be made later of Peripatetics who were, it would appear, scarcely more than Aristotelian editors and commentators.

Theophrastus of Lesbos. — Theophrastus (*circa* 372 -287 B.C.) a favorite disciple of Aristotle and chosen by him to be his successor at the head of the Peripatetic school, gave the theories of Aristotle a marked naturalistic interpretation; being apparently moved by the desire to bring reason and sense into closer union than, as it seemed to him, Aristotle had brought them. He did not, however, give up completely the transcendence of reason, but treated motion, in which he included, as Aristotle had not done, genesis and destruction as a limitation of the soul, and treated "energy" not merely as *pure* activity, or actuality, but as akin to physical activity. He affirmed, practically, that there was no motion that did not contain an "energy." This was equivalent to giving an absolute character to motion, whereas with Aristotle the absolute was unmoved. The alleged motions of the soul (Aristotle had denied motion to the soul) were of two kinds: corporeal — *e.g.*, desire, passion, anger, — and incorporeal, *e.g.*, judgment and the act of cognition. He retained Aristotle's notion that external goods are a necessary concomitant of virtue and an essential to happiness, and "held that a slight deviation from the rules of morals was permissible and required when such deviation would result in warding off a great evil from a friend or in securing for him a great good." "The principal merit of Theophrastus consists in the enlargement which he gave to natural science, especially to botany (phytology), in the fidelity to nature with which he executed his delineation of Human Characters, and next to these things, in his contributions to the constitution and criticism of the history of these sciences."[1]

[1] Ueberweg's *Hist. of Phil.*, Vol. I. p. 182.

Strato of Lampsacus. — A pupil of Theophrastus and the next leader, after him, of the Peripatetic School (281-279 B.C.) was Strato of Lampsacus. Strato discarded the doctrine of the real transcendence of reason, and held that there could be nothing in the human intellect which had not already been in sense. "He placed the seat of sensation not in the members of the body, nor in the heart, but in the seat of the understanding; gave to sensation a share of the activity of the understanding; made the understanding inter-convertible with thought directed upon sensible phenomena, and so came near resolving the thought of the understanding into sense."[1] This was done in the attempt to derive from Aristotle's conception of nature as a power working unconsciously towards ends a perfectly simple organic (even materialistically so) conception of the universe. Strato did not, it would seem, busy himself with experimental fact, but erected his theory upon a purely speculative basis. The theory of Strato is obviously a forward step in the direction taken by Theophrastus.

Dicæarch of Messene. — Dicæarch went still further and reduced all particular forces, including souls, to a single omnipresent, natural "vital and sensitive force." Here we have the naturalistic conception of organic unity in perfect simplicity. Dicæarch is said to have devoted himself more to empirical investigation than to speculation.

§ 16.

Three Leading Post-Aristotelian Schools of Philosophy. — We come now to three leading post-Aristotelian

---

[1] Ritter's *Hist. of Phil.*

schools of philosophy which, though standing in peculiar opposition one to another, yet are really to be regarded as belonging to the same organic movement of thought, and to have a common logical and psychological point of origin. They are known as the *Stoics*, the *Epicureans*, and the *Sceptics* (among whom may be included the *Academicians*).

§ 17.

The Stoics: Zeno, Cleanthes, Chrysippus, and Others. The Stoic school was founded near the beginning of the third century B.C., by Zeno, a native of Cittium in Cyprus. Having spent twenty years or more in the study of philosophy with teachers of the Cynic and Megarian schools, and of the Old Academy, — Crates, Stilpo, Diodorus, Xenocrates, Polemo, — he opened a school at Athens, in a place known as the Painted Porch, ποικίλη Στοά — whence the name of the school — and gained numerous disciples. He became noted for the simplicity of his habits of living, the temperateness and terseness of his speech, and the austerity of his manner, which, however, is said to have "relaxed at a dinner party." He won great respect from the Athenians, "who gave him the keys of their walls ... honored him with a golden crown and a brazen statue."[1] In obedience to what he believed a sign or omen, signifying that he should end his life, he strangled himself. His successor at the head of the Stoic School was Cleanthes, a water-carrier, who is

[1] Diogenes Laertius, *Life of Zeno*, pp. 259 and following.

described by Diogenes Laertius as industrious, attentive to the teachings of his master, and wholly devoted to philosophy, but as not intellectually strong, and very slow of mind. He did little or nothing more as a philosopher than to sanction by his influence the teachings of Zeno, being intellectually incapable of developing them to any great extent. He wrote numerous books and a *Hymn to Zeus*, which has been called the "most important document of the Stoic philosophy." The next president of the Stoic school was Chrysippus of the Soli, or Tarsus, in Cilicia (or Cicilia), who was born about 280 B.C. "He was a man of great natural ability, and of great acuteness in every way, so that in many points he dissented from Zeno, and also Cleanthes, to whom he often used to say that he only wanted to be instructed in the dogmas of the school, and that he would discover the demonstration for himself."[1] He acquired great fame as a dialectician,[2] was vastly industrious, writing five hundred lines a day, compiling (largely from the poets) more than seven hundred books, and, it is supposed, expanded portions of the teachings of the earlier Stoics, without, however, departing very essentially from the doctrines put forth by Zeno. "By Chrysippus the Stoic teaching was brought to completeness; and when he died, in the year 206 B.C., the form was in every respect fixed in which Stoicism would be

---

[1] Diog. Laert., *Life of Chrysippus* (Trans. in Bohn's Class Lib.).

[2] "This philosopher used to delight in proposing questions of this sort: The person who reveals the mysteries to the uninitiated commits a sin: the hierophant reveals them to the uninitiated: therefore the hierophant commits sin. . . . Again, if you say anything, what you say comes out of your mouth; but you say a wagon: therefore a wagon comes out of your mouth." Diog. Laert.

handed down for the next following centuries."[1] Other eminent Stoics were Aristo of Chios, who repudiated all philosophy but ethical philosophy; Herillus of Carthage, who declared knowledge to be the chief good, and opposed Zeno in some points; a certain Dionysius, who inclined to the doctrines of the Cyrenaics, etc.

Stoic Conception of the Nature and Parts of Philosophy.[2] — It is characteristic of the Stoic philosophers that, dividing philosophy into logic, physics, and ethics,[3] they laid the chief stress upon ethics, conceiving the real as that which acts on, or can be acted on by, us. The historical source of this we are to look for, most probably, in the conditions of the education of philosophers, as well as the general conditions of the times. The Stoics were, (in other words) intellectual descendants and representatives of the earlier Cynic schools, with a large infusion, no doubt, of the dialectico-sceptical spirit of the Megarian school and the Academy. The general relations between logic, physics, and ethics they conceived as follows: The chief good is virtue; virtue is "life according to nature" (a saying of Speusippus and Xenocrates); a true life according to nature, must depend upon the having a right conception of nature; but a true conception of nature is reached only in a certain way — by a certain method, and by the application of a certain standard, or criterion. The science of the good is ethics; of nature, physics; of methods and the criterion of knowledge, logic. Hence,

[1] *Zeller's Stoics, Epicureans, and Sceptics.*
[2] *Life of Zeno*, pp. 274-276.
[3] "Cleanthes says there are six divisions of reason, according to philosophy: dialectics, rhetoric, ethics, politics, physics, theology." Diog. Laert.

though ethics is highest, and in one sense, first, it is in another sense last, presupposing physics, which, in turn, presupposes logic. Zeno and Chrysippus compared philosophy to an animal; logic being bone and sinews, physics the flesh, and ethics the soul.

Stoic Logic. — With the Stoics logic is the science not only of thought but of expression — a corollary of their leading thought (taken in its simplicity) that the end of man is action, *i.e.*, to be really and externally what he is virtually and internally. The Stoic logic, therefore, included much that now falls in the domain of grammar; but it also included what now belongs to formal logic, and the theory of cognition, in the narrower sense, or theory of the sources of ideas and the criteria of knowledge. By some of the Stoics, however, logic was declared to have for its parts, — rhetoric, "the science conversant about speaking well concerning matters which admit of detailed narrative" and dialectic, the science of arguing correctly in discussions, which can be carried on by question and answer [Chrysippus] ... a knowledge of what is true and false, and neither one thing nor the other,[1] etc. Dialectic has two parts: one dealing with ideas, and the other with the expression of ideas.

Origin of Ideas.[2] — All ideas, according to the Stoics, originate from sensation, or the working of the mind upon what is given in sensation. The soul, Zeno held, is in sensation affected by external objects, as wax is by the seal that is pressed upon it. Perceptions ($\phi\alpha\nu\tau\alpha\sigma\iota\alpha\iota$)

---

[1] Diog. Laert.
[2] Diog. Laert., *Life of Zeno*, pp. 277 and following.

are impressions upon or in the soul (τυπώσεις ἐν ψυχῇ). Chrysippus preferred to say that perceptions, both external and internal, are changes of the soul (ἑτερώσεις ψυχῆς), to regard perception as active rather than passive; *i.e.*, as a *grasping* (κατάληψις) of the object instead of a being impressed by it. Perceptions remaining in the soul after the act of perception become memories, which taken in their unity, or as a whole, become experience, this in turn being the basis of judgment, or belief transcending sensation. From perceptions there arise *spontaneously* conceptions or general notions which the Stoics termed "common ideas" (κοιναὶ ἔννοιαι, or προλήψεις). General notions may be *produced*, by a consciously directed act of the mind. As to the special processes (as distinguished from media or sources) by which ideas are gotten, the Stoic theory is as follows : "All our thoughts are formed either by direct perception or by similarity, or analogy, or transposition, or combination, or opposition. By direct perception we perceive those things which are objects of sense; by similarity those which start from some point present to our senses; as for instance, we form an idea of Socrates from his likeness. We draw our conclusions by analogy adopting either an increased idea of the thing as of Tityus or the Cyclopes; or a diminished idea as of a pigmy. So, too, the idea of the centre of the world was one derived by analogy from what we perceived to be the case of the smaller spheres. We use transposition when we fancy eyes in a man's breast; combination when we take in the idea of a centaur; opposition when we turn our thoughts to death. Some ideas arise from comparison, — for instance, from a comparison of words and places."[1]

The Criterion of Truth in Ideas.[2] — According to Chrysippus and others the criterion of knowledge is perception : we *know* only what we *perceive* (by sense) ; only those ideas contain *certain* knowledge for us which are ideas of real objects. (General notions contain no reference to reality, are merely subjective.) What ideas these are, can be known with certainty only by the wise man. But real perceptions, or the ideas of real objects (φαντασίαι καταληπτικαί), possess greater distinctness than others, a certain power to compel belief or assent. That other ideas might also possess such distinctness and power to compel assent, the Stoics did not deny.

System and Logical Method. — The Stoic theory of knowledge and of conceptions included the idea of a science as a system of ideas. But to only one branch of systematic method did they give but little attention; viz., deduction, in the theory of which they made some improvements. They particularly emphasized the syllogism, the doctrine of which they held to be the most important part of dialectic, on the ground that it shows what is capable of demonstration, aids in forming the judgment, and gives scientific character to our knowledge. On the subject of propositions and argumentation, the Stoics laid down numerous distinctions, some of which now seem trivial, useless, or irrelevant to what is known as formal logic.[3] They laid particular

---

[1] Diog. Laert., *Life of Zeno.* (Trans. p. 278.)
[2] *Ibid.*, p. 276.
[3] *Ibid.*, pp. 282–289.

stress upon hypothetical and disjunctive syllogisms. It is, however, not quite correct to say [1] that the Stoics *introduced both* the *hypothetical* and the disjunctive syllogism. The former, or a near approach to it, may be found explained in Aristotle's *Prior Analytics*.[2]

The Categories. — The categories admitted by the Stoics are (besides the supreme conception of Being, or, rather, according to the Stoics, Something) four in number: subject-matter, or substance, τὸ ὑποκείμενον; quality, τὸ ποιόν; condition, τὸ πὼς ἔχον; relation, τὸ πρός τι πὼς ἔχον. Quality seems to correspond, in general, to Aristotle's "form." Real quality is of two kinds: common, or general (κοινῶς), and peculiar, or special (ἰδιῶς). Examples of τὸ πὼς ἔχον are size, motion, color, etc. Right and left, sonship and fatherhood, are examples of τὸ πρός τι πὼς ἔχον. The four categories have a natural interrelation. Substance cannot exist apart from quality, *i.e.*, real substance is definite. Condition presupposes quality, and relation condition. Zeller has pointed out three regards in which this theory of categories differs from Aristotle's:[3] the number of the categories,[4] their relation to each other, and their relation to a higher conception. To these may be added a fourth: the categories of the Stoics are not so purely logical, or conceptual, as the Aristotelian categories. The Stoic "substance" is, as we shall immediately see, matter either universal or particular; quality is purely material in origin, being due to a tension caused by air currents.

[1] As Zeller (and Benn after him) says.
[2] See above, p. 125.
[3] See *Zeller's Stoics, Epicureans, and Sceptics*, p. 95.
[4] Aristotle's "action" and "passion" are preserved in the Stoic "active" and "passive" principles of the world, *i.e.*, "matter" and "force."

Physics, or the Theory of Nature.[1] — The physics of the Stoics is also their metaphysics, for, though they could not avoid palpable inconsistencies with fact in so doing, they held material being to be the whole of being. This idea is in harmony with their sensational theory of knowledge, apparently a misconception of the Aristotelian, and, of course, with their ethical doctrine that reality is that which acts on us or is acted on by us. God, the Soul, the Good, virtue, vice, emotion, judgments are to the Stoics material, though time, space, place, expression are admitted to be immaterial. Substance, τὸ ὑποκείμενον, is either universal matter or the matter of individual objects. Quality, τὸ ποιόν, is due to air currents circulating through bodies. The world has a double nature; matter is capable of acting as well as being acted on; in other words, the world is a duality of matter and force. Matter, the passive principle, is without any distinctive quality. The active principle, inherent in the passive, matter, is reason, or God, conceived, however, as material. By whatever name called, — mind, soul, reason, logos[2] (λόγος), fate, law, nature, providence, — God is the all-pervading fire, the soul and seminal principle of the world, and is distinct from it only in abstraction: the distinction between them is a distinction without a difference. The world is, therefore, a living thing, pervaded by soul, — in different degrees in different parts. It is one, finite, and spherical. Exterior to it is a boundless (incorporeal) vacuum, there being no vacuum *in* the world. The world was produced by God out of his own substance, and will be

---

[1] Diog. Laert., *Life of Zeno*, pp. 307, 318.
[2] An idea common in the latest period of Greek philosophy.

absorbed again into that. Immediately afterwards a new world will be created, and so on *in infinitum*. In the creation of the world were generated, first, the four elements, fire, air, water, and earth, which are, all, "essence without any distinctive quality." "The fire is highest, and that is called æther; in which first of all the sphere was generated in which the fixed stars are set, then that in which the planets revolve; after that the air, then the water; and the sediment, as it were, of all is the earth, which is placed in the centre of the rest."[1] The water has a spherical form and the same centre as the earth; so, too, has the air surrounding it. Water and earth constitute the body of nature, fire and air its soul. The successive worlds that are by the Deity put forth from, and taken back into, his own substance are in all respects similar. Throughout all changes law abides. The world is, by virtue of the unity of matter and force, an organic whole. There is perfect adaptation of means to ends. Plants have their end in animals, animals in man, the whole, as a whole, in gods and men. Imperfection and evil are only apparent, attach not to the whole (which is organically perfect), but to the details of the constitution of things. The soul of man is material. "Whatever influences the body and is influenced by it in turn, whatever is united with the body and again separated from it, must be corporeal. How can the soul be other than corporeal? Whatever has extension in three dimensions is corporeal, and this is the case with the soul, since it extends in three dimensions over the whole body. Moreover, thought and motion are due to animal life. Animal life is matured and kept in health by the breath

[1] Diog. Laert., *Life of Zeno*, p. 309.

of life. Experience also proves that mental qualities are propagated by generation, and that they must be consequently connected with a corporeal substratum."[1] The central seat of the soul is the breast. The parts of the soul are the five senses, the generative power, the power of speech, and the intellect. The last-named is the principal part, and is the seat of personal identity. The emotions, or "passions,"—classified as grief, desire, fear, and pleasure—were termed by the Stoics "perturbations," and were declared to be merely judgments. Error in thought is a consequence of these perturbations. Being a part of the universal soul, the individual human soul is not free in will, though it is subject to moral responsibility. The soul, though corporeal, lives after death, but will at the end of the world (cycle) cease to be as an individual, being dissolved in the universal soul whence it sprung.

Ethics: its Parts.[2]—Ethical speculation was extensively practised by the Stoics. According to Diogenes, — Chrysippus and others, but not Zeno nor Cleanthes, divided ethics into "the topic of inclination [or natural tendency], the topic of good and bad, the topic of the passions, the topic of virtue, the topic of the chief good, and of primary estimation, and of actions: the topic of what things are becoming, and of exhortation and dissuasion." We shall treat here of the Chief Good, the Nature of Virtue, the Classes of Virtue, the Classes of Goods, the Wise Man, and the Stoic attitude towards the Popular Religion.

The Chief Good: Life according to Nature.— Nature

---

[1] *Zeller's Stoics, Epicureans, and Sceptics.*
[2] Diog. Laert., *Life of Zeno*, pp. 290–307.

working as an artist produces in each thing a certain inclination, or tendency, to preserve a certain form of existence. "The first and dearest object" of every animal (man included) is the preservation of its own existence and its consciousness of its own existence. This is its life according to nature; this is virtue and the chief good, — for virtue and the chief good can be only life according to nature. But what, precisely, is life according to nature? On this point there was a difference of opinion among the Stoics. By "nature" must we understand our human or our universal nature, or both? Zeno, it appears, had adopted, or, at least, emphasized, merely the first of these three conceptions of nature; but in the course of the development of Stoicism as a theory the second and then the last became predominant, the last being held by Chrysippus. "Chrysippus," says Diogenes,[1] "understands that the nature in a manner corresponding to which we ought to live is both the common nature, and also human nature in particular, but Cleanthes will not admit of any other than the common one alone as that to which people ought to live in a manner according; and repudiates all mention of a particular nature." In the "life according to nature" is included also, we shall find, life in and according to a social order, for *nature* is but a synonym for *reason*, and society is but a natural off-spring of reason, the common nature of mankind.

Nature of Virtue. — Now a life according to nature is a life determined by that which takes cognizance of reason in the world, viz., real knowledge. Virtue, in

[1] Diog. Laert., *Life of Zeno*, p. 291. This is a point in which Cleanthes *did* get beyond Zeno, who apparently stood nearer to the Cynics.

other words, is knowledge. With the Stoics the distinction made by Aristotle, and even by Plato, between virtues based on knowledge, on the one hand, and on the other, natural and acquired virtues, or virtues based on habit "joined with reason," does not hold. Strictly speaking, the emotions have nothing to do with virtue: they are, if any thing, mere hindrances to it, "perturbations," from which the wise or virtuous man is entirely free. Virtue is, rather, a condition of apathy (ἀπάθεια). But though virtue is in its origin intellectual, it is in actuality something more than that: it is action,— action based on knowledge. The Stoic conception of virtue differs considerably, it thus appears, from the Socratic conception and the conception held by Plato and Aristotle. The Stoics differ from Socrates, also, in holding that wrong-doing must be classed among things voluntary. They assert that vice is the result not of ignorance merely but of emotional perturbation, and that man has and must exercise control over the emotions, — generally by suppressing them. There are no degrees in virtue[1] (but then, at the same time, a distinction is made by the Stoics between an action that is merely *fitting*, καθῆκον, and one that results from a virtuous disposition, κατόρθωμα); and there is no mean between virtue and vice, a "stick must be either straight or crooked."[2] According to Cleanthes (with whom, however, Chrysippus disagrees at this point) virtue cannot be lost, "on account of the firm perceptions which it plants in men."[3]

Classes of Virtue.[4] — Regarding the classification of

[1] Ueberweg's *Hist. of Phil.*, Vol. I. p. 200.
[2] Diog. Laert., *Life of Zeno*, p. 305.
[3] *Ibid.*   [4] *Ibid.*, pp. 292, 293.

the virtues, there was a difference of opinion among the Stoics. One divided virtues into speculative and practical; another into logical, natural, and ethical. Some said there were four virtues; others, and among them Cleanthes and Chrysippus, more than four; one, Allophanes, asserted that there was but one virtue, viz., prudence. Aristo thought that what was considered a variety of virtues was more properly a variety of objects with which virtue, in itself one, was concerned. Chrysippus held that there were distinct conditions of soul constituting distinct virtues. Those, or at least some of those, who held that there is a plurality of virtues, held also that some of the virtues are "primitive" and some "derived"; that the "primitive" virtues are "prudence, manly courage, justice, and temperance," and that, "subordinate to these as a kind of species contained in them are magnanimity, continence, endurance, presence of mind, wisdom in council."[1] That the "virtues reciprocally follow one another and that he who has one has all"[2] was admitted even by Chrysippus. Cleanthes, Chrysippus, and other Stoics agreed in thinking that virtue could be taught.[3]

Classes of Goods: the " Summum Bonum." — Virtue, we have seen, was with the Stoics the chief good, or *summum bonum*. The Stoics did not admit that, as Aristotle had held, there was any thing to be added to virtue to constitute happiness, or the highest good; nor, as they admitted no degrees in virtue, did they admit degrees in goods: "All goods are equal . . . every good is to be desired in the highest degree . . . and

[1] Diog. Laert., *Life of Zeno*.   [2] *Ibid.*, p. 304.
[3] *Ibid.*, p. 292.

admits of no relaxation and of no extension."[1] Some things, however, are good in themselves ("final goods"), and others are good because they lead to final goods ("efficient goods"), others still are both efficient and final. The Stoics acknowledged another distinction which may, perhaps, be regarded as a softening (required by practical necessity) of their rigid rule concerning goods. All things are good, bad, or indifferent. Things positively bad are the vices, the diametrical opposites of the virtues: folly, intemperance, cowardice, injustice. Things indifferent are things that are "neither beneficial nor injurious, such as life, health, pleasure, beauty, strength, riches, good reputation, nobility of birth, and their contraries, death, disease, labor, disgrace, weakness, poverty, and bad reputation, baseness of birth, and the like."[2] Of things indifferent some, it is evident, are objects of preference (προηγμένα), because they "concur in producing a well-regulated life," and others are things to be avoided or rejected (ἀποπροηγμένα), because they are of the opposite character. "Every good is expedient, and necessary, and profitable, and useful, and serviceable, and beautiful, and advantageous, and eligible, and just: expedient inasmuch as it brings things which by their happening do us good; necessary inasmuch as it assists us in what we have need to be assisted; profitable inasmuch as it repays all the care that is expended on it, and makes a return with interest to our great advantage; useful inasmuch as it supplies us with what is of utility; serviceable because it does us service which is much

---

[1] Diog. Laert., *Life of Zeno*, p. 292.   [2] *Ibid.*, p. 296.

praised; beautiful because it is accurate in proportion to the need we have of it and to the service it does; advantageous inasmuch as it is of such a character as to confer advantage on us; eligible because it is such that we may rationally choose it; and just because it is in accordance with law, and is an efficient cause of union."[1]

The " Wise Man." — Now he who is the personal embodiment of *virtue* — since all virtue is the same, we need not say here *perfect virtue* — and who alone possesses absolute goods, and is worthy to have the advantage of all those "indifferent" things which are objects of "preference" is the *wise man*. The wise man is he who, being perfect in his knowledge of the laws of the universe, above all passion, and completely governed by reason, is perfectly self-contained and self-satisfied, — a fit companion for the gods, yes, even for Zeus himself. But the idea of the perfectly virtuous and self-sufficient individual man was in part necessarily abandoned by the Stoics. For, in the first place, they were obliged to admit that in reality there had been, and was, no such man; even the most exemplary men, Socrates, Diogenes, Antisthenes, had made great *improvement* in virtue; and, in the second place, though by their affinity, historical and logical, with the Cynics they were inclined to regard the individual as self-sufficient, they were obliged to admit that by the very fact of his possessing reason the wise man is bound to his fellow-man, that he must and will have friends, in whom he may see the reflection of himself. They asserted, indeed, that the

[1] Diog. Laert., *Life of Zeno*, p. 295.

wise man was the only person worthy to have friends. Again, the wise man will marry and beget children (Zeno held that there should be "community" of wives and children among wise men); he will also, according to Chrysippus, take active part in affairs of state, for he will desire to restrain vice and excite men to virtue.[1] And yet to realize as fully as possible the conception of individual independence, the Stoics made the wise man a citizen of the world, not binding him too closely by ties of family, friendship, or nationality. This idea hit the mean between the crudeness of Cynicism, pure and simple, and the practice of ordinary social life in a nation or a state. (The best political constitution is a mixed one, "combined democracy and kingly power and aristocracy.") Towards the universe, as a whole, and the power therein, the attitude of the wise man is that of resignation and obedience. In this attitude he is but acting out his own true nature. "The virtuous man . . . will honor God by resigning his will to the divine will; the divine will he will think better than his own will; he will remember that in all circumstances we must follow destiny, but that it is the wise man's prerogative to follow it of his own accord; that there is only one way to happiness and independence, — that of willing nothing except what is in the nature of things and will realize itself of our will."[2] But the Stoics affirmed, on the other hand, that "a wise man will rationally take himself out of life, either for the sake of his country or of his friends, or if he be in bitter pain, or under the affliction of mutilation, or incurable disease."[3]

[1] Diog. Laert., *Life of Zeno*, p. 303.
[2] *Zeller's Stoics, Epicureans, and Sceptics.*
[3] Diog. Laert., *Life of Zeno*, p. 306.

The Stoics and the Popular Religion. — The Stoics did not approve of the ordinary forms and instrumentalities of religion. To them the world was full of the Deity. Their philosophy was thus a religious, or at least a theological, philosophy. They gave the names of gods to "fruits, wine, and other gifts" of the gods, did not forbid the worship of ancient heroes, and on the hypothesis that God was everywhere accessible, practised the "art of divination" and prophecy, though there was not perfect unanimity among them in regard to this last point. They had a peculiar over-fondness for rationalizing the ancient myths, or giving them plain and consistent meanings.[1] To them there was reason in everything.

Historical Sources of Stoicism. — The chief historical sources of Stoicism have already been in part indicated. In logic and dialectics the Stoics were followers of Aristotle and the Cynics. Their neglect of induction is quite in keeping with their subjective individualistic tendencies generally. In physics they were followers of Heraclitus, Socrates, and Aristotle; their fire, or logos, or world-spirit being Heraclitic, their teleology being Socratic (not Aristotelian), their 'active' and 'passive' principles, 'matter' and 'force' being *quasi-*Aristotelian. In ethics they followed Socrates, the Cynics, and the philosophers of the Old Academy, their leading doctrine, 'Follow nature,' having been practiced by the Cynics and enunciated by certain philosophers of the Academy (Xenocrates, Speusippus, and Polemo). On the whole, the Stoics cannot be credited

[1] See *Zeller's Stoics, Epicureans, and Sceptics.*

with a large degree of intellectual originality; they were, rather, apostles of moral force, a certain (limited) ethical individuality.

Result. — It remains to examine (briefly) the connection, coherency, and validity of the leading Stoic conceptions. A distinct breach in the Stoic system is involved in the fact that whereas reason is held to be universal and knowable, and sense is held to be the source and criterion of knowledge, it is denied that there is a rational universal element in sense. Another incoherency, closely akin to this, is that while sense is held to be the only source of knowledge, the processes of thought are treated as something essential. An obvious inconsistency in the Stoic physics is the position that only material things are real and the admission that certain immaterial things, *e.g.*, time, space, expression, are real. Of a similar character is the idea that the soul is corporeal. Here the Stoics are about on a level with the Hylozoists. The conception of organic unity is given here too simple a form. The unity of body and soul cannot be that of simple identity or of materialistic organicity (if we may be allowed such a word); it is a unity in which difference is contained, an ideal, or speculative, unity. There is, too, an unexplained paradox, to say the least, in the Stoic idea that, though the individual is merely a part of universal reason and is subject to necessity, he is morally responsible. In the cardinal ethical doctrine of the Stoics, Live according to nature, there is, as the development of thought in the history of the school proves, a certain instability and inconsistency. Is nature the individual human nature, the universal nature, or a union of the two?

The later Stoics, as we have seen, took the last-mentioned view of the case, thus solving the conception. The mere individual in himself is practically nothing and becomes nothing if he be absorbed in the bare universal. Again, virtue is declared to be the only good, and yet there are admitted to be, besides things that are positively bad, a class of things that are "indifferent," some of which are "objects of preference," and useful and pleasant to the wise man; and an act fittingly done is to be distinguished from one done with right intention. Further, the sphere of the wise man is said to be pure reason, and yet he is subject to emotion, at least to the extent of having to repress and suppress it. Moreover the wise man is self-sufficient, but he needs friends and should take an active part in public affairs, and is dependent upon and benefited by the possession of external goods. Furthermore, all virtuous men are absolutely virtuous, all bad men are absolutely bad; but Socrates, Antisthenes, and Diogenes, who are not perfect, are not bad. Finally, the wise man is a fit companion for Zeus, and yet his attitude towards the universal order should be that of resignation and submission. In general, the Stoic system is full of paradox: instead of harmonizing or reconciling the natural antithesis of sense and reason, the individual and universal, it brought the members of the antithesis into sharper opposition, and this, too, in spite of the obvious unity aimed at by the conception of the world as an organic whole and of the individual as being universally self-sufficient.[1]

[1] See below, p. 246.

§ 18.

Epicurus and his School. — Epicurus, the founder of the Epicurean School, was born in Samos, in the year 342 or 341 B.C. Stimulated to inquiry (according to one account) by the reading of Hesiod, and failing to get satisfactory answers to his inquiries (concerning chaos) from his instructors, he began, at the age of fourteen, the study of philosophy. At the age of eighteen he went to Athens, and remained there as a student of philosophy until, at the age of thirty, he began teaching it, first at Mytelene, then at Lampsacus, and finally (about 306 B.C.) at Athens, where he taught for thirty-six years. His knowledge of and regard for other philosophers was slight. He had received some instruction in the doctrines of Plato, and thought him "golden," and in those of Democritus, whom he derisively called Leocritus (humbug?), but whose physical theories he borrowed freely; had perhaps been a pupil of Xenocrates and Nausiphanes, a Democritean, who had been a pupil of Pyrrho, the Sceptic; he ridiculed Aristotle as a debauchee, glutton, and vendor of drugs; called Protagoras a "porter," Heraclitus a "disturber," the Cynics the "enemies" of Greece; declared that the Dialecticians (the Stoics?) were "eaten up with envy." He is said to have thought highly of Anaxagoras, though it is hard to see why; there are no traces of any influence of Anaxagoras upon his thinking. The same may be said with regard to his admiration of Plato. His opinion of other philosophers is indicative of his attitude towards things in general, which is negative. His criticism of other philosophers, it would appear, and doubtless, also, the character of his doctrines, excited towards him hostile feeling and comment, and there were those who spoke of him as an extreme voluptuary; but Diogenes Laertius declares him to have been a man of excessive modesty (a modesty that caused him to "avoid affairs of state"), of filial gratitude, of philanthropy and piety; to have been warmly regarded by very numerous friends, and honored by his country with brazen statues. He died in 270 B.C., made cheerful in spirits, in the midst of great physical suffering, by the "recollection" of "his philosophical contemplations." He bequeathed the garden in which he had met his disciples in philosophical converse to the surviving members of his school and to all coming after them who should choose to "abide and dwell in it" and maintain his doctrines. Between him and the members of the school there was a very strong personal tie, and his personality, as well as his dogmas, was deeply impressed upon their minds. His dogmas embodied in brief statements, and, regarded as common intellectual possessions ($\kappa \upsilon \rho \iota \alpha \iota\ \delta \acute{o} \xi \alpha \iota$), were committed to memory by his disciples and were handed down traditionally. Diogenes Laertius[1] speaks of the "perpetual succession of his school, which, when every other school decayed, continued without any falling off, and produced countless numbers of philosophers, succeeding one another without any interruption." In his productivity as a writer he almost rivalled Chrysippus. He boasted of the originality of his writings, of the

[1] See *Lives of the Philosophers* (Bohn's Class. Lib.); *Life of Epicurus*, pp. 424-479.

perspicuity of their style and freedom from rhetorical constraints and ornaments. But he was guilty of a neglect of true rhetorical method which has justly brought down upon his style the condemnation of critics, ancient and modern. Of eminent Epicureans there should be mentioned the following: *Hermarchus of Mytelene*, president of the school after the death of Epicurus; *Metrodorus and Polyænus of Lampsacus; Apollodorus; Zeno of Sidon; Lucretius*, the Latin poet, who has followed Epicurus closely in essential points in his poem *De Rerum Natura*. Among the immediate personal disciples of Epicurus were several women,[1] a fact that gave occasion to rival schools for disagreeable gossip about the Epicurean school.

The Parts of Philosophy. — Epicurus divides philosophy into three parts: Canonics, Physics, and Ethics. Canonics is the science of the criteria of truth. It contains nothing of dialectic, for Epicurus declared that the "correspondence of words with things was sufficient for the philosopher." Epicurus regarded it as scarcely more than a mere introduction to physics, which in turn was held subsidiary to ethics, for Epicureanism, like Stoicism, Cynicism, and indeed most of the other post-Socratic systems in ancient philosophy, was primarily (and one-sidedly) ethical in its aim. There seems, in fact, to have been a strong tendency to make, or, rather, a habit of making, two parts of philosophy, Physics (*including* Canonics) and Ethics.[2] It will be seen in detail, as we proceed, how the physics, very largely, and the canon-

---

[1] The Leontion of Landor's Imaginary Conversation, *Epicurus, Leontion, and Ternissa*, bears the name of one of these.
[2] Diog. Laert., *Life of Epicurus*, p. 434.

ics less so, are determined by the leading ethical doctrines of Epicurus, viz., that the end of human existence is pleasure. It cannot be said, however, that there is a deduction of the parts of his system from the notion of pleasure, and to attempt such a deduction here would convey a wrong idea of the tone and mode of his thinking.

Canonics: Criteria of Truth in Ideas.[1] — The criteria of truth in ideas are, according to Epicurus, the "senses," preconceptions, or anticipations (προλήψεις), or "recollection of an external object often perceived anteriorly," and the "passions." "But," says Diogenes, "the Epicureans, in general, add also the perceptive impressions of the intellect." Of these criteria the senses are primary: "Every notion proceeds from the senses, either directly or in consequence of some analogy or proportion, or combination." The senses are entirely pure of all influence of memory, reason, or any other mental operation: they merely receive impressions from external causes, adding nothing, subtracting nothing. Each sense and sensation, furthermore, is independent of every other. One sensation cannot be a criterion for another resembling it or differing from it. The senses are, therefore, their own guarantee: reason cannot pronounce upon them; rather are the senses the foundation of reason. An error in perception must, therefore, not be attributed to the senses, but to judgment, or inference, (wrongly added preconceptions or "perceptive impressions of the intellect") attending sensation.[2] An example of a preconception or anticipation is the idea that arises in the mind immediately upon pronouncing the word "man"

[1] Diog. Laert., *Life of Epicurus*, pp. 435, 436. [2] *Ibid.*, p. 435.

in the sentence, "Man is such and such a nature." The idea is one we "owe to the preceding operation of the senses," and it is to be depended upon as a correct one. Such an idea is a necessary condition to every perception or judgment. (That is, "representation" is a condition of "presentation" and judgment.) "To be able to affirm that what we see at a distance is a horse or an ox, we must have some anticipation in our minds which makes us acquainted with the form of a horse or an ox. We could not give names to things if we had not a preliminary notion of what things were." The certainty of our judgment depends upon our properly applying our anticipations. "Error and false judgment always depend upon the supposition that a preconceived idea will be confirmed or at all events will not be overturned by evidence." The passions are pleasure and pain, the former being natural, and the other foreign, to human nature. They are the criteria of ethical judgment; *i.e.*, (according to Epicurus), judgment employed in determining what things should be chosen and what avoided. "Opinion" ($\delta\acute{o}\xi a$) and "supposition" ($\dot{v}\pi\acute{o}\lambda\eta\psi\iota\varsigma$) are partly true and partly false: true when supported, not contradicted, by evidence; false if contradicted by any evidence. It is often necessary to suspend the judgment. There is a certain degree of truth and objectivity in dreams.

Canonics: Method in the Study of Nature.[1] — Now as to method in the study of nature, we must proceed "from the known to the unknown." First, there must be an exact notion for each term, or there will result mere "verbal demonstration *in infinitum.*" Leading

---

[1] Diog. Laert., *Life of Epicurus*, pp. 437, 438, 456, 459, etc.

terms must represent indemonstrable notions ; *i.e.*, notions true according to some one or more of the criteria. We must be able to bring into our investigation, when necessary, the "impressions we receive in the presence of objects." We may pass to the unknown by analogy and by induction, but it is necessary to be on our guard against false analogies and against accepting unverified induction as equal in value to immediate certainty. Proper analogies are those founded on appearances, and are to be held superior to hypotheses. Now appearances may be susceptible of different "explanations," and it is a rule, made and insisted on by Epicurus, that we must guard against supposing that there is only one way of explaining phenomena. Phenomena may have many different causes and require as many different explanations. The Epicureans gave little attention to deductive logic as such.

Physics: Aim and General Character.[1] — Besides the principles of method laid down in the canonic, physical speculation must be conditioned by the idea that man's chief end is happiness, and that, therefore, he requires to know only so much as will preclude all ground for disquietude of soul, — the fear of death, of dæmons, of mysterious and unforeseen events.

First Principle. — The fundamental conception (material principle) of physics is, according to Epicurus, that nothing can come of nothing : the All has always been, and always will be, such as it now is, since there is nothing into which it can change, nor is there anything which, entering it, can cause it to change. The uni-

[1] Diog. Laert., *Life of Epicurus*, pp. 438–466.

verse is a material universe. Our senses bear testimony to the existence of bodies; and reasoning upon the testimony of the senses (for the senses, we have seen, are the foundation of reason) we infer the existence of space, for if there were not "that which we call vacuum, or space, or intangible nature, there would be nothing in which the bodies could be contained or across which they could move, as they really do move." We cannot, in other words, perceive, or conceive by the aid of inference or analogy, any universal quality or thing that is not body, or quality of body, or vacuum.

Atoms. — Bodies perceptible to the senses are composite and dissoluble. But there must be something "solid and indestructible" that remains after their dissolution; because if we suppose bodies to be divisible *in infinitum,* we are brought to the absurdity of "reducing everything to nothing," and consequently of saying that something can come of nothing. Composite bodies, then, have as their element the atom. The atom, though not cognizable by the senses, must have magnitude, it being solid and destructible, and a part of that which has magnitude. But since the process of division of bodies may conceivably be carried to an indefinite extent, we must assign to the atom the smallest possible dimensions. And in order to account for sensations and differences of quality in bodies we must suppose that atoms differ in magnitude. Again, it is impossible to account for the vast variety of form in bodies without supposing a great, an incalculable, variety in form among atoms. In any particular finite body the number of atoms is finite: in the entire universe the number is infinite, for the universe, not being limited by anything, is infinite, and body and vacuum are consequently infinite, because "if the vacuum were infinite, the number of bodies being finite, the bodies would not be able to rest in any place: they would be transported about, scattered across the infinite vacuum for want of any power to steady themselves, or to keep one another in their places by mutual repulsion : if, on the other hand, the vacuum were finite, the bodies being infinite, then the bodies clearly could never be contained in the vacuum." Furthermore, atoms have weight. Finally, the motion and the dissolution of sensible bodies (which can be caused only by a knocking together of the atoms) presuppose motion of the atoms. The atoms, in fact, must have been continually moving and with an equal rapidity from all eternity, since the vacuum offers no more resistance to the lightest than it does to the heaviest. Because of the different weight of the atoms, some of them move downward, some are pressed upward. Because of the "reciprocal percussion of the atoms, some of them have a horizontal movement to and fro." An atom has not any movement perceptible to the senses. The motion of the atoms is not due, as Democritus held, merely to natural necessity, *i.e.*, to their weight, but to a certain power of selfmovement, the ability, as it were, to "swerve a little" from a straight, fixed, and otherwise necessary, line of movement. Among the arguments employed by Lucretius (who may be regarded as an authority for the Epicurean physical theories) is the following : " If all motion is ever linked together, and a new motion ever springs from another in a fixed order, and first beginnings do not, by swerving, make some commencement of motion to break through the decrees of fate that cause follow not cause from everlasting, — whence have all living creatures here on earth, whence, I ask, has been wrested from the fates the power by which we go forward whither the will leads each, by which we likewise change the direction of our motions, neither at a fixed time nor fixed place, but when and where the mind itself has prompted? For, beyond a doubt, in these things his own will makes for each a beginning, and from this beginning notions are willed through the limbs."[1] There is, however, no other cause of motion in the atoms than that which is contained in themselves. The distances of the atoms from one another vary, some being great, others small.

Properties of Bodies. — The properties of bodies, such as forms, colors, magnitude, weight, are not particular substances (as the Stoics asserted), nor can it be said that they have no reality at all. They cannot be conceived as independent of the bodies, and must be conceived when we form an idea of bodies. Of these there are two classes: attributes, which constitute by their union the "eternal substance and essence of the entire body"; and accidents, which are not entirely inherent in bodies, but which, nevertheless, cannot be ranged among the incorporeal and invisible things. "These last, as they are not necessarily inherent in the idea of a body," can be conceived only in the moment in which they affect the senses. (Here we have, or appear to have, the modern psychological distinction between primary and secondary qualities of bodies. Democritus had made the same, or a similar, distinction.)

[1] Lucretius, *De Rerum Natura* (Munro's Trans.), p. 34.

The Visible Universe. — Of the worlds in distant space we must reason very much as we do regarding bodies that we "observe under our own eyes." Worlds and all other objects that may be compared to those objects "under our own eyes" have each been separated from the infinite by a movement peculiar to itself,[1] and they will be destroyed, some more, others less, rapidly. Epicurus did not believe that any worlds were formed by violent motions and crashings of other worlds, but by a flowing together of atoms to form a nucleus, and a gathering of "germs" about the nucleus thus formed. The number of worlds is infinite; but it is not reasonable to suppose that the worlds are identical in form, or that there are worlds of every possible form. There is no increase or decrease of body in the universe as a whole. The earth is suspended in the air. Lucretius explains why the earth does not drop or sink from its place in the centre of the world, as follows: "In order that the earth may rest in the middle of the world, it is proper that its weight should be lessened, and that it should have another nature underneath it, conjoined from the beginning of its existence and formed into one being with the airy portions of the world in which it is embodied and lives." The sun and the moon are in size what they appear to the senses to be. They are not reabsorbed into the whole. We must "beware" of supposing that the heavenly phenomena — "the motions and courses of the stars, the eclipse, their rising, setting, etc." — are "produced by any particular being which has regulated or whose business it is to regulate,

[1] See Zeller.

for the future, the order of the world, a being immortal and perfectly happy: for the cares and anxieties, the benevolence and the anger, far from being compatible with felicity are, on the contrary, the consequence of weakness, of fear, and the want which a thing has of something else." The truth is that these phenomena are governed by a "kind of necessity"; they have an order that was given them at the first organization of the universe. And yet we must not try to explain these phenomena in accordance with any idea of uniformity of cause: of supposing that there is but "one single mode of production" and of rejecting "all other explanations which are founded on probability." The eclipses of the sun and moon, for example, may be due to the fact that these bodies extinguish themselves, or to the fact that other bodies interpose between them and us; lightning may be the effect of a "shock and collision of the clouds," of the lighting up of the clouds by the winds, of the mutual pressure of the clouds, or of the pressure of the winds against them, or of various conditions. Susceptible of explanation upon the principle of a "plurality of causes" (to employ a modern phrase for a very old idea in the history of philosophy) are, likewise, the difference in the length of days and nights, clouds, thunder, hurricanes, earthquakes, winds, hail, snow, dew, comets, falling stars, etc. Regularity in celestial phenomena should not be made any more of than the little coincidences daily occurring immediately about us, a fact, the full appreciation of which would bring the perfect quietude and confidence of soul that characterize the wise man.

The Gods. — Nature, we have just seen, is, to the

Epicureans, in no sense controlled by a divine power or by divine powers. The Epicureans, nevertheless, believed in the existence of gods and treated of them in that branch of their philosophy called physics. Of the gods, philosophers — but not the οἱ πολλοί, whose ideas of the gods are mere "opinion" and are impious — have distinct knowledge through anticipations, προλήψεις. The gods are infinite in number and dwell in the vacant spaces between the worlds, in immortality and perfect felicity, without concern for the universe about them. Prayer and divination are, consequently, discarded by the Epicureans as the offspring of ignorance and fear. Epicurus says, however, that it is better to follow the fables about the gods than to be a slave to the 'fate' of the natural philosophers [Stoics], better to believe that the gods are to be moved by gifts and honors than to believe in an inexorable necessity.

The Human Soul.[1] — The human soul is a "bodily substance composed of slight particles diffused all over the members of the body, presenting a great analogy to a sort of spirit": it is composed of "atoms of the most perfect lightness and roundness," "wholly different from those of fire" (Democritus had said that the soul was composed of fiery atoms). The soul cannot be incorporeal, for it would then be, like the vacuum, incapable of 'doing' or 'suffering' anything," and merely a "condition and place of movement." In the soul is the seat of sensation, though doubtless sensation depends in part upon the body. There are "reciprocal bonds of sympathy uniting soul and body by virtue of which the soul takes cognizance of the changes that take place in

[1] Diog. Laert., *Life of Zeno*, pp. 441-443, 447, 448, etc.

the body which is its envelopment, and then reflects these into the body as sensible affections." "But there are certain affections of the soul of which the body is not capable." The irrational part of the soul, only, is diffused over the whole body, the rational part, as the emotions of joy and fear prove, having its seat in the chest. On the death and dissolution of the body the soul leaves it and dissolves and no longer has power of sensation or motion. Sensation is explained by Epicurus as being produced by the impact upon the organs of sense of infinitely small, thin, film-like emanations from bodies, which having the same arrangement and motion as the atoms in the bodies glide with infinite rapidity through vacant space, escaping all obstacles. These are termed images. "One must admit that something passes from external objects to us in order to produce sight and the knowledge of forms; for it is difficult to conceive that external objects can affect us through the medium of the air which is between us and them or by means of rays, whatever emissions proceed from us to them, so as to give us an impression of their form and color. This phenomenon, on the contrary, is perfectly explained, if we admit that certain images of the same color, of the same shape, and of a proportionate magnitude pass from the objects to us, and so arrive at being seen and comprehended. These images are animated by an exceeding rapidity, and, as, on the other side, the solid forming a compact mass, and comprising a vast quantity of atoms, emits always the same quantity of particles, the vision is continued, and produces in us one single perception which always preserves the same relation to the object. Every conception, every sensible perception which has to do with the form or other attributes of these images is only the same form of the solid body perceived directly, either in virtue of a sort of actual and continual condensation of the image, or in consequence of the traces which it has left in us." Hearing is produced, not by the air, but by "some sort of current" which, by virtue of the affinity of the small bodies composing it with one another and their identity in nature with the object from which they emanate "puts us very frequently into communication of sentiments with this object, or at least causes us to become aware of the existence of some external circumstances." Perception, in this case, depends on a "sort of sympathy" between subject and object. The case of smell is similar. — The human will is free, and man is accordingly a proper subject of moral praise and blame.

Ethics: First Principle, Pleasure. — All good and evil, says Epicurus, are in sensation : that which is the privation or absence of sensation, *e.g.*, death, is nothing to us. The first good is pleasure, it being that to which all human "choice and avoidance" have reference, "for the sake of which we do everything," "the beginning and end of living happily" (*i.e.*, well), that without which we are unsatisfied and seek it, with which we are satisfied and desire nothing. The desire of pleasure is connate with us, and it is inherent in animals. *No pleasure is intrinsically bad*; but not every pleasure is always worthy of being chosen, for the "efficient causes of some pleasures bring with them a great many perturbations of pleasure," and the choice of such pleasures would contravene the law that pleasure is the chief good. Even some pains are better than some pleasures, because of the greatness in degree of the pleasures consequent upon the choice of them. The pleasure, therefore, that is the chief good, is of a certain sort.

Kinds of Pleasure. — Now pleasures are in kind either bodily or mental, and they are either "motions" [the Cyrenaic doctrine], *e.g.*, cheerfulness and joy, or "states," *e.g.*, freedom from fear or bodily pain. The pleasure that is the chief good is not the bodily pleasure of the debauchee, but the "freedom of the body from pain and the soul from confusion," "the sober contemplation which examines into the reasons for choice and avoidance, and which puts to flight the vain opinions from which the greater portion of the confusion arises which troubles the soul." But though the pleasures of the mind or soul are superior to those of the body, the pains of the soul are worse than those of the body, since the body is "sensible to present affliction while the soul feels the past, present, and future." The noblest pleasure is inseparable from prudence and the other virtues; but, nevertheless, not the virtues but pleasure is the chief good. "We choose the virtues for the sake of pleasure; not on their own account." Justice and injustice have no independent existence; they have significance only as means and hindrances to pleasure. "Courage does not exist by nature, but is engendered by a consideration of what is suitable." "Friendship is caused by one's wants," and "arises from a community of participation in pleasures." It appears, then, that the highest pleasure is not, as the Cyrenaics declared, a motion, but a state; *e.g.*, contentment, freedom from ambition, from fear and apprehension. Specifically, the highest happiness of which human life is capable is a freedom from all apprehension relative to death and eternity, a state of the soul born of the knowledge that death is "no concern either of the living or of the dead, since to the one it has no existence and the other class has no existence itself."

The "Wise Man." — Epicurus "said that injuries existed among men either in consequence of hatred or of envy or of contempt, all of which the wise man overcomes by reason; also that a man who has been once wise can never receive a contrary disposition, nor can he of his own accord invent such a state of things as that he should be subjected to the dominion of the passions; nor can he hinder himself in his progress towards wisdom; that the wise man, however, cannot exist in every state of body nor in every nation; that if the wise man were to be put to the torture, he would still be happy; that the wise man will not only feel gratitude to his friends, but to them equally whether they are present or absent. . . . Nor will he marry a wife whom the laws forbid. He will punish his servants, but also pity them, and show indulgence to any that are virtuous. The Epicureans do not think that the wise man will ever be in love or that he will be anxious about his burial, or that love is a passion inspired by the gods. . . . They also assert that he will be indifferent to the study of oratory. Marriage, say they, is never a benefit to a man, and we must be quite content if it does no harm; and the wise man will never marry and beget children . . . still, under certain circumstances of life, he will forsake these rules and marry. Nor will he ever indulge in drunkenness, nor will he entangle himself in affairs of state. Nor will he become a tyrant. Nor will he become a Cynic . . . or a beggar. And even though he should lose his eyes, he will still cling to life. The wise man will be subject to grief. He will also not object to go to law. He will leave books and memorials of himself behind him; but he will not be fond of frequenting assemblies. He will take care of his property, and provide for the future. He will like being in the country; he will resist fortune, and will grieve none of his friends. He will show a regard for a fair reputation to such an extent as to avoid being despised; and he will find more pleasure than other men in speculations. . . . The wise man may raise statues if it suits his inclination; if it does not, it does not signify. The wise man is the only person who can converse correctly about music and poetry; and he can realize poems, but not become a poet. . . . The wise man will also, if he is in need, earn money, but only by his wisdom. He will propitiate an absolute ruler when occasion requires, and will humor him for the sake of correcting his habits. He will have a school, but not on such a system as to draw a crowd about him. He will also recite in a multitude, but that will be against his inclination. He will pronounce dogmas.[1] He will be the same man asleep and awake, and he will be willing even to die for a friend." " It is possible for one man to be wiser than another." [2]

Friendship. — Independent as the "Wise Man" of the Epicureans is, he yet needs friends; and friendship is

[1] Zeller supposes that the long-continued existence of the Epicurean school was a consequence of the dogmatism (and conservatism) practised and cultivated by Epicurus himself.

[2] Diog. Laert., *Life of Zeno*, pp. 466-468 (trans. somewhat altered).

to him, next to freedom from fear of death, the greatest source of pleasure. If one cannot make friends, he should avoid making enemies. "The happiest men are they who have arrived at the point of having nothing to fear from those who surround them; such men live with one another most agreeably, having the firmest grounds of confidence in one another, enjoying the advantages of friendship in all their fulness, and not lamenting as a pitiable circumstance, the premature death of their friends." Epicurus's theory here agrees precisely with his practice.

The State. — Towards the state the Epicureans were somewhat shy. Epicurus himself, we have seen, avoided affairs of state; and he declared that the wise man would never busy himself greatly with these unless there were special reasons for so doing. But, as may be inferred from Diogenes's account of the Epicurean "Wise Man," they did not believe or advocate a haughty independence of and disregard for governmental authority; and they were not republican but monarchical in political sentiment. They adopted here as elsewhere an independence for the individual which did not overshadow or threaten the independence of any other individual.

Religion. — Substantially the same is the Epicurean attitude towards the universal order of things — an attitude of independence and easy freedom. Man, if he be wise, is not overawed by the contemplation of nature and the gods, but dwells in serenity and happiness. Nature is not an object of fear or worship; the gods are not reached by divination and prayer; rather, are they to be merely contemplated in their perfect immortality and felicity. Such contemplation is to man the source of the purest happiness.

Historical Sources of the Epicurean Theories. — In physics Epicurus was obviously a follower of Democritus; in ethics, of the Cyrenaics; though he departs somewhat from the doctrines of both schools. Democritus seems to have arrived at his doctrine of the atom by combining Eleatic and Heraclitean conceptions: Epicurus attempts to deduce the atom from what is given in sense as such. To the Cyrenaic doctrine of pleasure, Epicurus added an ingredient of subjective intellectualism, giving the theory a certain appearance of refinement but no higher ethical value. No such definite historical sources for the Epicurean canonic can be pointed out.

Result. — The logical key to the system of Epicurus, if system it may be called, is doubtless the idea of the easy and undisturbed independence and being-for-self of the individual. This idea, obviously, has most interest for Epicurus in its ethical bearings. His "Wise Man" is one who possesses independence, not by positively mastering all that might otherwise interfere with his independence, or by actively coöperating with others to secure for himself and all others the independence he seeks, but by withdrawing from the world into a place specially prepared for those whose aim is to realize the conception of the independent individual in quiet contemplation, and pleasant converse with those who are not inclined to oppose but mildly to second their thoughts and wills. With this view there is a certain natural, but not necessary, agreement in the doctrine of the atoms and empty space. The atom, like the human individual, is an independent entity and, to a certain extent, also, it, like the human individual, follows its "own sweet will," — it is self-moving, moves rapidly and without violent contact with other atoms, — the atoms "flow." As the *atoms* are independent of one another and human individuals likewise, so are man and the universe, man and the gods, the gods and the worlds surrounding them. There is, however, a certain mild sympathy between subject and object in the Epicurean theory of knowledge. Considered as a whole, then, the system of Epicurus, though possessing a certain kind of inner refined harmony, is not a really logical, close, concrete system; its parts, instead of having the ultimate synthetic interrelation that springs from a positive, definite, and all-penetrating conception, exist, as it were, side by side (as the atoms do in unlimited space), held together merely by the vague conception of quiet, passive pleasure.

§ 19.

The Sceptics. — Under the term *Sceptics* are here included the so-called *Pyrrhonists*, Earlier and Later (to whom alone, often, the term is applied) and the philosophers of the so-called *Middle* and *New Academies;* the attitude of these thinkers being essentially the same. The chief of the Pyrrhonists are *Pyrrho, Timon of Phlius, Ænesidemus, Agrippa,* and *Sextus Empiricus;* the leading Academicians are *Arcesilaus, Carneades,* and *Clitomachus.*

The Pyrrhonists: Lives.[1] — Pyrrho, the first of the Sceptics, was an Elean who had imbibed Democritean

[1] See Diog. Laert., pp. 402-423; Zeller; Ueberweg.

doctrines from a certain philosopher, Anaxarchus, whom he accompanied to India in the army of Alexander the Great. From Diogenes Laertius we learn that he was peculiar, even morbid, in temperament, being extremely indifferent and having no sympathy with general human nature. There is no reason to suppose that he especially admired any of the philosophers (Democritus excepted). He is said to have been highly honored by his country and much esteemed by certain philosophers, among them Epicurus. He died in 270 B.C., at the age of ninety. His eccentricity among the philosophers of his times appears in the one fact (among others) that he left behind him no written works. Diogenes says that he had many disciples but very few of them are now known. Of these may be mentioned Nausiphanes, the instructor of Epicurus, and a certain Timon of Phlius (320–230 B.C.), who had been a pupil of Stilpo, the Megarian, and succeeded Pyrrho as leader of the school. Timon had no successor. The Pyrrhonists did not possess the social qualities of other thinkers of their day. Considerably later than these men, *i.e.*, in the first and second centuries A.D., others, styling themselves Pyrrhonists, took up and elaborated the doctrines of Pyrrho and Timon. Of these we mention Ænesidemus of Cnossus (first century), a certain philosopher by the name of Agrippa, and the celebrated Sextus Empiricus (200 A.D.).

Theories of the Earlier Pyrrhonists. — The position of Pyrrho and of Timon, adopted and extended by later thinkers, is that there is no criterion of truth either in sense or in intellect; that, consequently, there is no knowledge, contradictories are equally true (or false), that the true, philosophic attitude of mind is complete suspension of judgment (ἐποχή). These men, in other words, finding in the realm of intellect the same contradictions that they, like the Eleatics, Heraclitus, Democritus, the Sophists, Plato, and indeed nearly all the earlier thinkers had pointed out in the realm of sense, developed to its limit a principle that had before them not received complete development, even in the theories of the Sophists. But Pyrrho and Timon did not entirely despair of arriving at truth of a certain kind : truth in life, or conduct, they believed accessible. They taught here that the truth is imperturbability of mind (ἀταραξία), which follows suspension of judgment "like a shadow," and unquestioning obedience to custom and tradition.

The Later Pyrrhonists: The "Tropes." [1] — By the later Pyrrhonists there were advanced against the possibility of knowledge certain special modes of view termed "tropes" (τρόποι). Ten of these, which are attributed to Ænesidemus, are (in substance) as follows : The denying of knowledge on the ground (1) of the differences in the feelings of animals as regards pleasure and pain, what is injurious or advantageous ; (2) the differences in the "nature and idiosyncrasies of men " ; (3) the "difference of the organs of sense " ; (4) the "disposition of the subject [the human individual], and the changes in general to which it is liable " ; (5) "difference in laws and established customs, belief in mythical traditions, conventions of art, and dogmatic opinions " ; (6) the "promiscuousness and confusion of objects " ;

---

[1] Diog. Laert., *Life of Pyrrho*, pp. 409–413.

(7) "difference as regards the distance, position, space, and objects in space"; (8) differences as regards the "magnitudes or qualities of things — heat or coldness, speed or slowness, paleness or variety of color," etc; (9) "frequency or rarity or strangeness of the thing under consideration"; (10) "the fact that all things are known by comparison with others." In all these cases it is, practically, held that there is ground for suspension of judgment in the fact that, owing to the differences and contrariety of things, it is impossible to apply the law of identity, or conception of uniformity; *i.e.*, it is impossible to *think* (in the strictest, narrowest sense of the term). For example, — to take the third "trope," — since an apple is yellow to the sight, sweet to the taste, fragrant to the sense of smell, *i.e.*, since sight, taste, and smell are different and incommensurable, it is impossible to believe that there is in reality anything such as we ordinarily believe an apple (say) to be — "what is seen is just as likely to be something else than reality." To take another example: since "the Persians do not think it unnatural for a man to marry his daughter, but among the Greeks it is unlawful" "and since the Egyptians embalm their dead, and then bury them, the Romans burn them, the Pæonians throw them into the lake," no positive conclusion regarding marriage or the disposal of the dead is possible. The five tropes of Agrippa are these: the disagreement in opinion among men; the logical necessity of proceeding *in infinitum* in the attempt to arrive at a fixed, first principle; the fact that no object is perceived independently, but always in its relation to something else; the necessity of starting always with hypotheses; the reciprocal nature of

proofs, *e.g.*, proving porosity by evaporation and evaporation by porosity.

The Impossibility of Demonstration, of a Sign, of a Cause, etc. — The possibility of demonstration was denied by the Sceptics on the ground that there are no true indemonstrable premises, and without such all reasoning aiming at ultimate certainty must be a *regressus in infinitum.* It was denied also that anything could be regarded as a sign or indication of anything else: the *invisible* obviously cannot be a sign, either of the invisible or the visible; nor can the visible be a sign of the invisible, since the two bear no relation to one another, and finally, there is no need of a sign for the visible. Again, the notion of *a cause* is a spurious conception. "Cause is something relative. It is relative to that of which it is the cause. But that which is relative is only conceived and has no real existence. . . . However, let us admit that there are such things as causes. In that case, then, a body must be the cause of a body or that which is incorporeal must be the cause of that which is corporeal. Now, neither of these cases is possible; therefore there is no such thing as a cause. In fact, one body cannot be the cause of another body, since both bodies have the same nature; and if it be said that one is the cause, inasmuch as it is a body, then the other must be a cause for the same reason. And in that case one would have two reciprocal causes; two agents without any passive subject. Again, one incorporeal thing cannot be the cause of another incorporeal thing, for the same reason. Also, one incorporeal thing cannot be the cause of a body, because nothing that is incorporeal can produce a body.

Nor, on the other hand, can a body be the cause of anything incorporeal, because in every production there must be some passive subject-matter; but as what is incorporeal is by its own nature protected from being a passive subject, it cannot be the object of any productive power. There is therefore no such thing as any cause at all. From all which it follows that the first principles of all things have no reality; for such a principle, if it did exist, must be both the agent and the efficient cause." Motion, the act or possibility of learning, the distinction between good and evil, were likewise found impossible by the later Pyrrhonists.

Pure Negativism of the Pyrrhonists. — Pyrrhonism reached its culmination when, it being objected (it would seem, by the Stoics) that the Pyrrhonists were inconsistent in declaring that they knew nothing and yet admitting common fact of experience, or were, even in terms self-contradictory in saying that they knew nothing, because they must *know* that they did *not* know, — the Pyrrhonists answered that they admitted fact merely *as such*, *i.e.*, not *as known* and *demonstrated fact*, and that in saying that they knew nothing they merely stated a fact, but did not logically *define* or *demonstrate* their position. "We confess," said they, "that we see, and we are aware that we comprehend that such a thing is the fact; but we do not know how we see, or how we comprehend"; or, "while we say that we define nothing, we do not even say that as a definition."

The Middle and New Academies.[1] — *Arcesilaus.* — Arcesilaus (third century B.C.) had been a pupil of the

[1] See Zeller; Ueberweg; Diog. Laert., pp. 163-170, 177-180.

Peripatetic Theophrastus, and of Polemo, Crantor, and Crates of the Old Academy. He was the founder of the Middle Academy, so-called. His philosophical energies were given chiefly to combating the theories of the Stoics. He denied validity to the Stoic idea of perception, or the "cataleptic representation" (φαντασία καταληπτική), basing his denial on the very obvious ground that a false representation *might* be of sufficient strength to compel assent, as well as a true one; and he reached the position that it was not possible to know anything with certainty — not even that we did not know. In this he agrees with Pyrrho. He was, also, in agreement with Pyrrho in holding probability to be the "highest standard for practical life." From Diogenes, who describes him as a "man of very expensive habits," a "sort of second Aristippus," we ought perhaps to infer that in ethics Arcesilaus sympathized with the Cyrenaics; we have, at all events, no reason to think that he was practically or theoretically an advocate of impassivity.

Carneades.[1] — Carneades, the founder of the New Academy (second century B.C.), industriously studied and combated the Stoic doctrines, gave little attention to physics, and was fond of disputing on ethical topics. He was a forcible speaker, and drew many persons, even from other schools, to hear him. He repeats with added illustration the arguments of Arcesilaus and the Pyrrhonists on the worthlessness of the senses and the intellect as criteria of knowledge. The Stoic theology was especially attacked by him. Neither the alleged *consen-*

---

[1] See Zeller's *Stoics, Epicureans, and Sceptics*.

sus gentium, nor the alleged design manifested in nature is to him a demonstration of the existence of God; mere agreement of opinion among the majority of the human race proves nothing, and the existence of danger and destruction, folly, misfortune, misery, and crime in the world is sufficient refutation of the supposed fact of a providence. But even admitting the appearance of order in the world, what necessity is there for affirming the existence of a world-soul? The very idea of a God, an infinite personal being, an *infinite* being possessing the intellectual and moral attributes of *man*, is untenable. How can God be subject to the changes of sensation, feelings of pleasure and pain? With what reason can he be called brave, magnanimous, prudent? We cannot conceive God as limited or unlimited, corporeal or incorporeal. In short, we cannot think of God under the forms of sense or of intellect without encountering contradiction; we have no right, therefore, to assert positively, as the Stoics do, the being of a God. And there are no *gods;* nor is divination conceivable, since to "know accidental events beforehand is impossible, and it is useless to know those that are necessary and unavoidable, nay, more, it would even be harmful." Any supposed cases of fulfilment of prophecy are merely cases of accidental coincidence. Further, the human will is free, for there is no proof of the existence of uniform causality in nature, and we know, as a matter of fact, that our decisions are free. Justice is mere expediency. We have no positive knowledge; our only guide is probability. Now, probability is of three grades: mere probability, unimpeached probability, unimpeached and confirmed probability. "The lowest degree of probability is when a notion produces by itself an impression of truth without being taken in connection with other notions. The next higher is when that impression is confirmed by the agreement of all notions which are related to it. The third and highest is when an investigation of all these notions results in producing the same corroboration for all." "Assent will be given to no notion in the sense of its being absolutely true, but to many notions in the sense that we consider them highly probable." On ethical questions Carneades was so fully non-committal that not even his nearest disciple got from him any positive view. In this he went beyond all Greek sceptical thinkers, for they, as we have seen, admitted that a norm of conduct was to be found in tradition and custom. Carneades is a representative, therefore, of the most completely developed philosophical scepticism in Greece.

Result. — The position of the Sceptics may be described, in a word, as similar to that expressed by the modern phrase "the relativity of knowledge" and is, more than any other in the history of ancient philosophy, allied to the well-known modern philosophical attitude denoted by the phrase. But it would, most probably, be wrong to suppose that the ancient agnostics held to the idea of a real thing-in-itself behind the (supposed) relative and irreconcilable phenomena. They gave up the idea of causation (as we have just seen) with all others, the very idea which, when applied to explain the origin of knowledge, gives rise to the thing-in-itself. By way of general comment, interpretative and critical, we have to notice, in the first place, that there is a certain evasion on the part of the philosophers we have just been considering of the obligation to think everywhere and always as best we can, and a dogmatic assumption that thought has for its only presupposition and principle the notion of identity. In other words, if the Sceptic admits a thing as a fact, must he not accept the consequences of inference from the fact, must he not ask what the fact means? "Facts" are, indeed, not ultimate for philosophical thought but they must be given a meaning, and there is properly speaking, therefore, no such thing as a universal suspension of the judgment. Thought can have no other object than truth or reality; and is there not a certain demand upon thought in facts recognized as *facts, i.e.*, something immediately before the mind, whatever be their content, whether sensible or supersensible? Again, how is suspension of judgment, pure negativity in thought possible? This state of mind, if reflected upon, contains its own negation. It is double-sided; but the Sceptics saw only that side which could present itself in the act of withdrawing, or abstracting, from contradictory phenomena. If the Sceptic's principle is Thought, he must *think* and let phenomena fall into his scheme as best they may. This the Sceptics did not do; nor did they, on the other hand, take "facts" for what they were worth and by a fair induction, supplemented by reflection, draw a meaning out of them. The nearest approach made to this is contained in Carneades's doctrine of probability, which seems not to have been thought of as a *way to the truth* for mind, but only as a way to a comfortable mental attitude or a theory adapted to "practical purposes"; which, in other words, contained no other necessity than that which implied the impotency of mind and not the irrational and non-existent character of the thing regarded as the object of knowledge. The Sceptical doctrine, though valid as against uncritical dogmatism (*e.g.*, Stoicism), is not valid as against the position that in human experience, subject and object, thought and phenomenon, are, by the very nature of the conditions of experience, correlative : not mere identity but identity in difference is the law of real thought. We are not at liberty to ignore fact ; we are at liberty, and, in fact, obliged, to follow conceptions, and, among them, the conception of pure thought, to their consequences. Making allowance for a natural difference between sense and thought as forms of mental activity, the meanings of fact should tally with the positings of thought. It might perhaps be said of the theory of the ancient Sceptics, as it was said by a modern Sceptic of his own theory, that it was unanswerable but convinced nobody. But even this need not be said. The Sceptic is not at liberty to suspend the judgment : for on the one hand, he must make the most of facts, and on the other, he must deduce the consequences of a suspension of the judgment, namely, he must accept and understand the fact of mere subjectivity. And this is the service of Scepticism — that it brings this fact to light.

§ 20.

The Common Ground of the Stoics, Epicureans, and Sceptics. — Widely distinct as the schools of which we have just been speaking may seem to be, a comparison of them with each other and with the schools preceding them brings to light a very important point of agreement among them. As distinguished from the thinkers of the first period of Greek philosophy, the period of the nature-philosophers, these three schools, together with Plato and Aristotle, have their principle in the subjective (mind) instead of the objective (nature). But with Plato and Aristotle, the subjective embraces positively the objective in its sway; with the later schools the subjective stands in a somewhat doubtful relation to the objective, preserving a *quasi*-independence, either in the midst of the objective, as with the Stoics, or in retirement from, and a negative attitude towards, the objective, as with the Epicureans and Sceptics. A relatively higher value is placed upon the particular individual subject than had been placed upon it by Plato and Aristotle, and the universal subject has a tendency to become purely transcendent. The sources and avenues of knowledge are supposed to lie in those things which are characteristic of man as an individual, *i.e.*, in the senses chiefly, and the highest end of conduct is seen in that which has primary, if not sole, reference to the general individual as such. The philosophy of the Stoics, the Epicureans, and the Sceptics is, in tendency, if not in actuality, the philosophy of the individual as such determining itself: it is Socraticism developed on its narrower side and is the most advanced stage then yet reached by philosophy in this direction. In Scepticism the pure abstract individual is hardly distinguishable from the abstract universal, and Scepticism is therefore at the very threshold of a philosophy of self-determination. In Stoicism and Epicureanism the practical renunciation of all outside the individual self is incomplete. They are, therefore, slightly less advanced stages of the thought that constitutes the essence of Scepticism. In the stress laid by all these schools upon the individual, lies their strength as well as their weakness. But they only *implicitly* posited the individual as the universal.

§ 21.

Philosophy in Rome: Eclecticism.[1] — In the schools we have just been considering, thought appears to have reached a natural limit or, rather, turning-point : ceasing (with Aristotle) to be thought for its own sake and in its true universal character (the Thought of Thought), it has become thought for action's sake ; it is no longer the thought of the universal but is the thought of the individual. Beyond this limit, or turning-point, thought gives place to action, or life. In this direction nothing, it would seem, is to be expected of philosophy but a repetition of itself or a passing into exhortation and conduct. A complete return to a development of the earlier standpoint, that of Plato and Aristotle, seems practically impossible. The strained, paradoxical individualism of the Stoic doctrine and spirit, the evident one-sidedness of Epicureanism, and the destructive negativism of Scepticism are all — and particularly the last-mentioned — of a character to produce distrust of philosophy as a science, to disintegrate and scatter thought rather than concentrate it and give it the active consciousness of organic totality. Nor was there anything in the outward fortunes of philosophy to beget — directly — this consciousness. The Roman world — and all the world at this time was becoming Roman — was

[1] See *Zeller's The Eclectics.*

a world of action. Philosophers were Romans, or, if not, must think for Romans: in Rome, even philosophy must, literally, "do as the Romans do" and, as it happens, must be practical, in the narrowest sense. It must give up, to a large extent, its pretension to universality as regards the object of knowledge or the knowing subject. Philosophy, in other words, becomes "eclectic": the individual thinks whatever practical necessity or convenience for *him* requires or suggests, is governed by theoretical necessity neither as regards the source, origin, or consistency of his thought. He borrows ideas and combines them loosely; he borrows only such ideas as have a practical bearing, and gives them only such combination and setting as the practical demands or suggests. Differences as regards the amount of borrowing, the sources from which they borrow, and the manner of combining and setting borrowed ideas make the differences between the "Eclectics." The Eclectics do not, of course, constitute a school in any strict sense of the term. The greatest number of the so-called Eclectics are of Stoic persuasion; but we also find among them *quasi*-representatives of the Peripatetic School, the Academy, and the Cynic School. The Epicureans did not become Eclectics but remained a distinct sect. We begin with the later Peripatetics.

§ 22.

The Later Peripatetics. — The later Peripatetics were not to any great extent originators of philosophical conceptions or theories but were chiefly Aristotelian editors and commentators. Of these editors and commentators we may mention *Andronicus of Rhodes*, by whom, it is supposed, the works of Aristotle "were first properly collected and edited" (70 B.C.); *Boëthus of Sidon* (first century B.C.); an unknown author of a remarkable work entitled *On the Cosmos; Alexander of Ægæ* (first century A.D.); *Aspasius* and *Adrastus of Aphrodisias* (120 A.D.); *Aristocles of Messene*, and, particularly, the pupil of Aristocles, *Alexander of Aphrodisias* (200 A.D.), who was known as the Exegete κατ'ἐξοχήν (commentator *par excellence*). Most of these men in their interpretations and developments of Aristotle's doctrine incline towards a materialistic view of the universe, similar to that held by the earlier Peripatetics and by the Stoics. Their effort was directed towards removing apparent dualistic features of Aristotle's philosophy, such as the separateness of God and nature, of reason and the lower faculties, of knowledge considered as having for its object the universal, and the real as the individual. None of these identified God and nature; but they represented God as actively working in nature though preserving a distinct identity. They attained what is undoubtedly a very exalted conception of the Deity. By Alexander of Aphrodisias and others the soul was considered a product of the bodily organism. Alexander explained the universal as merely a *form* of knowledge; holding, on the other hand, that the individual is the only real. In doing this he did not solve the difficulty but merely put it a little aside, inasmuch as it does not appear that he asserted the organic unity of the universal and the individual. — We may, with sufficient propriety, class with these Peripatetics the celebrated physician *Galen* (Claudius Galenus), who lived in the second century A.D. He followed

Aristotle in logic, physics, and metaphysics, though inclined to keep physical speculation, as such, within narrow bounds. He seems to be an example of the "scientist" who is cautious in regard to making affirmations concerning the supersensible, though holding belief in the supersensible to be necessitated by religious and moral experience.

§ 23.

Later Academics. — Two Eclectic Academicians require to be noticed here : *Philo of Larissa* in Thessaly, who succeeded Clitomachus and was at one time teacher of Cicero, and *Antiochus of Ascalon*, a pupil of Philo, and at one time head of the Academy. These men flourished in the beginning of the first century B.C. They repudiated the Middle and New Academics, and regarded themselves as *true* Academicians.

Philo of Larissa. — Philo would accept neither the Sceptical, nor its opposite, the Stoical, theory of cognition. He advocated a doctrine of probability, or, rather, of a kind of conviction more firm than that resting on probability and yet not reaching perfect certainty; what might, perhaps, in current phrases of to-day be termed "moral certainty," "practical conviction," "intuition." His test of truth in ideas was, in other words, the self-evidence that belongs, or is supposed to belong, particularly to ideas of the moral consciousness.

Antiochus of Ascalon. — Antiochus, going a step further, denied that the moral consciousness could be satisfied with mere probability ; and, accordingly, attempted to refute the Sceptical theory of cognition. He thought that the senses are, when in a healthy condition, trustworthy, that, though suspension of judgment might be necessary in certain individual cases, it is not always required, and that the Sceptical theory was self-contradictory in its conviction of the impossibility of conviction, and in distinguishing between truth and error, and at the same time practically denying the distinction. In physics he agreed essentially with the Stoics. In ethics he held to a modified Stoicism and was in close sympathy with the Old Academy, placing the goods and virtues of the body along with those of the soul, among the perfect goods and virtues. He is, however, chargeable with what, in view of this, is an inconsistency, viz., the drawing a broad line of distinction between the wise and unwise. He was at one time teacher of Cicero, and of Varro, the great Roman scholar.

§ 24.

Later Stoics. — Leading Later Stoics are *Boëthus, Panætius, Posidonius, Varro, Cicero, Seneca, Musonius Rufus, Epictetus,* and *Marcus Aurelius.*

Boëthus. — Boëthus deviated from the doctrine of the original Stoics in that he gave as criteria of knowledge, reason, desire, and science, as well as perception, denied truth to the doctrine of the world-conflagration, denied also that God was the soul of the world, and that prophecy and divination were possible. Three of his reasons for the denial of the doctrine of the world-conflagration were the following: the world could not be destroyed by any cause acting within it, nor by any cause without, since there was only void without; God must become an idle being if the world were destroyed; "after the complete annihilation of the world [by fire] this fire must itself be extinguished for want of nourishment, and then the new formation of the world would be impossible."

Panætius. — Panætius (*circa* 180–110 B.C.), who was "the chief founder of Roman Stoicism," a friend of Scipio Africanus, the Younger, and afterwards head of the Stoic school at Athens, departed more widely than any of the later Stoics from the dogmatic spirit and the tenets of the earlier. He denied divination and the conflagration-theory. He gave to the soul a dualistic character, recognizing a vegetable element, to which he claimed that the reproductive function in man belonged, and accommodated the Stoic theology to the popular religion, and the Stoic ethical system to popular sentiment. From him were largely borrowed by Cicero the first two books of the celebrated treatise on Duties (*De Officiis*).

Posidonius. — Posidonius (first half of first century B.C.), another Rhodian who taught the Romans philosophy, substituted for the Stoic doctrine that the soul is rational, the Platonic doctrine that the soul is both rational and irrational in its parts. Posidonius held that reason cannot, as the earlier Stoics declared, be the cause of the passions, which, he thought, are by nature, *ir*rational, but that reason and the passions exist side by side in the soul as distinct faculties. He seems to have been led to this position by the common facts of experience, going to show that except in highly cultivated natures mere thought or will is not sufficient to arouse and control passion. By this view Posidonius relaxed the evident strain in the system of the earlier Stoics upon the faith of ordinary consciousness in its own immediate presentments.

Varro. — Varro rejected the scepticism of the Academy and Stoic one-sidedness. According to him happiness, or the end of life, is virtue plus the external goods conditioning it, and requires for its foundation a principle of positive knowledge. He is accordingly in sympathy with Antiochus and the Old Academy.

Cicero: Life. — Cicero (106-44 B.C.) holds a place in the history of philosophy not so much as an original philosophic thinker as one who, by his enthusiasm for noble ideas and his power of expression, and by the fact that he preserved from oblivion and gave form, order, and spirit to many doctrines of older thinkers, contributed to the spread and extended influence of philosophic conceptions and spirit among men. His interest in and study of philosophy, which seems to have had its origin in rhetorical or oratorical studies and ambition, began early and continued, so far as his political occupation permitted, throughout life, the last two or three years of his life being entirely devoted to the composition, or compilation, of philosophical works. His first teacher in philosophy was the Epicurean Phædrus, who was lecturing in Rome about the year 88 B.C. Though Cicero "seems to have been converted at once to the tenets of his master,"[1] he was soon after led to abandon them. At about the same time he studied dialectic (chiefly) with the Stoic Diodotus, without, however, accepting the Stoic doctrine as a whole. He was more attracted by Philo of Larissa, who came to Rome at this time. Philo, it seems, was a brilliant orator, roused in Cicero the highest enthusiasm for his subject,

---

[1] See Introduction to J. S. Reid's *The Academica of Cicero.*

and converted him from Epicureanism to the standpoint of the Academy. The next seven years (after 88 B.C.) were given to the study of philosophy, law, and literature. Two years at a later time were "spent in the society of Greek philosophers and rhetoricians." At this time he heard at Athens the Epicurean Zeno of Sidon, and, also, Phædrus, whom ten years before he had heard at Rome. He was influenced chiefly by Antiochus of Ascalon, whom he admired for his dialectical skill and the pointedness of his style. At Rhodes he met Posidonius, who seems to have been his model among the Stoics as Antiochus was among the Academics. Until quite recently it has been customary to attach comparatively little importance to Cicero as a philosopher because his philosophical works are, avowedly, chiefly translations and paraphrases of the writings of Greek philosophers; but there seems to be at the present moment a growing disposition to give him high praise for his enthusiasm for philosophical culture in an age and country not especially favorable to philosophy, and for preserving from oblivion, and infusing order and spirit into, the dogmas of the later Greek schools of thought. Of the early Greek thinkers, it should be said here, he knew little or nothing; nor was he master of the ideas of either Socrates, Plato, or Aristotle. He is, rather, a child of the individualistic and subjective thinkers of the later periods of Greek thought. The motive of Cicero's philosophical writing was, if not that of the original truth-seeker, that of the truth-lover and patriot who was desirous that his country should have the benefit, in its own tongue, of the thought of a more cultivated and thoughtful people.

Cicero's General Conception of Philosophy. — Entirely in accordance with the spirit of the age, and particularly with the spirit of the Roman people, Cicero looked upon philosophy chiefly as a thing having to do with practical life. Philosophy is the love of wisdom, and wisdom is the knowledge of things divine and human, "which comprehends the fellowship of gods and men, and their society within themselves." Ethics is thus given the first place in philosophy. Logic is recognized as having value because it supplies the method and the criteria of truth, and physics because it raises the mind above mean interests to the contemplation of the divine, and affords it high rational enjoyment. Cicero cannot in this respect be charged with anything like Cynic narrowness; he has a most genuine enthusiasm for science and learning, is indeed far superior to his age in this regard. But the wise and good man, if called upon by a danger threatening his country to make a choice between scientific studies and his country's good would, according to Cicero, feel obliged to choose the latter.

Theory of Knowledge. — In regard to knowledge as such and the standard of truth, the most impressive fact to Cicero's mind seems to have been that of the wide variety of opinion among men and of doubts that might be easily raised regarding our ability to know our own bodies, our souls, God, nature, etc. Cicero deems the proper attitude of mind to be that of the Academy, viz., doubt, or suspension of judgment, leaving room, however, for the acceptance of what seems highly probable. But as Cicero's interest was not, like that of Carneades, polemical, he looks upon doubt less as an end in itself than as a necessary preliminary to free undogmatic belief in what seems most probable. He agrees with the Sceptics in holding nothing as absolutely certain, but with the dogmatists, also, in holding as firmly as possible to the truth as far as it is, or can be, known by us. In other words, there must be a rational basis for action, and such basis must consist in the probable which is made a ground of decided and decisive belief. The highest probability belongs, according to Cicero, to the presentments of the moral consciousness, which are innate truth. Nature, he says, bestowed upon man a "mind capable of grasping all virtue, and, apart from any teaching, implanted in him rudimentary ideas of the most important matters, and began, so to speak, and included among his constitutional endowments, the groundwork, as we may call it, of the virtues."[1] The senses, also, and the *consensus gentium* are to be trusted.

Physics. — In physics Cicero's chief interest lies in questions relating to God, freedom, and immortality, questions having to him the highest ethical bearing. The ground for belief in God, the immortality of the soul, and the freedom of the will is, that such belief is innate and common to the race. God is the "creator, or, at least, the ruler of all things." "He is free and remote from all mortal mixture, perceiving and moving all things, and endued with eternal motion in himself." He is not declared by Cicero to be immaterial. The human soul has close affinity with God, and has on that account high worth, and high obligation resting upon it.

Ethics. — Cicero's position in ethics is indeed Eclectic;

---

[1] *De Finibus Bonorum et Malorum* (trans. by J. S. Reid), V. 21, 59.

even somewhat vacillating and inconsistent, but is on the whole, perhaps, Stoical, with a certain leaning towards the position of the Later Peripatetics. To him virtue is the highest, the only unconditional good; but there is a very evident desire on his part to unite to virtue as a necessary and universal concomitant the "expedient." The perfect austerity of the old Stoic ethics is not an element in Cicero's ethical ideal, argue as eloquently as he may against the allowing of expediency to take the place of virtue. The whole of the Second Book of one of his chief ethical works, the *De Officiis*, is taken up with showing how "the expedient" is to be attained. Virtue, the *honestum*, is, according to Cicero, one; but it is of four varieties, — wisdom (the highest virtue), justice, magnanimity (large-souledness), and moderation: "sagacity and the perception of truth," "the preservation of society by giving to every man his due and by observing the faith of contracts"; "the greatness and firmness of an elevated and unsubdued mind"; the observing of "order and regularity in all our actions." Cicero's divergence from the old Stoic conception of virtue is greatest in his idea of temperance, or moderation. To him this is grace and sweetness, polish of manner, as well as regularity and control of appetites; it is perfect fitness and adaptation of manner and conduct; it is culture, urbanity. He says that it is more easy to conceive than to express the difference between "what is virtuous" [in the broad sense], which he styles the *honestum*, and "what is graceful," or the *decorum*. In this there seems to be the manifestation of a tendency to allow the latter to swallow up the former. He finds that the Stoics are sometimes guilty of "subverting delicacy," as were the Cynics, and says, "Let us, for our parts, follow nature, and avoid whatever is offensive to the eyes or ears; let us aim at the graceful or becoming [*decorum*] whether we stand or walk, whether we sit or lie down, in every motion of our features, our eyes, our hands." The ethics of Cicero is, in short, the Stoic ethics refined, or humanized: pain and pleasure are to him not "indifferent," as to the old Stoics. This refinement, or humanism, also appears markedly in Cicero's conception of friendship, which he places next to wisdom among the things most valuable to man, and defines as nothing else than a complete union of feeling on all subjects, human and divine, accompanied by kindly feeling and attachment. Cicero did not attain, however, to the conception of a universal love towards men.

Seneca: Life. — The leading Eclectic Stoic of the next century is Seneca (3–65 A.D.). Seneca was educated in the school of the Sextians (a noted though short-lived sect in Rome that united a kind of Cynicism with Pythagorean rules of life, preaching a moral life and putting forth no speculative doctrines), and thence had in him a strong touch of asceticism, which appears particularly in his doctrine of the soul and its relation to the body. He was teacher and political counsellor of the wicked emperor Nero, and had weaknesses of character that were inconsistent with true philosophy and certainly quite discordant with the principles of Stoicism.

Seneca's Philosophy. — In Seneca, philosophy is practically reduced to ethics. He attached no importance to logic, and held to physics (in which he followed closely the Stoics of the Old School) chiefly for its ethical bearing. In his doctrine of the nature of the soul, Seneca gives up the simple monism of the Stoics for the dualism of Plato, keenly realizing what the older Stoics had not allowed themselves to recognize, the natural conflict between "passion and reason." "The body, or, as he contemptuously calls it, the flesh, is something so worthless that we cannot think meanly enough of it: it is a mere husk of the soul, a tenement into which it has entered for a short time, and can never feel itself at home, a burden by which it is impressed, a fetter or prison for the loosing and opening of which it must necessarily long ; with its flesh it must necessarily do battle ; through its body it is exposed to attack and suffering ; but in itself it is pure and invulnerable, exalted above the body, even as God is exalted above matter. The true life of the soul begins, therefore, with its departure from the body."[1] We have here an echo of Plato's *Phædrus*. Seneca was forbidden, by his materialistic conception of the nature of the soul, to posit unconditionally the immortality of the soul. Although giving theoretical assent to the Stoic ideal of the Wise Man, he seems to have felt obliged to doubt (as did most of the later thinkers who were in sympathy with the Stoics, but could not so completely abstract from environment) that the ideal was one that could be realized. He saw, rather, in the conditions of human life the necessity for self-criticism and internal conflict. Instead of the strong tendency manifest in the earlier Stoic doctrine to self-complacent individualism, there appears in Seneca a consciousness of human imperfection, which

[1] *Zeller's Eclectics*, p. 222.

bears fruit in a disinterested regard for men in general. "The real crown of his moral doctrine lies in the universal love of man, the purely human interest which bestows itself on all without distinction, even the meanest and most despised, which even in the slave does not forget the man; in that gentleness of disposition which is so especially antagonistic to anger and hatred, tyranny, and cruelty, and which considers nothing worthier of a man and more according to nature than forgiving mercy, and benevolence that is unselfish and disseminates happiness in secret, imitating the divine goodness towards the evil and the good ; which, mindful of human weakness, would rather spare than punish, does not exclude even enemies from its goodwill, and will not return even injury with injury."[1] It was by virtue of the influence of this mildness and sympathy that the rather heartless theology of the older Stoics became in Seneca a true religion. In Seneca, Stoicism verges upon its opposite.

Musonius Rufus, Epictetus, Marcus Aurelius. — Deserving of mention, though they seem to have contributed nothing to philosophy as a science, are *Musonius Rufus* (latter part of the first century A.D.), *Epictetus* (about the same time), a Phrygian slave who taught philosophy in Rome, and *Marcus Aurelius Antoninus*, the Roman Emperor (121-180 A.D.). Epictetus was a pupil of Musonius, and Marcus Aurelius a profound admirer of Epictetus ; so that there is a close historical connection between the three. They are also in essential agreement in their spirit and teachings. Completely possessed by the ethical idea, the whole force of their

[1] *Zeller's Eclectics*, p. 240.

philosophizing goes toward rendering the individual a, so to say, moral sphere, perfect in itself and without relation of dependence, positive or negative, to others. They teach the doctrine of an all-pervading, over-ruling Providence and of a kind but dispassionate regard for man. They belong to the noble class of conservators and disseminators of the ethical spirit. Epictetus and Marcus Aurelius taught a reverence for "the God (δαίμων) within." Their philosophy is, of course, of the Stoic type, with a tendency to simple Cynicism.

Cynics. — Later came philosophers of the pure Cynical type, who may be looked upon as Stoics reverted to the original prototype of Stoicism, *i.e.*, the Cynicism of Antisthenes and Diogenes, the most fundamental and permanent element of Stoicism being its disguised Cynicism.

§ 25.

General Character of the Second Period in the History of Greek Philosophy. — A review of Greek thought from the end of what was designated as the First Period discovers a common fundamental characteristic in the (more or less conscious) assumption that truth and reality are contained in *reason,* (mind, thought, νοῦς) regarded either as opposed or as indifferent to nature (the primary object of thought in the First Period) or as wholly above and beyond nature and phenomena generally or, finally, as above or higher than nature but embracing or at least constituting the essence of nature and phenomena generally. Hence the designation *Rationalism* (p. 34) for this period. It is perhaps hazardous to attempt a dogmatic and precise classification of thinkers and schools on the basis thus afforded for classification, but some such one as the following appears substantially correct. The representatives of the assumption or view that reason is opposed, or at least indifferent to, phenomena taken in their universal character are the Sophists, Socrates (?), the Cynics, Cyrenaics, the early Stoics (in ethics), the Epicureans, the Sceptics, the Eclectic Stoics, Academics, and Cynics; of the assumption that reason is wholly above and beyond phenomena, the Megarians; of the assumption that reason, though higher than nature, embraces it or constitutes its essence, Plato, the leading members of the Old Academy, Aristotle, the Peripatetics, the Stoics (in physics), and the Eclectic Peripatetics, — Plato and Aristotle tending toward a supra-rationalism, and the others toward a kind of rationalistic naturalism, *i.e.*, the identification of reason with nature. The general tendency of thought may be described as being toward the point of view of the first-named assumption, *i.e.*, toward subjectivism, away from universalism. But because of the contradictory character of the rationalistic standpoint as thus developed by the actual course of thought, a natural step for thought is to abandon this standpoint for another, the supra-rationalistic. The position of the Megarians is allied to the supra-rationalistic in all, perhaps, but as regards name. The One of the Megarians like the Being of the Eleatics was the object of thought, or reason, not of a power above reason. In Plato and Aristotle, in the idea of the good which is above science and being, or essence, and the thought of thought, which is above the heavens — we have a distinct suggestion of a higher standpoint than the ordinary use of the term *reason* in the period covers.

III. SUPRA-RATIONALISM (AND SUPRA-NATURALISM).

§ 26.

Standpoint and Schools of the Third and Latest Period in Greek Philosophy. — As a matter of fact it was just this supra-rationalism (and hence supra-naturalism) that became the standpoint of the thinkers and schools of the latest period of Greek thought. Such a standpoint was in part involved even in the common, non-philosophical consciousness of the time, — one century B.C. and several centuries afterwards, — which was filled with (supposed) intimations of and with aspirations towards the supra-natural : belief in magic, the existence of "dæmons," a prophetic character in dreams, and, of course, in the immortality of the soul, was rife ;[1] and it was but natural that an attempt should be made to find a real warrant, a philosophical basis, for such intimations and aspirations. It was natural also that such basis and warrant should, first of all, be looked for in systems of philosophy already in existence. As a matter of fact, it was found particularly in the systems of the Pythagoreans, Plato, Aristotle, and the Stoics ; and certain systems arose that were little more than professed rehabilitations of these systems, and having in common with one another, not only the same general aim but many doctrines, adopted from these systems. To the schools thus arising have been applied the names, *Alexandrian*, or *Jewish-Alexandrian* (Platonic and Aristotelian), *Neo-Pythagorean, Eclectic-Platonic, Neo-Platonic*, etc.

[1] See an interesting discussion on this point in A. W. Benn's *The Greek Philosophers*, Vol. II. ch. 4.

§ 27.

Jewish-Alexandrian Schools. — Of the philosophers of the Jewish-Alexandrian school we speak of Aristobulus (160 B.C.), who appears to have been the first to combine Jewish and Greek conceptions, and of Philo Judæus, a (Jewish) theologian of Alexandria, who flourished in the first part of the first century A.D., and, like Aristobulus, combined Jewish and Greek conceptions. Alexandria was at this time a meeting-place for the whole Mediterranean world, and a natural point of syncretism, also, for the ideas of that world.

Aristobulus. — Aristobulus held that the world is ruled by a divine power (not God but a "potency" of God), and that God is extra-mundane, visible only to reason (νοῦς). "In interpreting the [Jewish] seven days' work of creation, Aristobulus interprets, metaphorically, the light, which was created on the first day, as symbolizing the wisdom by which all things are illumined, which some of the Peripatetic philosophers had compared to a torch; but, he adds, one of his own nation (Solomon, Prov. viii. 22 seq.?) had testified of it more distinctly and finely, that it existed before the heavens and the earth. Aristobulus then endeavors to show how the whole order of the world rests on the number seven."[1]

Philo Judæus: General Attitude.[2] — Philo built up a philosophical system out of material borrowed from the Greek philosophers and treated in the spirit of the Hebrew, or, rather, Oriental conception of God as the

---

[1] Ueberweg's *Hist. of Phil.*, Vol. I. p. 227.
[2] Ritter and Ueberweg.

sole *being* and as remotely transcendent above the world. Naturally, therefore, he treats the logic and physics of the earlier philosophers (so far as these divisions of philosophy are concerned with mundane things and are within the general range of human intelligence) as of comparatively slight consequence, and converts philosophy into higher theology.

Theory of Knowledge. — Philo agrees with the Sceptics (Academicians) as to the inability of the human mind to attain to knowledge of the real, but instead of adopting their theory of probability, makes knowledge possible as a "gift" from God, a revelation. This knowledge comes to man when in a certain state of soul denominated "enthusiasm," a "reposeful divine rapture," in which the soul, liberated from sense and absorbed in itself, is fructified by God. In such a revelation is contained for man the knowledge of the *probable* ground of things: God is too high above human thought to be clearly apprehended by it even in a state of "enthusiasm." Man may by his own effort become *capable* of such a revelation, *worthy* of such a gift, through philosophic thought; the revelation itself is a gift. Philosophy is the highest form of human knowledge strictly as such. Other sciences, *i.e.*, grammar, rhetoric, geometry, etc., are but limited in power: they are merely propædeutic to the higher wisdom. They have value as media between sense and reason, but true knowledge is given not in sense-perception nor in demonstration, but in "immediate intuition," an activity or condition of the soul in which there is no coöperation of bodily activity. Knowledge of the individual object is the lowest form of knowledge, the highest form being concerned with the highest genus, being. Of being, however, we only know that it *is*, which is practically all that we know of God as he is in himself.

God. — According to this theory of knowledge, God is the sole self-existent being, without properties, unmixed, higher than virtue and science, than beauty and goodness; he has no name, is unknowable, simply *is*. And yet he is, if we must ascribe to him attributes, immutable, supremely happy, supremely good, universal reason, supra-sensible light; he is (like the Prime Mover of Aristotle) above and out of the world; present in it by his power, not by his substance, or essence.

The Logos. — The middle term between God and the world, *i.e.*, his power, lies in his energies, or potencies (which, though attributes, are distinct from him), which are emanations from him, and the totality and unity of which is the Logos (λόγος), or Word. The highest of these is creative power, second is the "ruling potency," third, the "fore-seeing," fourth, the "law-giving," etc. These are to be conceived as personal activities and, perhaps, beings (like the Ideas of Plato). Though God is the creator, the Logos is ruler, his minister, and "Second God." As related to both God and the world, the Logos (Word) has a double nature, which may be symbolized by an inward thought and an expressed thought in their union, or interrelation. The Logos (sometimes designated as Sophia) is thus an image of God and the archetype of the world, or, adopting the terminology of Plato, whom Philo here in a manner follows, the Logos is the Idea, the Idea of Ideas, the "place" (τόπος) of Ideas, the supra-sensible world. The

Ideas (or potencies), whose place and totality the Logos is, are ministering powers, angels, differing in degree of excellence and together constituting a hierarchy. When not illumined by the light of God, man may be illumined by that of the angels. The supra-sensible world, though gradated down to the sensible, is quite distinct from it.

The Sensible World and Matter. — The sensible world is a copy and reflection of the supra-sensible. It was created, through the instrumentality of the Logos, out of matter, which is purely corporeal, without form or property, inert, motionless, passive, potential, the source of imperfection in the sensible world, God being author only of that which is good. Matter, it thus appears, is in the system of Philo even more than in earlier systems a necessary, irreducible element.

Man. — Between the sensible and supra-sensible worlds stands man. By the world of sense man is seduced from God and put under the rule of material necessity and imperfection, but as a child of the Logos, as a rational being, capable of knowing (in part) and aspiring after divine excellence, he is subject to the law of justice and must be regarded as free. Man's supreme good is divine contemplation, or "mental peace and repose, and joy in God." This is also his virtue, for in virtue alone goodness lies. In virtue the pleasure of sense has no place and human science has only a subordinate one, virtue being a "gift" from God. The four virtues assumed by Plato are by Philo treated as but (lower) forms of one virtue, viz., "goodness after the pattern of divine wisdom." This wisdom is higher than prudence, which is earthly, merely. Three degrees of virtue are — to begin with the lowest — virtue resulting from (human) science, virtue resulting from an ascetic life, and virtue that is a natural "gift." The two first mentioned are human; the last is divine. These three are interdependent. A fourth kind of virtue is that having as its condition philosophic science; it is, however, a gift, as is natural virtue, with which on this account it is on a level. Other virtues or, rather, perhaps, conditions to virtue, are hope, repentance, and justice.

Result. — The most conspicuous historical sources of Philo's doctrines are the scepticism of the Later Academics, the Platonic theory of Ideas (of which Philo supposed Moses to be the real originator), and the Stoic ethics and physics. He owed much also to the Pythagoreans; was a debtor, indeed, to most of the leading earlier systems in the history of Greek philosophy. His theory of knowledge and virtue as gifts from God is original and distinctive, — a new growth in the history of Greek thought. Similar to it, perhaps, may seem Plato's idea that knowledge is the working of the Idea in man, or that we rise to the Idea of the Good by an act of soul higher than science, and Cicero's thought that there is in man an innate perception of virtue, God, and immortality. But the extremes of the system of Philo, owing to the Oriental remoteness of God from the world, are so distinctly separated that they are brought together only by an act of speculative imagination, or faith, whereas neither Plato nor Cicero steps outside the sphere of thought, or the *conception* of the *objective organic whole.* The point and principle of synthesis in the system of Philo is an unexplained subjective emotion (*i.e.*, aspiration towards God); in the systems of Plato and Cicero it is an intellectual effort to *grasp* (not *passively* apprehend) things mentally in their unity. According to Philo, spiritual knowledge is *given* to man; according to Plato and Cicero, man acquires such knowledge by means of a power possessed by himself, the function of which is just that of seizing upon the thing knowable. (By Plato the existence of such a power is deduced; by Cicero it is, rather, assumed.) Philo's place is therefore among mystical philosophers; he is a theologian who has based himself upon religious feeling without giving an intelligible account of it and of the process ("intuition") by which it reaches its goal, the knowledge of God. It may not inappropriately be added concerning him as a theologian that he practised an unliteral, allegorical interpretation of the Jewish Scriptures (analogous to the Stoic rationalizing of myths), and that because of his belief in the "impurity of matter," he did not conceive of the Logos as incarnated "nor identify the Logos with the expected Messias, to which course, nevertheless, he was powerfully moved by the practical and spiritual interest connected with redemption through the Messias."[1]

§ 28.

Neo-Pythagoreanism. — Pythagoreanism was revived in the first century B.C. by a certain *P. Nigidius Figulus.* The school thus originated is known as the Neo-Pythagorean School.

§ 29.

The Eclectic Platonists. — We must mention here the

[1] See Ueberweg.

historian *Plutarch* (*circa* 50–125 A.D.), who is placed among those Eclectics who kept most closely to the doctrines of Plato himself.

§ 30.

Neo-Platonism. — Platonism was revived by an Alexandrian named *Ammonius Saccas*, of whom little else is known except that he was the teacher of Plotinus (presently to be spoken of), and must have flourished in the early part of the third century A.D. He is said to have regarded the doctrines of Plato and Aristotle as substantially one and the same, and to have taught both in their purity. Other leading Neo-Platonists are *Plotinus, Porphyry, Jamblichus,* and *Proclus.*

Life of Plotinus. — Plotinus (*circa* 205–270 A.D.), a native of Lycopolis, in Egypt, studied philosophy eleven years in the school of Ammonius Saccas, and went, at about the age of forty, to Rome and opened there a school of philosophy, which was attended by a large number of persons of learning and eminence, both male and female. Here he taught for twenty-six years. He was of ascetic habits, was ashamed of his body, ate neither flesh nor bread, despised medicine, was averse to giving information of his personal history. He appears to have aimed at a philosophical culture that should, as far as possible, strip the outward individual as such of his attributes; and one of his practical projects was the founding of a state with a constitution such as that expounded in Plato's *Laws*. In the ascetic and mystic character of his ideals he resembled, it would seem, the Pythagoreans; and yet there can be no doubt that he regarded the theoretical as far above the level of the practical, — philosophical contemplation as above narrow moral discipline. His works, fifty-four in all, were arranged and edited by his pupil Porphyry, in a collection of six groups, of *nine* works each, whence the name Enneads (ἔννεα = *nine*).[1] Plotinus was a violent opponent of the pugnacious Christianity of his age; but both in his life and in his writings there stands out in full relief the desire and purpose to hold the mind above the things of mere sense and in the light of its own pure nature.

Dialectic. — Plotinus, as did his master Plato, particularly in the middle period of his philosophizing,[2] held philosophy or, rather, perhaps, the approach to it, to consist in a mental flight from this world to a higher region, in becoming "like God," an ascent to the Idea of the Good ; and in his opuscule, *On Dialectic*, he explains, after the manner of Plato, the method or mode of ascent to the Idea of the Good from the level of the born musician, lover, and philosopher, who are gifted, each in a particular way, with a finer perception than most men, of the harmony that lies veiled in the sensuous world. The perception which the musician and lover have of the harmony and inner truth of things is overpowered by "astonishment," the mere sensation of the beautiful ; and these gifted natures have first to be raised to a standpoint from which they can distinguish the *principles* of beauty (*e.g.*, concord, rhythm, figure) in objects of sense from the immediate environment of those principles. They may then contemplate

[1] See Ueberweg's *History of Philosophy* for the subjects, grouping, and chronological order of the works.
[2] See *Theætetus*, p. 176; also, *Phædrus* and *Republic*.

those principles in a higher grade of development (*e.g.*, beautiful pursuits and laws) and then pass on through the study of the sciences to dialectic, or the science of thought and being, which is the "immediate instrument" of the Good itself. The born-philosopher does not require to be disengaged from meshes of sense and feeling; he is *naturally* quick to perceive thought-distinctions, but is somewhat dubious and only in want of some one to "indicate the way." He passes readily from the particular to the universal, and, after having received a training in the sciences, finds dialectic to be his native element. What then is dialectic? "It is a habit enabling its possessor to reason about everything, to know what each thing is, in what it differs from other things, what the common something is in or of which it participates, where each of these is, if a thing is, what it is, what the number of beings is, and of non-beings (which are not nothing but different from beings). It also discusses the Good and the contrary of it, the Eternal and its contrary. All these things it discusses scientifically and not from opinion." "It employs division, obtains knowledge of the first genera of things, intellectually connecting that which results from them till it has proceeded through the whole of an intelligible nature, and again by an analytic process it arrives at that to which it proceeded from the first."[1] Dialectic is not merely the *instrument* of philosophy: "it is concerned with being and what lies beyond being: it knows the motions of the soul, what the soul admits and what it rejects"; it understands manner, virtues,

---

[1] *Select Works of Plotinus* (trans. by T. Taylor).

habits, passions, actions. It is the "most honorable part" of philosophy, but it presupposes, and is presupposed by, the other parts. It is not possible to know dialectic without knowing "inferior concerns"; but though these may be in a manner understood "without dialectic," the knowledge of them is perfected by dialectic. The first principles of dialectic have their origin in intellect and not in any faculty or activity of the soul relating particularly to "inferior concerns." Dialectic in its highest form stands above, and "surveys," logic, or the principles of the understanding, or dianoetic faculty, which immediately govern the sciences relating to inferior concerns. The foregoing, which, it is to be observed, is quite Platonic in quality, elevates us to the standpoint of Plotinus, the standpoint of speculation (vision), or pure thought, or self-consciousness. Another account of the steps leading to this standpoint (which should be added to the foregoing, not only because it is more scientific but also because the meaning of Plotinus's philosophy is easily missed without care in the attempt to approach his standpoint) is the following:[1] The standpoint of sense is, naturally and necessarily for most men, prior to that of thought. Some never get beyond this; considering the things of sense "as the first and last of things and apprehending that whatever is painful among these is evil and whatever is pleasant is good." "Others are in a small degree elevated from things subordinate, the more excellent parts of the soul recalling them from pleasure to a more worthy pursuit." "Others through a more excellent

---

[1] See *On Intellect, Ideas, and Being* (Taylor's trans.).

power and with piercing eyes, acutely perceive supernal light, to the vision of which they raise themselves above the clouds and darkness, as it were, of the lower world, and there abiding despise these regions of sense, being no otherwise delighted with the place which is truly and properly their own, than he who after many wanderings is at length restored to his lawful country." Concisely stated, the steps of progression in the love and knowledge of the beautiful are: first, love of sensible beauty; second, "love of the beauty of science and virtue and of beauty of soul"; third, love of the "cause of beauty of soul"; fourth, love of "that which is first and which is beautiful from itself." In this last alone is there complete satisfaction ("liberation from parturiency") for the soul that is in intellectual travail.

Reason, Intellect, or Nous: the Realm of Ideas. — Since the ascent to the realm of that which is "beautiful from itself" has been by a process of abstracting from the uniformities and types *in things*, and thinking more and more of the types *in themselves*, that which is "first and beautiful from itself" must be conceived as the realm of *pure types* or *forms*, which is intellect, or reason. Soul is not that which is "first and beautiful from itself," because, if it were, one soul would not be beautiful and wise, and another unwise and base (as now is the case); soul is subject to passions, or passive changing states: it is linked with the sensible world and, as thus involved (incidentally) in motion, is in "capacity" not in "energy" (Aristotle's distinction of δύναμις and ἐνέργεια). Soul is beautiful merely as participating in intellect, or reason; reason alone is in energy and always in itself, for itself, and from itself. In reason, things are known as they really are, and the knower and the known are one. Reason is the place of being, the totality of pure forms, and of knowledge. If intellectual perception were not a perception of being, then intellect were only a "capacity" or "possibility," but we must have that which is in energy, and intellect is seen to be such only when the objects of intellectual perception are in intellect itself. If they were elsewhere, or outside of intellect, or had no being, then intellect would only be in capacity not real intellect and the objects of its perception not being. Intellect is, then, both that which is and that which knows. And, further, in so far as sensible things participate in types, they are objects of intellect; and not only so, but since intellect, or reason, has only itself for its object, they are creations of intellect. Further, still, it is the same thing to perceive intellectually and to be. In intellect all things subsist collectively, or at the same time, and yet as one, just as in the seed are contained all the potentialities of the future plant. But there is in intellect no (temporal) process as in the growth (and reality) of the seed. Reason is eternally "present with itself." "It does not extend itself to the objects of its perception as if it did not possess them, or as if it acquired them externally or obtained them by a discursive process, as if they were not already present with it . . . : but it stands firmly in itself." For this reason, intellect, as distinguished from being, does not exist prior to being; if it did, we should have to say that intellect, by energizing and intellectually perceiving, generated beings. Rather, intellect is posterior to being, just as the energy of fire is posterior to fire; and yet, since intellect would lack in itself being (and hence would not *be* intellect) if it *became* its object or being, we say that being and intellect are one. Considered with reference to its contents the intelligible world is or contains in it "according qualities and quantities, numbers and magnitudes, habitudes, actions, and passions, which are according to nature, motions, permanencies, both universal and particular," "sameness, difference, the stable, essence, quality, art." On the contrary, there is in the intelligible world no art that has to do with sensible things. "Neither will the agriculture be there which is conversant with a sensible plant; nor the medicine which saves the health of the body, or which contributes to strength and a good corporeal habit. For there is another power, another health, there, through which all animals are sufficiently corroborated." Rhetoric, military art, œconomics, politics, and all natural objects are there merely by participation. "Geometry, however, by being conversant with intelligibles must be arranged in the intelligible world." The soul in its real essence is there and the true sciences and justice and temperance.

The One, The First, The Good. — In intellect, or reason, there is a certain duality of the knower and the known, even though these be in a manner one, and therefore, says Plotinus, reason is not the Absolute (The First, The One, The Good). The Absolute is what is One simply and without qualification. It is prior to being and intellect. It is in itself neither intelligible nor intellective. It is intelligible in the sense that, being that which alone is absolutely perfect, its presence with or to intellect or reason is essential to the perfect being and activity of intellect. If this, which is prior to intellect itself, had intellectual perception, it would have to have present with it another thing, and hence would not be sole and first, but "many" and second. The One is not one among many, nor one in or through many: it is absolutely sole. The thought of it is wholly unlike the thought of anything else. To attain to the perception of the One it is requisite to abstract totally from the world of sense, *i.e.*, "to commit one's soul to, and establish it in, intellect." One then perceives that which is absolutely formless and distinctionless, and it may be, becomes weary of the vision and wishes to descend again to the world of sense. "When the soul directs its attention to that which is formless, then being unable to comprehend that which is not bounded, and, as it were, impressed with forms by a former of a various nature, it falls from the apprehension of it and is afraid it will possess nothing from the view. Hence it becomes weary in endeavors of this kind, and gladly descends from the survey, frequently falling from all things till it arrives at something sensible, and, as it were, rests on a solid substance; just as sight, also, when wearied with the perception of small objects, eagerly turns to such as are larger." Nevertheless, the Absolute, or First, is to be approached only in the manner described. All intellectual perceptions proper, however pure of sense, are but conditions to the apprehension of the One. In speaking of the One we necessarily apply names to it that designate not anything that is really in the One itself, but, "something which happens to us because we possess something from it, the One meantime subsisting in itself. It is necessary, however, when speaking accurately of the One, neither to call it that nor this. But we, running, as it were, externally around it, are desirous of explaining the manner in which we are affected about it. At one time, indeed, we draw near to it, but at another time fall from it by our doubts about it. . . . Doubt especially arises because the perception of the highest Good is not effected by science [*i.e.*, natural, or mathematical science] nor by intelligence [the knowledge of pure types] like other intelligibles, but by the presence of him. All concrete or synthetic doctrine extends only so far as the way and progression to him." The act of perceiving the One is a complete merging into it, a perfect union of knowing subject with known object, a union which is of the nature of the One and is hence necessarily a perfect union of the knowing subject with itself. It is only after separating from the One that intellect has before it the distinction of subject and object. The One is distinct from, though present with, all else.

Intellect, Reason, or Nous as an Emanation. — The One being thus prior for thought to all things else is the absolute prius of all things else. But in what way? How does the (our) thought of the One lead to that of intellect, soul, and sensible things? How do all things else follow from the One? When we try to hold or, we may just as well say, lose, ourselves in the conception of the One, or pure formlessness, we find spontaneously arising the thought of the opposite. This fact is the foundation of Plotinus's theory of the "generation and order of all things after the first." "The One being perfect in consequence of not seeking or possessing, or being in want of anything . . . becomes, as it were, overflowing,[1] and the super-plenitude of it produces something else. That, however, which is generated from it (being still under its influence) turns towards it (to become or to partake of, the One) and is filled, and was generated looking to it. But this is intellect and the permanency of it about the One produced being, but its vision intellect. When, therefore, it is established about the One in order that it may see it, then it becomes at once intellect and being."[2] In this vision of the One intellect has the consciousness of power and of itself. The One, that is to say, having produced by its overflowing an energy which it causes to turn back towards it and look at it sinks down (for that intellective power) into the realm of being, and being and intellect are thus organically distinguished and joined — immanent the one in the other by the presence of the One — as knower and known. Intellect viewing being in a light reflected from the One — seeing being by vision that it has immediately on leaving the One — sees being as one (a form of One) rather than many, and one with itself (intellect): it therefore sees itself. Viewing being as being, *i.e.*, as established and independent, it sees it as many (rather than one). In the latter form it is discursive and scientific, not pure intellect. "By logically analyzing the conception of self-consciousness we obtain, first of all, Nous itself, or Reason, as the subject, and Existence as the object of thought. Subject and object, considered as the

[1] In all other natures *desire* or *want* is the cause of their putting forth energy.
[2] *On the Generation and Order of Things after The First* (Taylor's trans.).

same with one another, give us Identity; considered as distinct they give us Difference. The passage from one to the other gives Motion the limitation of thought to itself gives Rest. The plurality of determinations so obtained gives Number and Quantity, their specific difference gives Quality, and from these principles everything else is derived."[1] Such is the deduction of the primary ideas from the One and from Nous and Being. The intelligible world does not fall below the notion of organic unity. The intelligible world is an "image" of the One. It is an organism of eternal types and forms. Now, since form must have realization in matter, there is in the intelligible world a universal substratum, "incorporeal matter." This is the bond of union among the Ideas, or distinct forms, of the intelligible world. It is cognized by "indefinite" reason.

Soul. — Out of the superabundance of the Intellect, or Nous, comes soul,[2] which is an "image" of Nous, as this is of the One. It partakes of the permanent, abiding nature of Nous but has in it also the negative of permanence, the principle of motion. Nothing, however, intervenes between soul and Nous: though distinct, they are continuous one with the other. Soul, imitating Nous, looks back to its origin (as the Demiurgus of Plato's *Timæus* looks to the Idea) and generates an image of itself; viz., visible nature which also is a kind of soul. From both of these are generated souls, rational and irrational. The "procession," or going

---

[1] Benn's *The Greek Philosophers*, Vol. II. p. 321.
[2] See *On the Essence of the Soul, a Discussion of Doubts relative to the Soul.*

forth of souls, from Nous is neither a voluntary nor a compulsory act, but "resembles a physical leaping or the natural tendencies to wedlock, or the impulses to certain beautiful actions to which we are not excited by a reasoning process." Each individual soul has inherent in it the universal law that carries it naturally to its particular end at the time appointed by the law itself; or, to state the same fact in a different way, each soul is suspended from an intellect which rules its course (as, according to Aristotle, the Heavens are "suspended" from the Deity, or Prime Mover). "Souls fall from the intelligible world, in the first place, indeed, into the heavens, and there receiving a body they proceed through it into terrene bodies so far as their progressions are more extended in length. And some of them proceed from the heavens into inferior bodies, but others pass from certain bodies into others: these being such as have not sufficient power to raise themselves from hence on account of the great weight of oblivion which they have attracted and which draws them down by their oppressive influence." Souls differ either inherently or from the diversity of the circumstances into which they are introduced or from fortune and education. That natural and, as it were, free necessity which conducts all beings to that condition of existence to which they are adapted, "coördinating and weaving together even the smallest things," is a kind of universal justice awarding their deserts to those who have done good or evil, whether in this life or a preëxistent state.

Soul and Body. — As being an "intelligible nature and divine allotment" the soul is not body nor the harmony in incorporeal natures, nor the entelechy, or perfection, of the body. The soul is "present with" the body; and, as the One is with intellect and intellect with the soul, it is not *in* the body; rather the body is in it, as the air is and shines in the light. As intermediate in nature between the perfectly indivisible (the One and intellect) and the divisible (the sense world), the soul is present with the body as whole and as part. The whole soul is in each part, but has a difference of function in the different parts by virtue of its adaptability to differences in the organs of the body. If the soul were not (as thus) an organism, all synthesis of the findings of the separate senses would be an impossibility and so, likewise, would all distinguishing and mental registering of sensations, for there will be no locating of them. The order and beauty of the cosmos, to take a quite analogous case, show that there must be a single power which wisely connects and governs all things in it. This power is the soul of the world. The soul in the body, by virtue of its (relative) divisibility, supplies all parts of the body with life and "power of sensation"; by virtue of its indivisibility it "conducts all things wisely." In the case of the sense of touch the whole body is present as instrument with the soul; in that of the other senses only limited parts of the body. The central seat of sensation is the brain. Though the sensitive soul is bodily in nature, it is, to some extent, "judicial," or intellective. The phantasy, or imagination (in the widest sense), is permeated by reason; impulse and appetite are not entirely beyond the influence of reason and phantasy. Memory has its roots partly in the intellect, partly in the phantasy. The soul is throughout, therefore, dominated by reason, or intellect. But because of the natural deterioration of intellect that takes place in the passing of intellect into soul, the intellect in the soul is not pure, or intuitive, but discursive, or rationalistic, intellect. Only rarely does the soul while in the body attain to the summit of intellect and merge into the Divine Being. It always possesses, however, though it does not always energize according to them, the innate ideas which it brought with it from the intelligible world. The soul, after its separation from the body, retains its powers, and has, if it has been deeply attracted by its bodily life, a recollection of everything done or suffered in the body. Evidence of the truth of the supposition that memory is not purely bodily in origin and will continue after death is to be found in the fact that the soul remembers, while in the body, some things that are not bodily in their origin. "In course of time after death the recollection of other things from former lives will arise, so that some of the bodily recollections will be dismissed and be despised. For, the soul becoming in a greater degree purified from the body will recollect those things, the remembrance of which she lost in the present life." The intellect, as well as the memory, undergoes a process of purification after death. Then the ratiocination and the use of discourse which are made necessary now by the irregular diversity of beings, or existences, give place to a pure intuition. "If, however, souls live in the intelligible world without (discursive) reasoning, how can they be any longer rational? They are still rational because they are able to employ a reasoning process whenever circumstances render it necessary. It is necessary to assume a ratiocination of this kind . . . we must not think voice is employed by them there so long as they entirely subsist in the intelligible world. But where they have bodies in the heavens they do not use the dialect which they employ here through indigence or ambiguity; but performing everything in an orderly manner and according to nature they neither command anything to be done nor consult about it. They also mutually know the objects of their knowledge through a conscious perception; since even here, likewise, we know many things through the eyes, pertaining to those that are silent. There, however, every body is pure and each inhabitant is, as it were, an eye. Nothing, likewise, is there concealed or fictitious, but before one can speak to another the latter knows what the former intended to say." The Plotinic spirit-realm is thus completely determined, or organized, according to the conception of pure self-consciousness.

The Individual Soul and the Soul of the World. — The individual soul is *en rapport* with the soul of the world and receives influences from it; but is, by virtue of its rational part, a different soul from that of the universe — just as the soul of the child in the womb is different from that of the mother. The soul of the world, which produces the beauty and order of the cosmos, is (in part, at least) transcendent. Man may rise to a true sense of his own inherent worth and dignity by the contemplation of the soul of the world as manifested in the cosmos.

The Sensible World and Matter. — The sensible world begotten and fashioned by the soul of the universe, is an "imitation" of that soul immediately and of the intelligible world indirectly, for the soul receives from the intelligible world the principles of all things. These principles, or forms, it is the function of the soul to objectify. The result, the objectification of forms, is just the world of sensible objects. Form, however, requires for its objectification that in which it shall receive real existence, and this is termed matter.[1] Sensible objects as such are constantly passing into and out of existence. Since form is intelligible, and as such permanent, these changes must be due to the matter of such objects. Corporeal matter takes on now one form, now another, is potentially all things and "always some different thing." All theories, therefore, that represent matter as fixed, or determined, in any respect, as are the elements of Empedocles and atoms of Democritus, or as having form, as do virtually the "seeds" of Anaxagoras, are false. Matter is absolutely without quality of any sort — without even magnitude — all qualities, or determinations, being given to it by form, which alone possesses definiteness or distinguishableness. If matter possessed magnitude, for example, the creator would be subservient to that, and "his production would not possess the quantity [nor the quality?] which he wished it should, but that which matter is capable of receiving." "Every form possesses magnitude and the quantity which it contains is accompanied with reason (*i.e.*, with a productive principle) and subsists under this. Hence in every genus of things quantity is defined together with form. For there is one magnitude of a man and another of a bird." Matter is indefinite and perceived

---

[1] See Plotinus's *On Matter*.

by the indefinite reason. "If, however, everything is known by reason and intelligence, but here reason indeed says what it is requisite to say about it, and wishing to become intelligence is not intelligence but, as it were, a privation of intellect,— if this be the case, the conception of matter will rather be spurious, and not genuine; be composed of an imagination which is not true and another kind of reason (compare Plato's 'spurious reason' in the *Timæus*[1]). What, therefore, is the indefiniteness of the soul? Is it not all-perfect ignorance, such as the absence of knowledge? Or does the indefinite consist in a certain negation in conjunction with a certain affirmation, and is it like darkness to the eye, obscurity being the matter of every invisible color?" The notion of matter is not exactly that of nonentity, if it be possible to think nonentity. The soul is pained, shrinks, at the thought of indefiniteness, and instinctively affirms seeming nonentity as a kind of entity. But matter is, nevertheless, not magnitude nor quality of any sort but merely the capacity for the objectivity of the quality that is in form. Form, in other words, just as, seemingly, about to pass into nothingness suddenly develops into magnitude and every other quality. Matter is merely then the subject of the qualities and has no reality if there be no form. But as far as matter is concerned, there is between matter and form no relation prior to their union, matter being entirely "indifferent to quality." Matter is mere externality, or otherness. When we term it the infinite, or indefinite, we can mean only that it is not something possessing the

---

[1] *Timæus*, p. 52. See above, p. 92.

attribute of indefiniteness, but the indefinite itself. Corporeal matter is "perfect poverty," "necessarily evil," and the cause of evil.

Virtue.[1]—The world of sense is, for man, evil; for it is the world of indefiniteness and change, whereas man is, by his very essence, — intellect and soul, — pure and permanent. He must fly hence and become like God; in this lies his virtue. It is doubtful if all the so-called virtues *are* virtues. Temperance and fortitude, for example, imply that man is subject to fear; but pure reason knows no dread. The so-called "political virtues"[2] are founded on deliberation, but deliberation is not a purely intellectual act or function. Temperance, fortitude, prudence, and justice possess, indeed, a certain efficacy in assimilating man to the divine; but God has no need of any of these virtues as such. Assimilation is of two sorts: one requiring an approach of two things towards each other in quality; the other, that one of the two things approach in similitude the other, this other ranking as "first" and remaining unchanged. The assimilation upon which perfect virtue depends is assimilation to that which is unchanged. Such assimilation must result in a purification of the soul of all passion, and in making necessary sensations of pleasure remedies and means of liberation from pain, in causing the irrational part of the soul to be obedient to the rational part. In accordance with this idea, the "political virtues" must be transformed so that wisdom "will consist in a contemplation of what intellect contains";

[1] See *On the Virtues.*
[2] That is, the virtues described by Plato and Aristotle as necessary to the good citizen, the member of the ideal state.

true justice will be that "energy of one thing towards itself in which there is not another and another" (*i.e.*, the unity of self-consciousness); temperance, inward turning to intellect; fortitude, apathy, according to a similitude of that to which the soul looks (*i.e.*, the One shining in Reason), and which is naturally impassive" (*i.e.*, pure reason). The virtue and end of man is that perfect felicity which is to be found only in intellectual contemplation. The soul's growth in this virtue is its return to God, the source from which it ultimately emanated, the One. The proper virtue of the individual soul is of like nature with the "virtue" of all else that emanates from the One. Nous, Soul, Nature have their being and produce their works in acts of "contemplation"; that is to say, in their natural aspiration and return towards the One.[1]

Historical Sources of the System of Plotinus. — If we say that the system of Plotinus is, historically considered, an attempt to mediate between, or "reconcile," the systems of Plato and Aristotle, rather, however, from the standpoint of the former than of the latter, we shall indicate at one and the same time the main historical sources and the essential character of the system in itself. In the one we have the Idea of the Good which Plato affirmed (in the *Republic*[2]) to be above both knowledge, or science, and essence, or being. In the conception of reason and being as the unity of subject and object we have the God of Aristotle, and in the intelligible world Plato's realm of Ideas given rather the psychological character of Aristotle's God. Plotinus's

[1] See *On Nature, Contemplation, and the One.*
[2] See above, p. 87.

theory of the soul, with its doctrines of preëxistence, the imprisonment of the soul in the body, and its immortality, is Platonic and not Aristotelian; but Plotinus's arguments relating to the unity of the soul, its relation to the body, the unity of subject and object, etc., seem to be traceable to Aristotle's *De Anima*. In Plotinus's account of the sensible world and of matter, we find a combination of Platonic, Aristotelian, and Stoic views combined. Again, Plotinus's ethics, if such it may be termed, is, in its subjectivity, asceticism, and impassivity, somewhat Stoic; in its purely theoretic tendency, Aristotelian; in its purism, enthusiasm, and aspiration towards supra-mundane perfection, Platonic. Finally, in the deduction from the One of all things else, we have an attempt similar to that of the Pythagoreans to deduce all things else, from mere number up to self-consciousness, from the primal One.[1] Plotinus himself very frequently speaks with veneration of the "ancient philosophers," and freely acknowledges obligations to them.

Result. — Notwithstanding, however, the obvious indebtedness of Plotinus to earlier philosophers, it seems clear, even from our brief sketch of his real system, that he had a standpoint and a full, firm grasp upon the philosophical conceptions that he had borrowed, that were quite his own. By bringing together Plato's Idea and Aristotle's Thought of Thought, he, in the first place, openly converted the former from an idea, or thought-object, to a conception, or thought-function, or, better, a thinking-subject, and so made the Idea more distinctly an intelligent, synthetic power, — the One, that is to say, is Plato's Idea become inner, spiritual; and, in the

[1] See above, p. 7.

second place, made the latter, Thought of Thought, which is a more or less dual self-consciousness, more distinctly absolute spirit. Viewed externally, or as idea, the One of Plotinus seems, indeed, but a mere abstraction, indistinguishable from mere matter; but, comprehended from within, it is the opposite of that, — it is pure intellectual power, absolute self-determination. If it seems to lack content, we have to remember that its content is merely held in abeyance, is to be developed by the system: the One is in reality fulness of power, which goes forth spontaneously — overflows — into existence, or concrete actuality. Psychologically considered, Plotinus possesses a certain unique excellence that even places him, in a certain respect, above both Plato and Aristotle — the one a master of dialectic thinking and the other of discursive reflection, — viz., a singularly sustained purity and loftiness of insight and peculiar power of keeping the mind's eye ever fixed in the direction of the sole truth. This appears particularly in his masterly attempt at a synthesis of the Idea and the Thought of Thought, and the completeness with which the conception of the One dominates his mental attitude; and constitutes a new force in the history of Greek thought. — As regards the perfection of the system of Plotinus as a system, one point seems to demand attention here. The system is a system of emanation, and there is, logically, no return of the first principle upon itself: the system is a straight line instead of circle, a fact that seems at first sight peculiarly inconsistent with the fact that its first principle is the One. The solution of the antinomy seems to lie in the consideration that, just because the One is absolute, it can be "mediated" by nothing else. A return into self is not necessitated. It overflows naturally, spontaneously, and is in no way dependent in its emanations. There is, it may be said, a certain "return" towards the One on the part of the soul and of nature in the act of contemplation; but the One is in no way affected by this, though the return may be considered as a natural, spontaneous consequence of the working of the One in the soul and in nature.

Porphyry and Other Commentators. — Mention may be made of Porphyry, the pupil and biographer of Plotinus, whose right to a place in the history of philosophy seems to rest chiefly upon his services in diffusing the opinions of Plotinus, and in expounding in an attractive manner writings of Plato and Aristotle, particularly portions of the *Organon* of the latter. He taught piety and asceticism, and inclined to theurgy. — Three other important commentators on Aristotle are *Themistius* (fourth century A.D.), *Simplicius*, and *Philoponus* (sixth century A.D.).

Jamblichus. — Jamblichus (fl. 306–337), a pupil of Porphyry, "attempted a speculative justification of superstition. He imitated Pythagoras more than Plato, his philosophy resting rather on mystical speculations with numbers than on Platonic ideas. In his system not only did all the gods of the Greeks and Orientals (excepting the Christian God) and the gods of Plotinus find a place, but he also took a quite peculiar pleasure in adding to the number of superior divinities from the resources of his own fancy."[1] Above even the One of Plotinus, Jamblichus supposes an unknowable essence.

[1] Ueberweg.

Below the One are the intelligible world, the world of thinking beings, including Nous, Power, and Demiurge (Creator). Next in rank is a triplicity of souls, and last the sense-world. Jamblichus blended with theology Neo-Pythagorean number-speculation. He defended image-worship, theurgy, and prophecy. His ethical creed is contained in the idea, held by Plotinus and Porphyry, of purification. He is said to have been the intellectual ideal of Proclus, the last great thinker of the school of the Neo-Platonists and the last great mind in the history of Greek speculation.

Proclus:[1] *Life.* — Proclus (412–485 A.D.) carefully prepared himself for the profession of forensic oratory and afterwards gave attention to the sciences — particularly to geometry, preparing commentaries on the works of Euclid, — gaining probably in this way much of that fine intellectual power and that appreciation of scientific method and form which place him among the master-dialecticians and system-makers. He was especially noted for his moral and spiritual excellence; for the possession not merely of the "political virtues," but also of the "theological," or "religious," virtues. "He seems to have held the view that the pupil of theology ought to avail himself of every branch of enlightenment, but the philosophical specially, as a means to a higher intelligence, in that he is to purify himself by virtue, to make himself master of physics, and by logical exercises prepare himself for a knowledge of the divine. His object is to construct a complete system of theology on a train of consequential reasoning."

---

[1] See Ritter and Ueberweg.

He mastered the whole course of Greek philosophy, prepared commentaries on the *Parmenides* and *Timæus* of Plato, and Plato's theology generally, and taught philosophy at Athens.

The Philosophy of Proclus. — The philosophy of Proclus may be described in general terms as substantially the same in content with that of Plotinus, differing from it in scientific rigidity and symmetry, as regards form, and by a more marked theological aim. Immediately below the One there is in the system of Proclus not, as in that of Plotinus, the intelligible world, or reason and being, but a "plurality of unities" which mediate between the One and what is below them, the One being otherwise entirely out of relation to that which emanates from it. These unities are gods. They are "followed by the triad of the intelligible, intelligible-intellectual, and intellectual essences. The first of these falls under the concept of being, the second under that of life, the third under that of thought. Between these three essences, or classes of essences, there exist also, notwithstanding their unity, an order of rank; the second participates in the first, the third in the second. The intelligible in the narrower sense of the term, or Being, includes three triads, in each of which the first two terms are "limit" and "illimitation," the third terms being in the first triad, the union of the two first or "being"; in the second, "life"; in the third, ideas or that which has "life in itself." In each of these triads, the first or limiting term is also denominated by Proclus (who follows in this particular the precedent of Jamblichus) "Father"; the second or limited term, Power; and the third or mixed term, "Reason." The intelligible-intellectual sphere falling under the concept of life contains, according to Proclus, feminine divinities, and is subdivided into the following triads: One, Other, Being, the triad of original numbers; One and Many, Whole and Part, Limitation and Illimitation, the triad of gods who hold together; and the triad of 'perfecting Gods.' The intellectual essences, lastly, falling under the concept of reason are arranged according to the number seven, the first two terms in the triad, or the terms which correspond respectively with Being and Life being subject to a threefold division, while the third term remains undivided."[1] The human soul, according to Proclus, does not commune with God immediately but mediately, through dæmons, or spirits next in rank above it. The union of each order of being with that next above is effected by love. Holding, as he did, that the soul is farther removed from God and in closer connection with matter than Plotinus had conceived it, Proclus rejected the Plotinic (Stoic) doctrine of apathy. The relation of the individual to the universal in the system of Proclus is mystical. The system is theological rather than philosophical in its aim. — As an illustration of his application of the "geometrical method," — probably under the influence of Euclid, — we give the seventh Proposition in the "Elements of Theology"[2] with its demonstration. "Everything productive of another is more excellent than the nature of the thing produced: For it is either more excellent, or worse, or equal. Let it be, in the first

[1] Ueberweg, Vol. I. p. 258.
[2] Translated by Thomas Taylor.

place, equal. That which is produced from this, therefore, will itself also either possess a power productive of some other, or it will be entirely barren. But if it be barren, it will on this account be worse than its producing cause: and because of its inefficacy it will be unequal to that which is prolific and possesses a productive power. But if it be productive of other natures, it will either produce that which is equal to itself (and this will be the case in all things, and all things will be equal to each other and nothing will be more excellent than another, since the productive nature always constitutes the thing produced equal to itself) or that which is unequal. But in this case, it will not be equal to its producing cause; for it is the property of equal powers to fabricate equal effects. But the productions of these are unequal to each other, since in this hypothesis the producing cause is equal to that which is prior to itself. It is requisite, therefore, that the thing produced should not be equal to its producing cause. But neither can the producing cause be ever worse than the thing produced. For if the producing cause confers essence on the thing produced, it bestows power also, according to essence. And if it is productive of all the power which that posterior to itself possesses, it can also make itself such as its production. But if it can do this, it will also make itself more powerful; for impotence cannot hinder, since a fabricative power is present, nor defect of will. For all things naturally desire good. Hence if it can form anything else more perfect, it will also perfect itself before it perfects that which is posterior to itself. The thing produced, therefore, is neither equal to nor more excellent than its producing cause, and hence the producing cause is entirely more excellent than the nature of the thing produced."

Result. — Neo-Platonism was the last of the schools of Greek philosophy. Notwithstanding the opposition of its leaders to Christianity, this school by its attempt to unite philosophy and religion and by the encouragement it gave to popular super-naturalism was the point of transition from pure ancient Greek pagan speculation to Christian Theology. It had a large influence on the Church in the Middle Ages.

PHILOSOPHY.

Empirical Psychology;
or, The Human Mind as Given in Consciousness.

By LAURENS P. HICKOK, D.D., LL.D. Revised with the co-operation of JULIUS H. SEELYE, D.D., LL.D., President of Amherst College. 12mo. 300 pages. Mailing Price, $1.25; Introduction, $1.12; Allowance, 40 cents.

THE publishers believe that this book will be found to be remarkably comprehensive, and at the same time compact and clear. It gives a complete outline of the science, concisely presented, and in precise and plain terms.

It has proved of special value to teachers, as is evidenced by its recent adoption for several Reading Circles.

John Bascom, *Pres. of University of Wisconsin, Madison:* It is an excellent book. It has done much good service, and, as revised by President Seelye, is prepared to do much more. (*Feb. 3, 1882.*)

I. W. Andrews, *Prof. of Intellectual Philosophy, Marietta College, O.:* This new edition may be confidently recommended as presenting a delineation of the mental faculties so clear and accurate that the careful student will hardly fail to recognize its truth in his own experience. (*April 6, 1882.*)

Hickok's Moral Science.

By LAURENS P. HICKOK, D.D., LL.D. Revised with the co-operation of JULIUS H. SEELYE, D.D., LL.D., President of Amherst College. 12mo. Cloth. 288 pages. Mailing Price, $1.25; Introduction, $1.12; Allowance, 40 cents.

AS revised by Dr. Seelye, it is believed that this work will be found unsurpassed in systematic rigor and scientific precision, and at the same time remarkably clear and simple in style.

G. P. Fisher, *Prof. of Church History, Yale College:* The style is so perspicuous, and at the same time so concise, that the work is eminently adapted to serve as a text-book in colleges and higher schools. In matter and manner it is a capital book, and I wish it God speed.

Lotze's Philosophical Outlines.

Dictated Portions of the Latest Lectures (at Göttingen and Berlin) of Hermann Lotze. Translated and edited by GEORGE T. LADD, Professor of Philosophy in Yale College. 12mo. Cloth. About 180 pages in each volume. Mailing Price per volume, $1.00; Introduction Price, 80 cents.

THE German from which the translations are made consists of the dictated portions of his latest lectures (at Göttingen, and for a few months at Berlin) as formulated by Lotze himself, recorded in the notes of his hearers, and subjected to the most competent and thorough revision of Professor Rehnisch of Göttingen. The *Outlines* give, therefore, a mature and trustworthy statement, in language selected by this teacher of philosophy himself, of what may be considered as his final opinions upon a wide range of subjects. They have met with no little favor in Germany.

These translations have been undertaken with the kind permission of the German publisher, Herr S. Hirzel, of Leipsic.

Outlines of Metaphysic.

THIS contains the scientific treatment of those assumptions which enter into all our cognition of Reality. It consists of three parts, — Ontology, Cosmology, Phenomenology. The first part contains chapters on the Conception of Being, the Content of the Existent, Reality, Change, and Causation; the second treats of Space, Time, Motion, Matter, and the Coherency of Natural Events; the third, of the Subjectivity and Objectivity of Cognition. The Metaphysic of Lotze gives the key to his entire philosophical system.

Outlines of the Philosophy of Religion.

LOTZE here seeks "to ascertain how much of the Content of Religion may be discovered, proved, or at least confirmed, agreeably to reason." He discusses the Proof for the Existence of God, the Attributes and Personality of the Absolute, the Conceptions of the Creation, the Preservation, and the Government, of the World, and of the World-time. The book closes with brief discussions of Religion and Morality, and Dogmas and Confessions.

Outlines of Practical Philosophy.

THIS contains a discussion of Ethical Principles, Moral Ideals, and the Freedom of the Will, and then an application of the theory to the Individual, to Marriage, to Society, and to the State. Many interesting remarks on Divorce, Socialism, Representative Government, etc., abound throughout the volume. Its style is more popular than that of the other works of Lotze, and it will doubtless be widely read.

Outlines of Psychology.

THE Outliues of Psychology treats of Simple Sensations, the Course of Representative Ideas, of Attention and Inference, of Institutons of Objects as in Space, of the Apprehension of the External World by the Senses, of Errors of the Senses, of Feelings, and of Bodily Motions. Its second part is "theoretical," and discusses the nature, position, and changeable states of the Soul, its relations to time, and the reciprocal action of Soul and Body. It closes with a chapter on the "Kingdom of Souls." Lotze is peculiarly rich and suggestive in the discussion of Psychology.

Outlines of Æsthetics.

THE Outlines of Æsthetics treats of the theory of the Beautiful and of Phantasy, and of the Realization and Different Species of the Beautiful. Then follow brief chapters on Music, Architecture, Plastic Art, Painting, and Poetry. An appendix to this volume contains a brief biography of Lotze.

Outlines of Logic.

THIS discusses both pure and applied Logic. The Logic is followed by a brief treatise on the Encyclopædia of Philosophy, in which are set forth the definition and method of Theoretical Philosophy, of Practical Philosophy, and of the Philosophy of Religion. This volume is about one-fifth larger than the others, and makes an admirable brief text-book in Logic.

Latin Text-Books.[2]

		INTROD. PRICE
ALLEN & GREENOUGH:	Latin Grammar	$1.12
	Latin Composition	1.12
	Cæsar (7 books, with vocabulary; illustrated)	1.25
	Sallust's Catiline	.60
	Cicero (13 orations, with vocabulary; illustrated)	1.25
	Cicero de Senectute	.50
	Ovid (with vocabulary)	1.40
	Virgil (Bucolics, and 6 Books of the Æneid)	1.12
	Preparatory Course of Latin Prose	1.40
ALLEN	Latin Primer	.90
	New Latin Method	.90
	Introduction to Latin Composition	.90
	Latin Reader	1.40
	Latin Lexicon	.90
	Remnants of Early Latin	.75
	Germania and Agricola of Tacitus	1.00
BLACKBURN	Essentials of Latin Grammar	.70
	Latin Exercises	.60
	Latin Grammar and Exercises (in one volume)	1.00
COLLAR & DANIELL:	Beginners' Book in Latin	.00
COLLEGE SERIES OF LATIN AUTHORS.		
CROWELL	Selections from the Latin Poets	1.40
CROWELL & RICHARDSON:	Brief History of Roman Lit. (BENDER)	1.00
GREENOUGH	Virgil:—	
	Bucolics and 6 Books of Æneid (with vocab.)	1.60
	Bucolics and 6 Books of Æneid (without vocab.)	1.12
	Last 6 Books of Æneid, and Georgics (with notes)	1.12
	Bucolics, Æneid, and Georgics (complete, with notes)	1.60
	Text of Virgil (complete)	.75
	Vocabulary to the whole of Virgil	1.00
GINN & CO.	Classical Atlas and Geography (cloth)	2.00
HALSEY	Etymology of Latin and Greek	1.12
	Classical Wall Maps (three or more), each	3.50
KEEP	Essential Uses of the Moods in Greek and Latin	.25
KING	Latin Pronunciation	.25
LEIGHTON	Latin Lessons	1.12
	First Steps in Latin	1.12
MADVIG	Latin Grammar (by THACHER)	2.25
PARKHURST	Latin Verb	.35
PARKER & PREBLE:	Handbook of Latin Writing	.50
SHUMWAY	Latin Synonymes	.30
STICKNEY	Cicero de Natura Deorum	1.40
TETLOW	Inductive Latin Lessons	1.12
TOMLINSON	Manual for the Study of Latin Grammar	.20
	Latin for Sight Reading	1.00
WHITE (J. W.)	Schmidt's Rhythmic and Metric	2.50
WHITE (J. T.)	Junior Students' Latin-English Lexicon (mor.)	1.75
	English-Latin Lexicon (sheep)	1.50
	Latin-English and English-Latin Lexicon (sheep)	3.00
WHITON	Auxilia Vergiliana; or, First Steps in Latin Prosody	.15
	Six Weeks' Preparation for Reading Cæsar	.40

Copies sent to Teachers for Examination, with a view to Introduction, on receipt of Introduction Price.

GINN & COMPANY, Publishers,
BOSTON, NEW YORK, AND CHICAGO.

Greek Text-Books.

		Intro. Price.
Allen:	Medea of Euripides	$1.00
Flagg:	Hellenic Orations of Demosthenes	1.00
	Seven against Thebes	1.00
	Anacreontics	.35
Goodwin:	Greek Grammar	1.50
	Greek Reader	1.50
	Greek Moods and Tenses	1.50
	Selections from Xenophon and Herodotus	1.50
Goodwin & White:	Anabasis, with vocabulary	1.50
Harding:	Greek Inflection	.50
Keep:	Essential Uses of the Moods	.25
Leighton:	New Greek Lessons	1.20
Liddell & Scott:	Abridged Greek-English Lexicon	1.90
	Unabridged Greek-English Lexicon	9.40
Parsons:	Cebes' Tablet	.75
Seymour:	Selected Odes of Pindar	1.40
	Introd. to Language and Verse of Homer, { Paper / Cloth	.45 / .60
Sidgwick:	Greek Prose Composition	1.50
Tarbell:	Philippics of Demosthenes	1.00
Tyler:	Selections from Greek Lyric Poets	1.00
White:	First Lessons in Greek	1.20
	Schmidt's Rhythmic and Metric	2.50
	Oedipus Tyrannus of Sophocles	1.12
	Stein's Dialect of Herodotus	.10
Whiton:	Orations of Lysias	1.00

College Series:

- Beckwith: Euripides' Bacchantes.
  Text and Notes, Paper, .80; Cloth, $1.10; Text only, .20.
- D'Ooge: Sophocles' Antigone.
  Text and Notes, Paper, .95; Cloth, $1.25; Text only, .20.
- Dyer: Plato's Apology and Crito.
  Text and Notes, Paper, .95; Cloth, $1.25; Text only, .20.
- Fowler: Thucydides, Book V.
  Text and Notes, Paper, .95; Cloth, $1.25; Text only, .20.
- Humphreys: Aristophanes' Clouds.
  Text and Notes, Paper, .95; Cloth, $1.25; Text only, .20.
- Manatt: Xenophon's Hellenica, Books I.-IV.
  Text and Notes, Paper, $1.20; Cloth, $1.50; Text only, .20.
- Morris: Thucydides, Book I.
  Text and Notes, Paper, $1.20; Cloth, $1.50; Text only, .20.
- Seymour: Homer's Iliad, Books I.-III.
  Text and Notes, Paper, .95; Cloth, $1.25; Text only, .20.
- Smith: Thucydides, Book VII.
  Text and Notes, Paper, .95; Cloth, $1.25; Text only, .20.

Sanskrit.

Arrowsmith:	Kaegi's Rigveda, (*translation*)	$1.50
Elwell:	Nine Jatakas (*Pali*)	.60
Lanman:	Sanskrit Reader	1.80
Perry:	Sanskrit Primer	1.50
Whitney:	Sanskrit Grammar	2.50

Copies sent to Teachers for Examination, with a view to Introduction, on receipt of Introduction Price.

GINN & COMPANY, Publishers,
BOSTON, NEW YORK, AND CHICAGO.

SCIENCE AND HISTORY.

NATURAL SCIENCE.

		INTROD. PRICE
Everett:	Vibratory Motion and Sound	$2.00
Gage:	Elements of Physics	1.12
	Introduction to Physical Science	1.00
Hale:	Little Flower-People	.40
Hill:	Questions on Stewart's Physics	.35
Journal of Morphology	(per vol.)	6.00
Knight:	Primer of Botany	.30
Williams:	Introduction to Chemical Science	.80

PHILOSOPHICAL SCIENCE.

Davidson:	Rosmini's Philosophical System	2.50
Hickok·	Philosophical Works	.00
Ladd:	Lotze's Outlines of Metaphysic	.80
	Lotze's Outlines of Philosophy of Religion	.80
	Lotze's Outlines of Practical Philosophy	.80
	Lotze's Outlines of Psychology	.80
	Lotze's Outlines of Æsthetics	.80
	Lotze's Outlines of Logic	.80
Seelye:	Hickok's Mental Science (Empirical Psychology)	1.12
	Hickok's Moral Science	1.12

POLITICAL SCIENCE.

Clark:	Philosophy of Wealth		1.00
Clark & Giddings:	The Modern Distributive Process	(retail)	.75
Macy:	Our Government		.70
Political Science Quarterly		(per vol.)	3.00
Seligman:	Railway Tariffs and the Interstate Law	(retail)	.75

HISTORY.

Allen:	Readers' Guide to English History		.25
Andrade:	Historia do Brazil		.75
Fiske-Irving:	Washington and His Country		1.00
Halsey:	Genealogical and Chronological Chart		.25
Journal of Archæology		(per vol.)	5.00
Judson:	Cæsar's Army		1.00
Montgomery:	Leading Facts of English History		1.00
	English History Reader		.60
Moore:	Pilgrims and Puritans		.60
Myers:	Mediæval and Modern History		1.50
	Ancient History		1.40

Copies sent to Teachers for Examination, with a view to Introduction, on receipt of Introduction Price.

GINN & COMPANY, Publishers.

BOSTON.   NEW YORK.   CHICAGO.

www.ingramcontent.com/pod-product-compliance
Lightning Source LLC
Chambersburg PA
CBHW031901220426
43663CB00006B/716